THE TWO BACKPACKS

UNDERSTANDING TEENS AND WHAT THEY CARRY

DR. JORDAN LAUER

HALLA CRANN

Published by Halla Crann Publishing

The Two Backpacks: Understanding Teens and What They Carry

JordanLauer.com

ISBN (Hardcover): 979-8-9985757-0-9
ISBN (Paperback): 979-8-9985757-1-6
ISBN (eBook): 979-8-9985757-2-3

Cover design: Bryana Anderle (YouPublish.com)
Editorial and art direction: Chad Harrington (YouPublish.com)

For permissions or inquiries, contact: JordanLauer.com

Printed and bound in the United States of America

FOR ASHLEY, MAX, GRACE, AND LIAM.
YOU INSPIRE ME TO WANT TO KNOW
MORE, DO MORE, AND BE MORE.

Contents

Foreword

The first day of class is the same at all levels. A student eagerly awaits the learning ahead; she looks around and imagines new partners and friendships; she envisions meeting her teachers, rich discussions, rigorous analysis, and deep personal reflection. Day one is a day of possibility.

Unless, of course, one feels the exact opposite. Which is certainly possible, and probably likely. And there's the possibility that both scenarios hold true for the same student. That's the essence of *this* book. Our students, to borrow a phrase from Whitman, contain multitudes. We deny their experience if we view our work as simply a surface level exercise. Inside our young people there is a battle over competing values and interpretations which educators need to understand. The end goal is not influence, but empathy. By making genuine connections with students, teachers develop trust. Through this bond, we can then hope to teach; anything achieved in class without trust is luck or decoration.

As an administrator, I seek new ways to engage students in their education. I've worked in all tiers, from elementary to high schools, and though conversations are different, the needs are the same. Our students today exist in a world which we, as their elders, never experienced. Sure, there are elements of the "childhood experience" that, at first glance, appear similar to our own. But the landscape transforms each day. When I was 13, I had the internet on a large computer on a desk in my room, but it wasn't in my pocket or on my bedside table. I had conflicts with peers on the playground, but they ended (or at least paused) when we went back to class, and they never continued as anonymous slander on social media. If we rely solely on personal experience, we do a disservice to our students and to the families who trust us with their care. To empathize with our students, to truly listen to understand, we must turn inward and recognize our differing experiences first.

I walked into the first lecture of my doctoral program like the student I described in the first paragraph. I care deeply about the work of educators as much as I care for my own learning. I anticipated meeting like-minded educators and, luckily, I was right. What I brought to the classroom, which I figured made me unique, was the impending arrival of my second child. My wife was in her third trimester when classes started. I was equal parts excited and terrified. *Late nights writing? Later nights comforting a newborn? Dirty diapers? Deadlines? Relentless fatigue?* The stress was all imagined, but it was very real. It was during introductions when I learned that (1) I wasn't the only doctoral candidate anticipating a newborn, and (2) my personal struggle was no more significant than any other student's. We are all weathering our own storms. We must all release our egos just a bit in order to understand. That's the power of the Two Backpacks. The one we see, and the one we must seek.

With wit and sincerity, Dr. Lauer brings to life the competing influences on the minds of our young people. Through anecdotes, research, personal experience, and insight, he helps us see the weight students carry. To help them unburden themselves, we educators must first unburden ourselves. Let go of preconceptions and opinions; welcome insights and fresh ideas. There are many here. The work isn't going to be easy, but it will be worth it.

Dr. Colin Hunt
March 2025

Seeing the Second Backpack

Shortly after the COVID-19 pandemic started to fade and restaurants had reopened to allow patrons to dine inside, I was sitting at a small table with my wife at our favorite local restaurant. The restaurant is well-liked by locals and has a very "dive" feeling to it—wood paneling on the walls and all—and it is a wonderful cross-section of my local community. As we had been contained in our house for the past several months, my wife and I were both taking in the smells, sights, and sounds of our local spot. We were mystified by the sensory overload we were experiencing in the very close quarters of the establishment, and more importantly to us at the time, the feeling of community we had not felt in what seemed a lifetime.

We missed people, missed hugs with friends, missed the muted roar of a room full of conversations and laughter, and missed adding our voices and laughter to that roar. More importantly, we missed what being around others does to us individually and as a couple. Connection with others enhances everything, fosters creativity, and gives perspective. We both had missed who we were when we were part of a collection of people, simply enjoying being exactly where they were.

Within earshot of my wife and I was a table of late-30s to mid-40s women. Nothing about this was noteworthy as we sat at our table, other than being in proximity to people outside of our close family and friends again. What stole my attention and brought me out of my post-containment reverie at this particular dinner was the conversation the table of women were having. After their initial small talk and pleasantries, the women started discussing their individual lives and how things were going at home, especially during the COVID-19 shutdown. Being annoyed at their husbands, sharing both living and working space, the unique experience of working remotely, the amazing and odd habit of wearing "comfy pants" with a dress top during remote meetings, and being home with their children twenty-four hours a day, seven days a week.

Once the topic shifted to behavior, and the monumental task of attempting to understand their preteen and teenage children, my interest was genuinely piqued. I am not attempting to be creepy with that statement but being an educator of fifteen years and a parent myself, this topic was right in my professional and personal wheelhouse. Having children is difficult in itself, and with both my wife and I being educators, we are constantly surrounded by them and all of their successes, quirks, amazing abilities, and maddening behaviors. We are also consistently in various parts of schools with adults who spend their professional lives amongst teenagers. Teachers, when together discussing their students, naturally tend to discuss the frustrating behaviors they witness: missing work, not studying, teenage drama, apathy, and cell phones… cell phones… cell phones!

Cell phones are a real problem in schools, but there is a bitter irony listening to a veteran teacher complain about phones while scrolling on their phone and pausing mid-sentence as an unexpected notification is displayed, only to realize they were in a conversation and now cannot remember what they were saying or even the topic being discussed. That, dear reader, is the crux of the phone issue within the classroom.

Teachers, historically trending as more studious teenagers during their time in school, often fail to understand why students do not care about even the most engaging lesson, not to mention disruptive behaviors they may display while in class. I have always attempted to understand why certain students act, behave, and feel the way they do. I feel it is an important part of my job to understand the emotional side of what my students are feeling and how that affects their performance in school. I am far from alone in this feeling as a teacher, but often when these observations are shared with other teachers, especially the more seasoned, it is met with eyerolls or curt dismissals of, "they just need to apply themselves or they will never be able to get a job!"

This reaction can be worrisome, but it is far from unfathomable. Teaching is hard! I know, I know… many of your thoughts immediately jump to holiday breaks and summers off for teachers, but as someone who is "in the arena," the job is… exhausting. At times, even crushing, but the teaching profession does have the ability to be exhilarating and uplifting. It is hard because you are constantly trying to prove to teenagers why the lesson you are sharing with them is important and applicable to life. Now remember that historically, teenagers struggle to think that anything—unless that thing is directly affecting them negatively or positively in the right-now—is important (we will discuss this in more detail later).

Teachers are also dealing with 25–35 unique personalities, mood swings, silly and immature behaviors, missing work, grading, defiance, mandated professional requirements, and parents who think their little angel could, or would, never fail to turn something in or curse at one of their friends in the middle of class. We also stress and hope these same teenagers decide to care enough to try on the day of the state mandated standardized test, which often is factored into our professional evaluation. All of that I just listed is just from one class in a typical seven class school day!

Exhausting!

With all that teachers must do to complete one class and then repeat it six more times just to get through the day, it is understandable to receive eye-roll reactions from other teachers when attempting to connect teenage behaviors to personal feelings and experiences. If you manage people in your profession or know someone who manages people, you have most likely heard similar statements about adults who are "not applying themselves" in the workplace.

Due to experiencing and understanding the frustration and unwillingness to look for a deeper meaning behind the issues most decried by teachers, I continued to search for true understanding of modern teenagers. but it wasn't until that post-COVID evening that I realized I needed to work harder to grasp why teens behave, think, and feel the way they do when they have experienced adults laying out the proper path right in front of them.

The table of women had moved to discussing their own children and many of the similar behaviors that "drove them nuts." I don't want you to think that during this conversation I was merely ignoring my wife while on a dinner date. With my back to the table in mention, I was able to let her know that they were fretting about their own kids, and as we are both educators, and have two teenage children of our own, she was also interested in eavesdropping on a bit of the gossip. (Like the sages of old always said, "The couple that eavesdrops together, stays together.") One woman was talking about how she could not understand how her son did not even seem to care about the things he openly expressed his love for. She explained to her friends, "Jack LOVES and is so good at soccer, but anytime we try to tell him he should go outside and practice, he either rolls his eyes or completely flips out on us!" All of the friends at the table agreed, chipping in anecdotes about how their teens also seem to "flip out" at small and random requests. One friend even exhaustively emphasized the point saying, "It's gotten to where my daughter is so moody I have to do a mood check to decide what I'm going to ask her because I don't want a screaming match to break out right when I get home!" She continued to explain, "I used to have to do that with my momma when I was a kid to make sure I didn't get a beatin'… but I'm the parent!"

The expressed lack of understanding of their own flesh and blood really struck me and ushered in the realization that these same statements echoed through my mind and had been said before in school break rooms or faculty meetings where one teacher may stand up, after a new directive is explained from the administration about dealing with student behavior in a more progressive way than previously, and declare, "but I'm the teacher!!"

I must also say that the women at the table near us expressing how little they understood their own children made me personally feel better. My wife and I have felt and said the very same things at times with our teenagers. She has even said to our friends in the past, "With me teaching 8th grade and Jordan teaching high school, I thought we would be prepared for raising teenagers, but we were not!"

We were not alone, and you never really know if your friends you share these feelings with are being truthful when they comfort you. Explaining, with that sympathetic look and pat on the knee, that all parents feel that way with teens, or if they are just taking pity on you during a frustrating time.

Adults, of any station, are shaken to the core when children whose care they are charged with question or defy them. It naturally brings into question their own roles and the very bedrock of the cultural system we as people rely upon. This is not meant to sound overly dramatic, and the shaken feeling often happens subconsciously, manifesting itself in anger as the adult attempts to reestablish their authority. We see this in the classroom—although hopefully at a much slower and more professional pace—and in our homes as very natural teenage defiance is interpreted as a threat and disrespect. This natural teenage defiance is a way for teens to distinguish the order of the world and find their own place in that order while also attempting to make sense of the situations around them.

The vulnerability and frustration of the mother yelling "But I'm the parent" opened a floodgate of emotions and the conversation at the table behind me moved through several topics: teen dating, performance in school, behavior around the house, and nonsensical acts that elicited both laughter, head shakes, and facepalms, such as one teen who decided to cook a frozen pizza while still in the box, nearly engulfing his entire kitchen in flames.

His rationale? Every time he ordered a pizza it was delivered both hot and in a box.

Facepalm.

The topic of cell phones and social media continued to be sprinkled throughout the parts of the conversation I could hear, and the mothers were utterly lost about what to do or even think about those issues. This same line of thinking, or more accurately, confusion and frustration, is also found throughout schools with teachers. We all love our phones, don't get me wrong, but when it comes to phones and teenagers, we are in uncharted waters. You hear teachers say, "all they care about is their phones" and "I fight them trying to be on their phone all day long." The same statements were made by the mothers about how monitoring cell phone use and misuse in their homes was a never-ending battle. Social media, and watching our students and children navigate that new minefield, produced the same refrain from both parents and teachers. One mother explained, "It's like she's two different people! One with us at home, and one on her dang Instagram account!" Another mother frustratedly responded, "Alexis can be so happy and then a text or some message will come across her phone, and her whole mood changes!" She then stated, almost embarrassed, as if allowing her daughter to have a phone had violated the parental duty of protection, "I feel like I should take her phone to keep her happy."

These statements struck me profoundly because I realized that some of the issues and stress that come from dealing with teenagers as a parent, teacher, or teenager are not coming from the age-old battle between two different generations. Rather, these are elements of us, as a people, existing in a new age, a time of connectivity and information with our children on the front lines. Smartphones and social media are the main weapons, and our children and students have targets across their backs. Teens are going through the turbulent waters of maturation with new elements of technology and connectivity that none of us—of a certain age—could even dream of when we navigated through the same tumultuous teenage years.

Previously, I stated that tension between teenager and adult was "natural." I am not attempting to give a pass to that defiance but rather to understand so it can better be confronted and understood to help the adult/teenager relationship. Adults have the values and beliefs that have been instilled in them by their parents and experiences. This belief or code allows humans to be predictable to each other, and with that predictability, we can cooperate and even compete in an orderly fashion to reach our goals. Shared beliefs help simplify the world and our roles in it, allowing us as people to know what to expect from each other.[1] Teenagers constantly challenge the set code because the young naturally evolve and have different experiences, which can threaten or change the current established belief systems of adults. This very dynamic causes a natural tension between adults and their belief in the established code and teenagers attempting to change that code to match their values. Since the accepted code and the values attached to it are challenged, making the world seemingly unravel at the seams to adults, it is easy to take a nihilistic approach to the world and plainly state that our society is ending or will end due to the apparent wants and values of youth. I said this is easy to do as an adult, and if you think about it, you actually hear this more and more from adults. Notice how many friends, family, or colleagues mention—almost flippantly—how our society is falling apart consistently, especially after some youth-generated movement is being discussed. It is easy to become nihilistic when a group—especially a group widely seen as not equal to the current majority—attempts to challenge and change your values and code. Being easy doesn't mean it is correct.

As adults, we are making the mistake of trying to put a square peg in a round hole. Applying the same parenting and teaching techniques that were used on older generations, frankly, does not reach modern teenagers as it may have in the past. The code for twenty-first century teens is changing from everything to information attainment, school importance, dating, career, and societal views. It is challenging coming to terms with this, as seasoned adults are supposed to have the answers since we have already been through this part of life, but with the explosion of technology, information, and connectivity, the journey through life for twenty-first century teenagers is very different than it was for previous generations. Step one is to accept that.

My revelation hearing this conversation on that post-COVID evening and combining my years of experience as an educator was thus: we simply do not understand, at an adequate level, Gen Z and the twenty-first century teenager.

> We simply do not understand, at an adequate level, Gen z.

It is an incredible act of hubris to presume we possess this understanding solely because all of us were once teenagers ourselves. This further revealed to me that each student walks into the classroom or our homes wearing two backpacks. The first backpack is filled with the standard folders, textbooks, pencils, knickknacks, and treasures of that student (a cleaning of my eleven-year-old's backpack with him revealed that everything I thought was trash, was in fact, a valued artifact that should be kept and protected). We can all see and interact with this backpack, and it is normal for them to have. The second backpack every teen carries is invisible, but it is far from empty. It is unique to each child and contains the multitude of emotional elements that have made that student who they are today. It is filled with self-image issues, worries of being bullied and the agony that follows, taking care of mom who hopefully gets out of bed today, wondering which version of dad walks

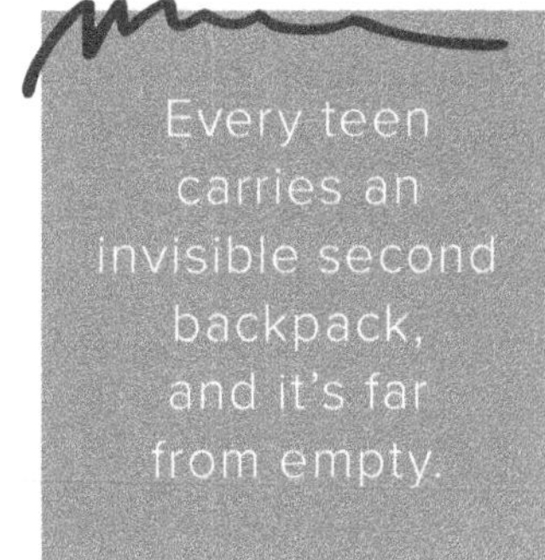

through the door this evening, relationship issues, intimate desires, academic stress, trust issues, eating disorders, anger issues, peer pressure, and so much more. The weight slumps their shoulders, is constant, and cannot be neatly packed in a locker or hung on a hook. Our youth are dealing with issues previous generations did not have, could not fathom, and could not prepare for as now-parents and leaders. Technology and social changes have amplified the challenges younger and older generations did have in common well beyond what older generations experienced. I realized we need to open and explore that second backpack by first, recognizing it exists, and second, understanding what it may contain so we have the possibility to lighten the load for our teenagers.

Hopefully, as you are holding this you have started the journey of accepting the fact that Gen Z has a very different journey than previous generations had and that all our children are wearing two backpacks. Accepting and being open to those revelations creates the long and winding road to producing a better understanding of modern teenagers. After hearing the conversation of the mothers in the restaurant and the revelation that followed, I realized there is a lot of work to be done. To start down the pathway of understanding, I set out to research many of the topics that make up and affect our teenagers today, so you did not have to.

The following chapters will cover topics such as breakthroughs in neuroscience so we can first understand how the brain functions, especially in our teenage years. This will help as adults to give a true scientific reason why the teens we interact with may seem moody, anti-social, forgetful, and disengaged to name a few. It is also impactful to investigate what causes behavior in general from a neural standpoint so we can cease to see it as purely random acts and instead become aware there are chemical and environmental motivations to all behavior. Examining the neuroscience and research will hopefully also help us understand why and how we often react the way we do to many of these teenage behaviors. How many times have you, as an adult, or even for my teenage readers, gone into a conversation resolved to not have it turn into a conflict and it quickly evolved into a screaming match? My guess: this happens more often than any of us would like to admit.

The impact of cellphones and social media will also be discussed. These items are unique to the twenty-first century teenager as companions to their development, and it is important to identify how they may both positively and negatively affect teens in terms of emotional development, peer relations, intimate relationships, and academic performance. Take a moment, and with as much clarity as possible, remember back to when you were a teen, with all of the emotions, fears, and changes you were experiencing on a daily basis. If you have those memories clearly in view, now imagine if the bully who tormented you—I believe we all had one in some shape or form—could follow you home and continue your torment. Sadly, with the connectivity provided by cellphones and social media, many of our teens face this issue daily. With cyberbullying, most adults' lack of experience with such a modern phenomenon and the nebulous nature of cyberbullying has led to a consistent pattern of adults overlooking or downplaying teenager claims of being bullied online.

Aside from attempting to impart the carbon-copy teaching, parenting styles, and values that were used in the past, it would also be disastrous to attempt to not understand the very real differences males and females naturally have in terms of maturity, academics, natural drives, and behavioral patterns. Therefore, the differences between males and females are also important to investigate and understand. How many of us either have or know children who are from the same family, experience the same parenting styles, and have the same opportunities as they grow, but because they are different sexes they act like, and legitimately are, completely different people?

Parents and teachers share a symbiotic relationship with each other. Each affects our teens. One helps to mold and guide them while at school, the other while they are at home, and both focus on and care for the hopes and well-being of our children. Because of this unique relationship between people who are basically strangers, the role teachers and parents play in teenage development begged to be understood. Adults in these roles make limitations and rules, often derided as oppressive, but rules are an ancient part of humanity. One of the most important allegorical stories in the Bible is the story of Moses and the golden calf. The tale reminds us that without rules, when we are left to our own devices, humans are quick to find the most convenient pleasurable pursuits and tend to worship qualities that may be beneath our true values. And those were fully developed adults! Attempt, at your own horror, to imagine how unchaperoned teenagers may behave in that same situation.

How do our actions affect modern teenagers for their long-term development and in the moment? Adults have an active role; we are not simply reactive agents to their behavior. Reactionary interactions are not sufficient to properly raise a teenager and be a part of their development. We must understand that every interaction with a teenager is molding who they are and possibly who they will be. As one student bemoaned at my door after walking down the hallway and receiving comments from every teacher about fixing their outfit to follow school dress code, "Man! It's like I have my own parents and then ten extra parents all telling me what to do and wear all the time!" Adults matter to teens, positively and negatively.

Emotions, how they are formed, and how the second backpack is filled with them will be investigated and explained. What creates and forms the emotions with which teens walk into our homes and classrooms? How can we understand and navigate those emotions to help teens feel understood and accepted? Hopefully with understanding, we can stop creating the easy path for natural defiance (and subsequently, punishment) by demanding they act as adults assume they should. What is anger specifically as well, and how do we as adults feel and deal with it compared to how our teenagers do? As one student stated to me in a moment of anger that left me speechless (anyone who knows me, especially my wife, will explain that rendering me speechless is almost an impossible task in itself), "With all the shit I have gone through just this morning, do you really think I care AT ALL about the French Revolution or an English essay?!" I felt small and ineffectual after hearing this. Prior to this I felt my subject and I were important. Firstly because it is my career and I have worked hard at it, but secondly, and more importantly, because I do believe understanding history provides so many skills other than the obvious memorization of facts. History is a blueprint to us as a people, but I digress. At this moment, I realized I was attempting to talk about long past events and this particular student was carrying a second backpack bursting at the seams with emotions, hurt, and anxiety from his life in that very moment.

Finally, our current society, the events that are happening, and how they affect twenty-first century teenagers will be discussed. Society affects us all, but to sincerely understand how our teenagers are developing and growing, we need to pull back and see how the events of our world are aiding or harming that development. Has it been a peaceful time period? Is there division, war, and unrest? What social trends are guiding teen development? How are the adult generations handling and reacting to those trends? Technology, and how teens are ensnared and harassed by technology, is important to investigate as it often brings generational divides which creates increased tension and misunderstanding between generations.

We often see these same questions reveal themselves throughout history, especially in the art of the times. Artistic styles and themes reflect the world around the artist. Times of war create dark, violent, or revolutionary themed artwork, music, philosophy etc. J. R. R. Tolkien's masterpiece trilogy *The Lord of the Rings* reflected his time in World War I; with the orcs and forces of evil representing the very real forces of industrialization and war, while the hobbits, the Shire they cultivated, and the elves with the forests and valleys they occupied reflected pre-industrialized times of agriculture and respect for nature. Times of peace create bright pieces, uplifting music, literature and philosophy focused on progress and the future, or the nostalgic work of romanticism.

The world we live in matters!

Let me say that again so we all fully understand. The world we live in matters! It matters to the older generations who helped to form it, to developing youth who live in it and will inherit it, and to the future generations who will be affected by it.

Please, do not let the topics and the research scare you away. Research is a balm, capable of healing the wound of change emanating from the transition from childhood to the teenage years. My intention is to cover these important topics but to also explain them in an easily digestible manner with humor and hopefully entertaining anecdotes, stemming from and containing actual quotes from my students over my years of educating teenagers (all names used in any anecdote have been changed to protect those students and their families). I have and will continue to gladly perform the hard research, so you do not have to.

I hope that this book helps to open the door to the understanding that our youth are different than we originally believed. That means we must continue to work toward building an understanding of them and their needs. I hope this work also starts meaningful conversations about teens and the two backpacks they carry and how we can cease to think of teenagers as smaller empty vessels that are easily filled with our older values, beliefs, rules, and expectations. Together we can grow into the realization that they are both sophisticated and immature, complex beings who have their own unique set of values, beliefs, stressors, humor, and sources of joy. I hope it brings conversations between adults and teens. These conversations will be hard and often seem pointless at first, but if they are had, they will bear fruit. After all, are not the hardest endeavors often, in the end, the most fruitful and joyous?

This work has been an enlightening journey, and I appreciate you taking it with me. Now, let's begin to open and peer into the second backpack our teens carry.

2

Bruh, I'm Built Different!: The Teenage Brain

The brain is the organ of destiny. It holds within its humming mechanism secrets that will determine the future of the human race.

—*Wilder Penfield (1963). "The second career: with other essays and addresses"*

The twenty-first-century teenager may seem to be a separate species altogether with their attitudes, sureness of any opinion they develop, creativity, impulsivity, and behaviors. Even teenagers themselves believe they are quite different from other people in their lives. I cannot tell you the number of times I have been told, after telling a student to stop or they may get hurt, or that they need to study or they will fail, "Bruh! I'm built different, bruh!" The human brain is the same for all humans in terms of its structure and makeup. After all, by the age of two, human brains are already approximately 85 percent the volume of an adult brain.[1] So to all teenagers; you are in fact NOT built different... bruh.

So, if by age two our brains are already 85 percent of its fully mature mass, how, and in the name of all that is holy and sacred, why are teens so different in their thinking and behavior? That ever-frustrating difference for teenagers is when and how—"how" meaning the part of the brain that is maturing and the timing and speed of that maturation—their brain is developing and the effects of that variable development on every aspect of their behavior and lives. Moods, beliefs, affections, religious commitments, music tastes, food tastes, romantic preferences, beginning political ideologies, self-image, academic beliefs and work habits, are all some of the parts of teenage life that will be contemplated, experimented, and possibly decided during this pivotal period of life and brain maturation. The importance of the teenage years is exhaustively made clear by Dr. Robert Sapolsky in his book *Behave*:

> Think about this—adolescence and early adulthood are the times when someone is most likely to kill, be killed, leave home forever, invent an art form, help overthrow a dictator, ethnically cleanse a village, devote themselves to the needy, become addicted, marry outside their group, transform physics, have hideous fashion taste, break their neck recreationally, commit their life to God, mug an old lady, or be convinced that all of history has converged to make this moment the most consequential, the most fraught with peril and promise, the most demanding that they get involved and make a difference. In other words, it's the time of life of maximal risk taking, novelty seeking, and affiliation with peers.2

What!?! Seriously? Those all seem like really important parts of our life to me! To make them all start to be contemplated, experimented, and decided upon during such an unstable time period is absolutely terrifying.

As terrifying as that fact is for teens themselves to understand, parents and teachers need to know this is natural, normal, and we will survive! Even if we come out the other end looking like we were sucked into and spat out of a jet engine. Teens going through all of the aforementioned changes while their brain is not fully cooked yet is as natural as the unspoken rule that every eleven- to thirteen-year-old boy knows; one should avoid words that start with "s" at all costs when in public or around girls! (For those who don't know, any word spoken starting with "s" during the early years of puberty leads to the embarrassing "voice crack" where your newly deepened voice unexpectedly leaps back to how it sounded at age eight. One crack like that at the wrong time and you're cooked!) I believe I managed to not say the word "shirt" or "sure" for an entire year while in public.

A meaningful understanding of just how important the teenage years are to building who we will be the rest of our lives will function as a map as you navigate these perilous years (if you are a teen reading this) or help guide teenagers through this period (if you are an adult in their lives).

With crucial elements of life being decided during the teenage years, understanding the basic structure, functions, interaction of regions, and development of the brain is helpful to better understand how teens behave and feel. Knowledge of these brain elements reveal how teen development affects them; it also has the potential to reveal how they may affect us, the adults charged with their care, who often are left to tread in the wake of their lives.

Investigating if we can change our own brains (that, my friends, is a hot newish buzzword you may have become aware of from commercials or social media ads called *neuroplasticity*), the techniques that have success with teenagers, what the newest neuroscience has uncovered, social perceptions of neuroscience, and how to parent the teenage brain will also take us deeper into both the labyrinth of the modern teenager's brain and the depths of the second backpack.

Brain structure

I know you did not expect or want in the slightest an anatomy lesson covering the brain! For this brief explanation of brain structure, I promise a degree in biology or physiology is not required to follow along. I will also refrain from using heavy academic or neuroscience terms, so you do not have to have the ol' Google machine working overtime as you read. I don't expect you to be able to give a lecture over these topics. For any teacher reading this section, many of the terms presented will most likely be the same terms you have been inundated with the last handful of years during professional development and faculty meetings... if you were paying attention, because all of us use that time to try to catch up on planning and grading. Many of the recent neuroscience topics concerning teenagers have become woven into the pedagogy of education and parenting (we will discuss the popularization of neuroscience findings as both good and bad shortly).

My intention is to provide every reader with a deeper insight into how new science, research, and understanding of the teenage brain actually explains how the twenty-first-century teenager thinks, and why they may behave the way they do. Hopefully, this new research and information expels some fears of this tenuous time, allowing us all to be a bit more informed as the physical structure of the brain is important to understanding teens and how their brain operates. Therefore, to work to gain better understanding, let's do this together.

The brain, like any other part of our anatomy, has distinct parts and regions. Each part controls specific elements of our bodies and the functions of our minds. The most basic units of our brain structure we will be covering are the brain stem, the limbic region (comprising the hippocampus, and the amygdala), the cerebral cortex, and the prefrontal cortex. Now, to picture your brain, and how these parts interact and work together it's helpful to use the "hand model" expertly explained by Daniel Steigel.[3]

Use your hands to imagine your brain

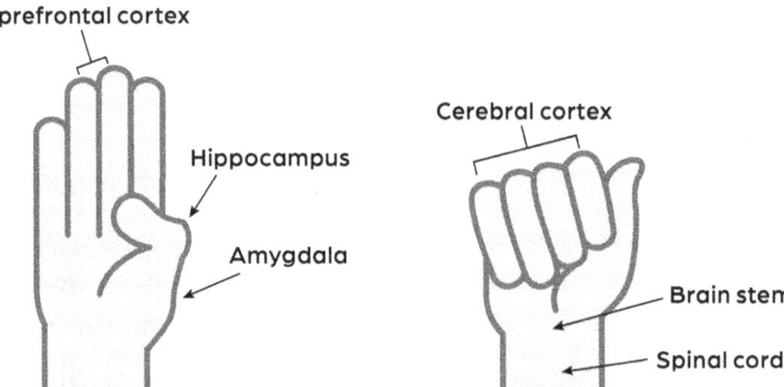

Hand model courtesy of Dan Siegel

Adapted from D. J. Siegel, Mindsight

As you are looking at the model above, your wrist acts as the spinal cord, coming from your backbone, which our brain rests upon. The open palm is the interior brain stem, and to visually orientate you, the back of your hand acts as the back of your head in this model. The limbic region, wonderfully performed by the thumb placed in your palm in this model, lies deep within the interior of our brain. To complete your own hand model, curl your fingers, making a fist with your thumb inside. Your curled fingers over your thumb represent your cortex. Your middle two fingers represent the prefrontal cortex, the star of the teenage brain, which we will discuss in detail later this chapter. The brain stem (wrist), the limbic area (thumb in the palm), and the cerebral cortex (wrapped fingers), are referred to as the "triune brain." These units of the brain integrate, or link together, their activities creating "vertical integration," meaning these units "talk" to each other and react based on what they are experiencing at the time.

Now that you can form your own brain using your hand, this can be used to impress your friends, coworkers, or family the next time you want to show how much you know about the brain of your children, students, or yourself.

> *Teens reading this; if you show the brain hand model to your parents, I promise they will be impressed. I would even dare to say they will be a bit relieved that you are paying attention and learning something. You may even want to lead with this bit of knowledge before you ask them for permission to do something, cash, or to buy you something! Food for thought.*

Let us investigate deeper into what functions each part of your new brain-hand model performs to understand how each part works and what job each carries out inside our brains.

The brain stem

The brain stem is in charge of many of our most basic and ancient functions. It is the part of our brain that keeps us going and helps to protect us. The brain stem controls our basic states of stimulation: sleep, hunger, sex, and our waking lives. This region of the brain is also responsible for the fight-or-flight response to stimulation. The fight-or-flight response is a physiological (body reactions) and psychological response to threatening or traumatic situations. This simple but powerful response system is a critical reason for the survival of our species throughout the centuries.

When you find yourself outside on a dark night because your dog, Fido, stood at the back door whining, with that adorable head tilt, alerting you he needs to use the bathroom, and a terrifying noise emanates from the woods near your house, your body reacts. The hair on the back of your neck stands up and your heart rate increases. Feeling these changes, and the anxiousness the influx of adrenaline into your system causes, you quickly gather up your dog and sprint into your house, regardless if old Fido went to the bathroom or not. In this instance you just experienced your flight response!

This response has also been found to be the cause of most anxiety or panic disorders due to overly frequent, intense, or inappropriate activation of the fight-or-flight response.[4] People with anxiety disorders often misinterpret, through no fault of their own, the very natural response to situations as a dangerous situation itself, causing deeper anxiety and even panic. Anxiety is not a disease itself. It is a tornado siren, blasting through the silence to tell you something in your life is off. Maybe you haven't slept enough, your diet is bad, you haven't actually connected with a real human being in a long time, or the only joy you feel is when that notification pops up on your phone saying, "Your package has been delivered." When those things are your reality, your brain will tell you something is wrong anytime you feel stressed, which for most of us can be all the time. Many will misinterpret this as anxiety of being around other people, driving, or just leaving your house. Remember, anxiety is the alarm, not the problem.

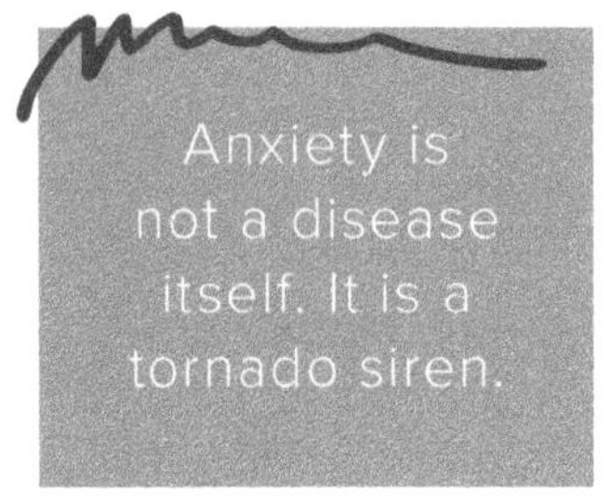

Recently, the fight-or-flight response has been adapted to include several other stages someone may go through when exposed to a dangerous or traumatic event including: freeze, flight, fight, flop, or friend.[5] These reactions can happen to physical stimuli but can also be responses to psychological stimuli, such as someone who is afraid of heights experiencing an increased heart rate and becoming sweaty as they exit the elevator onto the rooftop bar for a friend's wedding.

We all know what the first three reactions are in the fight-or-flight response, but many may not be familiar with what "flop" and "friend" are. To "flop" is much like freezing—think of when a cat notices another cat and it becomes rigid and statuesque—but instead of becoming rigid or statuesque, your muscles become loose, and your body becomes floppy. Interestingly, this reaction aids in reducing the actual physical pain and damage of what may be happening to you. Picture in your mind one of those slow-mo videos of a crash test dummy behind the wheel as the vehicle slams into a wall. The dummy's body is loose and flowing, moving with the impact. Compare this to how most humans would react in a similar scenario: arms and legs both locking as they press against the steering wheel and brake pedal preparing for impact. Your mind can shut down in this stage to protect itself from psychological pain as well.

The "friend" stage of our response system tells our bodies to react by calling for a friend or other people to help; this is why we often scream when we see something awful or terrifying. I always think of my wife riding in the car with me. As she scrolls her phone she looks up and sees the brake lights of the car in front of us (I have already seen the lights well before her) her brain thinks we are going to rear-end the other car, so she grabs my forearm resting on the console and draws in a sharp breath. She was in the "friend" stage hoping I can deliver us from danger by not hitting the other car. Of course this scares the bejeezus out of me, thinking that she has seen something I missed.

In this stage we can also attempt to "befriend" a person who may be dangerous by pleading, bribing, negotiating, or placating them. Our brain's prime directive is to keep us alive, and the "friend" stage is a perfect working example of that directive. In a dangerous situation we will offer, or promise, almost anything for a slim chance to survive.

The brain stem also identifies how we respond to threats to ourselves. This is the decision-making element of fight-or-flight. The threat is not immediately dangerous, and we are more in control in this instance. Our brain stem assesses the threat or perceived threat and then decides on one of the stages listed above. If our brain is in survival mode, it becomes reactive, where emotions and action guide our decisions.[6]

Hint: most teens are often in survival mode due to their thicker frontal lobe and developing brain, stress, and either environmentally or self-imposed external factors.

Finally, the brain stem is paramount to our internal motivational systems. These systems help determine when we need food and what food we may be craving, if we need or desire shelter, our reproductive urges (who we are sexually attracted to or when we are aroused by someone or some situation), and safety. This region of the brain works with the limbic area to force us to act on these motivational systems. When you are going about a busy day at home and all of a sudden, a deep desire to eat strikes you, that is your brain stem letting you know you should eat. Working in tandem with the limbic system to match craving with movement, almost immediately after feeling the urge, it seems as if you are magically teleported to the open refrigerator with all the delicious options laid out before you.

My limbic area and brain stem must be super active late at night as I find myself in front of my magic, teleporting fridge way more than I would like to be.

Story Time: A tale of two responses

Early in my career, I was working at a rural middle school teaching seventh-grade social studies. Across the hall from my classroom was the eccentric eighth-grade social studies teacher's class. As the bell rang to begin the next period, I lingered in the hallway for a few seconds to make sure no stragglers were coming out of the bathroom. As I started to pull my door closed to begin class, I overheard a commotion coming from the eighth-grade class across the hall. I stopped, aiming my attention across the hall to listen more closely. As the commotion became more pronounced, I suddenly heard the eccentric teacher bellow out, "Y'all stop it!" Upon hearing her startled plea, I rushed to her door and a wide-eyed student opened it for me.

I burst into the room to find two eighth-grade boys fighting on the far side of the room. They were more wrestling with each other in that clumsy middle dance that acts as a placeholder for when they get older and really start throwing punches. As I was working to get around the classroom's large rectangular tables, which were set up in a big square, another eighth-grade boy —Jaxon, who played football for me on the middle school team—sprang to action and wrapped up the larger boy like an octopus from behind, his arms and legs wrapped around and intertwined with the larger boy's arms and legs. As Jaxon wrapped him up, he also leaned backward and pulled the larger aggressor to the ground and off the smaller boy, whom our larger aggressor had pressed against a table and had received a few real punches.

For anyone who has ever been in a classroom when there is a fight, it is a pretty chaotic scene. This fight happened before seventh and eighth grade students had camera-equipped phones, and our school still had a policy where if a phone was seen during school hours it was put in the office safe for two weeks. Fights now consist mostly of amateur camera men/women standing around documenting the fight, hoping "it will be a good one" so they can share it with their friends or, God forbid, upload it to popular fight accounts on X or Instagram.

With the absence of cell phones, this was an old-school classroom fight. Some kids stayed where they were while others quickly moved away from the sloppy wrestling match, jeering the students, while the classroom teacher—who again was an eccentric veteran teacher of twenty-five years or more—yelled at the boys from behind her desk. This only acted as an accelerant for the combatants and spectators, adding to the noise and chaos of the situation. The young man who jumped out of his chair and wrapped up the much larger boy activated his "fight" response of fight-or-flight. He assessed the situation and decided to attempt to break it up. I asked him later that afternoon at football practice what his thought process was. He sheepishly looked at me, hoping he was not going to get into trouble and said, "Coach, I didn't really even think or know what I was doing. I didn't want them to fight or try to swing on me, so I thought I could just wrap one up and y'all would come help." He acted. His brain stem had him jump into the fray to stop the potentially dangerous situation.

The other response I noticed while Jaxon was stepping in was shocking to see compared with the other commotion happening in the room. A female student was sitting near where the brawl ended up. She grabbed her pencil pouch and binder to get up from her seat and move away with the rest of the students. A violent push from one of the boys put the fight right next to her. In that moment her brain stem activated her fight-or-flight response. Her response to what her brain identified as a threatening situation was to freeze. She sat back in her chair and looked straight ahead with her eyes wide, and her pencil pouch clutched tightly in her hand extended toward the combatants as if she was offering it to them. It was unsettling to see. As soon as the fight broke up, she blinked several times, relaxed, and went completely back to normal.

This one altercation provided two visceral examples of how our brain stems can activate our flight-or-fight response in very different ways. Freeze, flight, fight, flop, friend.

Limbic area

The limbic area, your thumb against your palm in the hand model above, includes both the amygdala and the hippocampus. It's tasked to work with our brain stems to create our emotional and behavioral responses. For our behavioral responses, our limbic area controls our most basic survival needs such as feeding, reproduction and care for our children, and the emotional interpretation of our fight-or-flight responses.[7]

Since we are discussing teenagers, we all know their emotions and control of those emotions, or lack thereof, are a constant area of concern. We have all felt those out-of-control emotional responses—even though many of a certain age when dealing with teens may believe, "we never behaved that way"—for situations that seemingly did not call for such an emotional explosion are all the work of this tiny area deep within our brains. The limbic area is where we explode into anger with little hope to calm down, especially for teenagers whose frontal cortex is not developed enough to fully apply logic to situations. We will discuss how and why those emotions occur later on.

The amygdala, as part of the limbic area, is the key to our emotional responses to many situations, such as fear, anger, anxiety, and pleasure. Its other role is to attach our emotions to our memories. This little guy provides our emotional responses often unconsciously, meaning, as the sentient masters of this world, we get very little say in how we react emotionally. Sweet irony! This is especially true for teens since their undercooked frontal lobe offers little help in regulating those reactions!

Isn't that fun?

The more an event is connected to a strong emotion (fear, hate, love), the easier we remember it. Fear creates some of our strongest memories. Fear-based memories can be cemented in our minds after only a few encounters with whatever scared us in the first place. We all have several memories, from almost any age, where we can vividly remember a terrifying situation.

You were chased or bitten by a dog at age five: memory is clear as day. The time you were separated from your parents in a store, fair, or amusement park: you can still feel your heart beating rapidly and the terror from thinking you wouldn't ever see your mom and dad again, or you can still smell the funnel cakes as you remember being jostled by the crowd as you squirmed through it, hoping for a glimpse of your parents.

Fear creating strong memories is an important evolutionary survival skill that creates emotional and physical responses based on that memory throughout the rest of our lives. As Dr. Jordan B. Peterson wonderfully pointed out, "The reason we have memories is to not remember the past. The reason you have memories is if you had something bad happen to you in the past you can figure out what was bad, you can figure out why it happened, and then you can't do that thing again in the future… it is very practical." You very well may still be terrified of dogs, or you develop deep anxiety anytime you are separated from your friends or family in large crowds due to these very old memories. That is evolution at work. An ancient vestigial skill that connects a current real-world event to something that produced fear previously in our lives and warns us to be alert and aware.

The other part of the limbic area is the hippocampus, and it functions as the main memory center of our brains. It helps us connect memories to our various senses. Have you noticed that when you smell a certain smell or hear a certain song, a specific memory floods into your mind? For me, smelling Chanel No. 5 brings the memories of my maternal grandmother, or Don McClain's "American Pie" awakens memories of being five and running around my house like a madman, wearing my Walkman listening to that song over and over.

The hippocampus transforms emotions and the events that caused those emotions into what is called our "episodic memories."[8] In simpler terms, the autobiographical memories of what has happened to us. So, as we said above, the amygdala connects an emotion to an event, and the hippocampus then stores that emotion-driven memory with all of its details into our long-term memory system so we can remember, learn, and react to situations that are similar. These memories act as a "mental time machine" allowing us to revisit past events or remember small details often in striking clarity.[9] The hippocampus puts the puzzle pieces of our minds together. It aids in integrating our experiences to have meaning: emotions, thoughts, body sensations, facts, and memories.[10] This "mental time machine" and experience integration very well could be a unique skill for higher functioning mammals.

Where is Your Brain?

Thinking Brain
Upstairs Brain
Ready to Learn

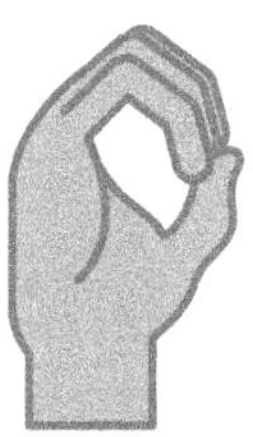

Yellow Zone
Caution Area

Feeling Brain
Downstairs Brain
Flipping Your Lid

The cortex and prefrontal cortex

The cortex is the outer layer of our brains. This section of our brains moves outside of the area of survival, bodily functions, emotions, and reactions to the arena of thoughts and ideas. In our hand model of the brain, it would be your fingers from the tip to the second knuckle. This region of our brain gives humans the unique skill of metacognition: to think about thinking and knowing what you know, and do not know.[11]

Our cortex allows us to say the phrase, "c'mon me, think this through" or it allows us to understand the question, "what are you thinking about?" Even if you were in a daze and may not have been aware you were actually thinking about something, once you hear the question, we can recall exactly what we were thinking and answer. This skill is one humans have always had, but it is a marvel that we are able to understand that we are thinking about something specific.

The prefrontal cortex in our model would be represented by your fingers from the fingertips to the first knuckle. This region of our brain is the key, the passcode to beginning the journey of understanding modern teenagers and how their second backpack is filled. The prefrontal cortex allows us to develop a sense of time—a human trait that somehow TikTok has found a way to completely turn off, if you know, you know—a sense of self, and our moral compass and judgments.

Located within the prefrontal cortex is a sub-region represented by the two middle fingers in our model, which make up the prefrontal region. This sub-region controls impulsiveness, allows us to possess and control both our insight and empathy, and enacts our moral compass and judgments based on the situation we find ourselves in. To be frank, this region and subregion are what make us human. We can hold back or act upon our impulsive thoughts. We can apply past experiences, history, and ideas to the situations we are experiencing or ideas we are thinking or being informed of. We can put ourselves in the situations of others, feel for them and, if we choose to do so, provide them with support and advice. We know our values, what is right and wrong, and apply those in the moment. We are multi-layered, complex, feeling, and thinking beings.

Adults, as you read this and think of the teenagers in your life, you may be screaming out, "Oh my god! My teen/student is missing their prefrontal region!" If you are a teen reading this, thinking of how you or your friends behave, your mind may be sadly declaring, "Aw man, my prefrontal region is broken." Do not worry, our teens possess a prefrontal region; for teens, worry not, your prefrontal region is present and is doing just fine.

The issue is a matter of development, and that in part begins to explain why teenagers struggle, to various degrees, with many of the skills just mentioned. Later in this chapter, we will dig deeper into how and why teenagers' brains are different and why that difference causes them to have issues with impulsivity, empathy, memory, deadlines, and risk assessment.

Neuroscience and what we can learn from it

We now have a working grasp on the structure of the brain in our quest to understand the modern teenager. We can, and should, step into the realm of neuroscience discoveries and insights. As a discipline, neuroscience is the study of the brain's development, structure, and function. We have already covered structure; now the focus shifts to the brain's development and functions. Our goal is to better understand teenagers and the items they carry in that ever-important second backpack. If we, as the adults in their lives, do not understand the basic functions and how the brain develops, we cannot hope to understand them on a meaningful level. Neuroscience can aid us in continuing the journey to that understanding.

Major advances in the field of neuroscience emerged in the 1990s and have exploded in recent years with advancements in neuroimaging and improvements upon previous findings. Many of the advances found their way to teenagers, the classroom, and pedagogy—the method and practice of teaching—as schools are the highest controlled concentration of teens in our country. Which makes the nation's schools a perfect laboratory for observation and understanding of this fascinating and unique time in our development. Some of the major findings of neuroscience during that period were emotions have a great impact on learning, the brain can both rewire itself and grow new neurons, short-term memory is not so temporary, sleep is important for memory, and the varying pace of brain development explains the behavior of teenagers. For now, let's discover what neuroscience has thus far found on brain development, how that development makes teenagers different, and what adults can do to support, making ALL of our lives easier.

Guards at the gate

Neuroimaging has provided intriguing discoveries on the effects of stress and pleasure on our brains. One of our previously discussed structures, the brain stem, is the brain's first sensory information filter system. The brain has filters that act as gatekeepers to the information that makes it to our neural highways. I like to imagine two guards, dressed in a regal uniform, with long spears turning aside to let needed information pass and stepping together and crossing their spears for any information that is not needed. In our waking world there are millions of pieces of sensory information every single second that could enter our brains. If this happened, we would quickly be driven insane due to sensory overload, but these guards only allow several thousand through at a time and only the most needed. The unflinching guard's name is the reticular activating system (RAS).[12]

The information the RAS admits the most frequently is sensory information most critical to survival, such as changes in our environment that could potentially be threatening. Once this information is allowed past the guards, it is sent to our lower brain—which we identified as the amygdala from our previous stroll through brain structure—and our fight-or-flight system is alerted.

Imagine you are out in the woods in the dark of night looking for your dog who ran off when you were letting him out. It's summer, and the woods are alive with the sounds of the night. There are crickets chirping, cicadas buzzing, off in the distance an owl hoots and is answered by a prospective mate further in the distance. Our brains take all of this in, but it is quickly moved to background noise as your RAS has admitted it, found it non-threatening, and passed it off to our cortex where we logically place each sound with its description. But as you are walking, calling out ol' Fido's name—most likely cursing him a bit for making you venture into the dark—even though you are making a lot of noise crunching through the brush and yelling, a few yards away you distinctly hear (almost feel) a stick snap in half. What do you do? You freeze and listen. You may whip around to the noise, but most freeze to make sure the sharp snap of the stick, which only could break if something or someone with weight stepped on it, doesn't turn into the snap of multiple sticks and the sound of something charging at you through the underbrush. Your pulse increases, you can hear your blood rushing through your ears, sweat lightly starts to bead on your skin and palms, and your muscles tense, waiting for action. That, my friends, was your RAS admitting this information, finding it a threat, and sending it to your amygdala and priming your fight-or-flight response. Dang it Fido!

How does knowing what the RAS does help us in understanding our main goal of knowing what is in the modern teenagers' second backpack? Teens' RAS can be activated by stress, fear, and embarrassment and that can cause unwanted behaviors and conflict within our classrooms or homes. The scene I described above is one of actual intentional danger, but for teenagers whose brains are still developing, it can activate for non-dangerous situations.

If you want your child to listen to and internalize what you are telling them, you first have to make sure they are not worried about punishment or embarrassment. For teenagers, these two outcomes are perceived as a threat and the information is sent to their amygdala priming their fight-or-flight response instead of being sent to their prefrontal cortex for logic and knowledge acquisition, as most information does in an adult brain. The fear of punishment for them is real, and their brain is doing its most ancient and primary function—protecting them from harm.[13] Simply put, if our teenagers experience fear, sadness, embarrassment, or anger toward a situation, they will be reactive and fail to internalize any information we adults find important.

We just became more informed about one thing that may be weighing down that second backpack and can now use that to lessen the load. For parents, this means that if you come into a situation where you want to talk to your teen about a life-lesson or something you need them to do, it is important to make sure all of the aforementioned emotions are abated. If you want to explain to them why it is important for them to pick up their rooms, at least occasionally, and you are not already hot under the collar yourself over the issue—which as a parent, I understand how sometimes it is easy to see a messy room and just lose it—it is helpful to take away that fear of punishment. Instead of bringing up the subject with no warning, take the time to let them know you are going to talk about it and that they are not in trouble. Calmly inform them that in twenty minutes you would like to talk about their room, and that they are not in trouble. That twenty minutes provides time for them to work through any fear they may still have. This time allows them to disengage their fight or flight response, activate their prefrontal cortex, and internalize the conversation. Maybe it will lessen conflict at home. Maybe you hear a rational, well-thought-out explanation from your teen, paving a path to a possible solution. Maybe it starts to build trust and understanding. Maybe at first it's a colossal failure and your teen screams at you for violating the sanctity of "their" room and slams the door in your face. It is at least a new way to approach a scenario that you may have been going round and round about, causing stress and conflict for you and your children. Trying, after all, is just us learning and attempting to better ourselves. Don't be afraid to try.

For teachers of modern teenagers, the information is much the same. If a student is filled with fear of punishment, embarrassment, or anger, their brains will not be open to accept the information of the lesson. You could have the best lesson in the world and if one of these feelings is filling their second backpack, they will remember very little or parts that are not important to the overall goal. It is important to know your students and to put work on the front end to limit some of those feelings or positively prime their RAS.

Story Time: Popcorn reading and a pop quiz

This story was shared with me by a seventh-grade teacher who explained how this scenario allowed her to better understand the pressure some teenagers feel while in class completing tasks adults feel are simple but for some teens can become agonizing and fear-inducing.

Working through a new unit in science class, Mrs. Ball wanted to make sure that her students read and understood the textbook material as the unit's subject was very technical. She decided to have her students "popcorn read" the section of the chapter. Popcorn reading is a frequently used technique where the teacher chooses a student to read a specific part of the text, and when that student finishes, they are often allowed to choose the next person to read or the teacher can select the next reader. Mentally, you most likely are already assessing the problems that can arise for some students using this strategy: fear of embarrassment, failure, and reading out loud.

Mrs. Ball planned on letting the kids read their section, and then she would explain a bit and select the next reader based on snaking up and down the rows of desks. Mrs. Ball selecting the readers would keep students from being picked by other students for not being the strongest reader (it happens). She explained the lesson for the day and asked the students to get out their textbooks and turn to the proper page to begin.

Eli was not a poor reader, but the thought of reading in front of his friends was terrifying. What happens if he stutters, cannot pronounce a word, or the worst outcome possible, his voice cracks?! Once Mrs. Ball explained how they were going to read, Eli started counting the number of sections and students before him so he could pre-read the section and make sure he was prepared. While his other classmates were reading their sections and Mrs. Ball was explaining what they had just read and the importance to their class, Eli was counting, sweating, and pre-reading.

The current reader was one student away from him, time for one more quick look through so he could sound professional and smart. As the student before him stopped reading and Mrs. Ball started explaining that section, Eli took a deep breath and waited. Mrs. Ball then stopped and said, "Eli, will you please read the next section?"

"Yes ma'am," he answered confidently.

"Thank you, Eli!" Mrs. Ball responded happily. "We are at the bottom of page 235. You may start when ready."

Eli started reading, and his plan worked perfectly. He knew all the words and how the section flowed. He finished and was very happy with himself and his performance. Then his plan blew up in his face. Mrs. Ball finished explaining what he had just read and told the class that they were about to have a pop quiz over the section they had read as a class. Eli was heartbroken. He had not paid attention to anything else that had been read because he was so worried about messing up and getting embarrassed or made fun of.

The only question he got correct on the pop quiz was the one over the section he read. His RAS was so primed in survival mode he did not even hear any of the other sections, nor Mrs. Ball's explanations.

This does have a happy ending for Eli though. Mrs. Ball, being a caring and connected teacher to her students, noticed how strange this was, and after talking to Eli and hearing what had happened, allowed him to review the section with her and retake the quiz. His score was much better on the retake.

The reticulating activating system (RAS) and novelty

Advances in neuroimaging answered a long-held question about our brains: what other information is allowed through the RAS when there is no threat. Imaging revealed the RAS loves novelty, different and interesting situations, and change associated with pleasure and sensory input about things that make us curious.[14] This is great news because we now have stimuli that we know our teens' brains will react to in a positive way to! We can create strategies to help shift away from teens' lower brain and make sure their prefrontal cortex is engaged. That creates learning and logical reactions... well, as logical as we can expect a teenager to be.

How do we apply these findings about novelty to our lives to help understand what is in our teens' second backpack? Novelty basically means something different and interesting. The RAS allows this input into our brains because, following its survival prime directive, it notices a change in the environment and alerts us. Now you have our teenagers' attention.

"I have my teen's attention? Say less. Mission accomplished!"

Getting the twenty-first-century teen's attention may seem like a victory in itself, but let's grow off that victory. Being alerted by novelty and opening that attention, and possibly lessening fear and anxiety, means progress is possible. To gain this attention and make things more novel as teacher you could: move seats around periodically, modulate your voice as you present, mark key points in different colors, play songs connected to the lesson as students enter the room, put posters up connected to a new unit, have something fun and different on their desk as they walk in, or ask them to make predictions about a clue you have posted. These will all activate the RAS to be alert to the change, and your students will pay attention and activate their prefrontal cortexes to process that change. These strategies can also make your lesson a long-term memory as students will be more willing to share the crazy song you played to start the new unit or what they predicted when a clue was put on the board when their parents ask about what they did in school today. Upon hearing about the crazy song or the posters around the room, the parents' RAS will be activated for curiosity, and a conversation based on your lesson will commence! Parents will naturally have questions about what the lesson covered and the connection the teacher created and your student, their child, will recite what they learned, cementing those facts into their memory. Boom! Learning.

Parents, you could change things up by leaving something novel in their room with a note that could start a conversation. Let's say your child loves pineapple, so you leave a whole pineapple on their bed with a note that says, "Let's have a fresh pineapple snack when I get home and talk about how your classes are going this semester." They would be alerted to the strangeness of a pineapple on their bed and are now actively intrigued. The note shares your intentions, is non-threatening, and gives them time to work through their very natural defensiveness about a parent wanting to discuss grades. Compare that strategy to how this conversation usually works.

The parent knocks on the door of the room, already starting to open it before being invited in because "it's my dang house!"

"We need to talk about your grades," the parent says sternly.

"What do you mean? My grades are fine," says the startled teen.

"Fine? You have a D' in algebra and a 'C minus' in English! Those aren't fine!" the parent says exasperatedly.

"I don't see what the big deal is." The teen rolls her eyes and grabs her phone to check a notification. "Everyone has a 'D' in that class because the teacher sucks, AND a 'C' in English isn't bad!"

"It's a 'C minus,' and none of those excuses are good enough." The parent moves closer and points at her daughter's phone in her hand. "That *thing* is the problem, and if you don't raise them, you will lose it until we feel you are focusing on school!

"You are so unfair! Get out and leave me alone!" the teen wails as she shoves her face into her pillow.

"Get those grades up by the end of the week or your phone is gone!" the parent shouts as she forcefully closes the door.

Does this exchange seem familiar? Have you had a similar conversation even though your intention was not to cause a conflict? That conversation probably will not have the desired effect of addressing grades and hopefully helping your child raise them. Applying a bit of novelty, with the idea about the note and pineapple, starts the process in a less threatening manner and creates an open conversation. Now, as a warning, any tense situation, especially with a teenager, can devolve into a conflict, but it is a better strategy to at least attempt to begin in a non-threatening manner. It is certainly worth a try, and now as a parent or teacher, you know it is backed by neuroscience as well. The conversations may be short or awkward. That is OK. Remember, teen amygdalae and RASes are ready to defend themselves, and their prefrontal cortexes are not developed enough to reason them to not be skeptical of the situation. It will be difficult. Take baby steps until the conversation you desire happens organically. It is well-known across schools of psychological thought that voluntarily—key word here—facing an obstacle that you fear, hate, or despise is curative to our mental distress and makes us stronger.[15]

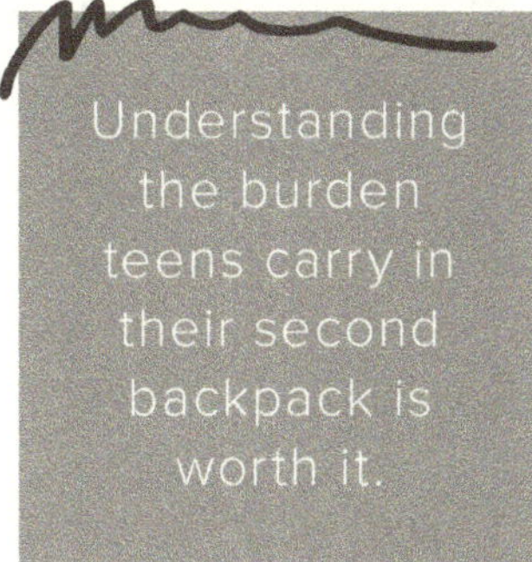

Understanding and lessening— God willing—the burdens twenty-first-century teens carry in their second backpack is worth the time.

3

Parents, Take the Wheel: Driving Development

The adolescent brain is like a sports car with an inexperienced driver—it has all the potential to go fast but requires guidance and skill to avoid crashing.

—Dr. Frances E. Jensen, The Teenage Brain

The biggest collective fear we have when getting behind the wheel of a vehicle is crashing. It is not only the possibility of injury but also the idea of losing control with such serious and possibly fatal consequences, often through some mistake of our own. We have all heard heartbreaking personal stories of tragic car crashes; sadly, a large number of us even have personal connections with these tragedies. We all also have some connection with lesser accidents: fender benders, animal strikes, backing into structures, and swiping that mailbox that appeared out of nowhere. Teenagers, and the way their brains work, seem to live a life of these metaphorical crashes, some smaller, some more serious. The adults in teens' lives are constantly grabbing the wheel to avoid as many crashes as possible, especially larger crashes that may lead to serious emotional change, physical harm, or social and legal consequences. We pray all the while with all our might that when we are not present, to grab the wheel, our teens can keep their eyes forward and the car on the road.

Why do we feel the need to grab the wheel and drive? Is it that teens are clearly in a state of being unable to handle the snares and treasures of growing up? Or is it that they merely do not want to grow up? (Those of a certain age read that last sentence and immediately had the old Toys R' Us jingle pop into their head. "I don't wanna grow up, I'm a Toys R' Us kid!") Both of those are correct, but it is not because our teens are making a cognizant choice. The real culprit takes us back to one of the structures of the brain we discussed in the previous chapter. The prefrontal cortex (PFC), and how it develops, is the source behind many of the behaviors of teenagers.[1]

The PFC, if you remember, controls our higher thinking functions. It is the reason that we can think through problems and is where the skill of metacognition—one of the human superpowers that sets us apart from other animals—is housed. How it develops, and the rate it develops, was found to directly connect to how teenagers think and behave. These scientific findings from the 1990s to the present have shown us that our teenagers are not merely little adults who are making rash, risky, or impulsive behaviors because they do not know any better. Teenagers, because of the PFC development during this stage, naturally cannot make many of the decisions that adults can. It is much like asking a two-year-old to ride a bike without training wheels. It is not that they do not want to ride the bike or are being difficult; they just cannot do it because their motor skills and coordination are not developed enough.

The prefrontal cortex: Cook at 350 degrees for 24 years

As with the other regions of the brain covered in the last chapter, there have been major developments, due to advances in brain scanning, in our understanding of the prefrontal cortex (PFC) and its development. These developments showed us that there are peaks in the amount of gray matter—the areas of learning, speech, and cognition—in different brain regions during separate stages of teen brain development.[2]

What does this mean? This revealed to us that other than our first three years of life, which was previously thought to be the primary window for gray matter growth, there was a second stage of gray matter development.

When? You guessed it: the teenage years!

This was a shocking scientific finding; the teenage brain was not a finished adult brain with teens carrying out risky or impulsive behavior due only to immaturity or hormones. Their brains were not done cooking yet, they were still developing. In fact, shocking as it may be to many, the frontal cortex does not become fully cooked until the mid-twenties![3] As Dr. Robert Sapolsky explains in *The Biology of Humans at Our Best and Worst,* "First, no part of the adult brain is more shaped by adolescence than the frontal cortex. Second, nothing about adolescence can be understood outside the context of delayed frontal cortical maturation."[4]

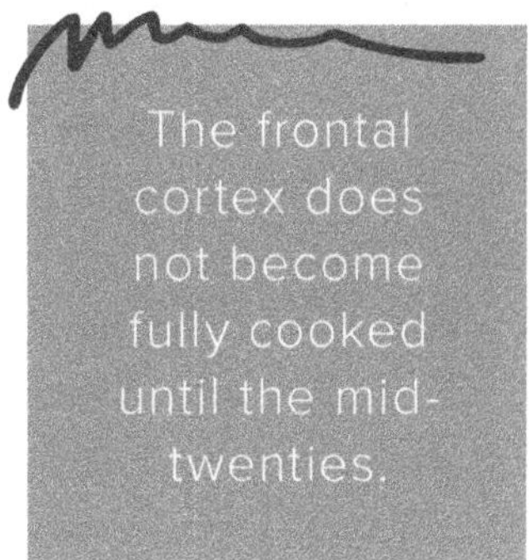

So how does the brain "cook" during early and teenage years? Our brains cook or develop by a process called "pruning": the gray matter cells increase in certain regions making them more dense, and then when gray matter cells are found superfluous, the cells are discarded by the brain, shrinking the amount of gray matter in that region.[5]It may be odd to think of our brain growing in power by making areas smaller (less dense), but the brain focuses on efficiency not density; therefore as a region develops, extra gray matter is shed and only the most efficient pathways are kept. This pruning allows the specific regions of the brain to specialize in the functions they control. The teenage brain has quick cooking in some regions and slower cooking in others. This fact is thought to explain many of the behaviors we associate with teenagers. Because their PFC cooks slower, teenagers have difficulty with processing information, memorizing, regulating impulsivity, and planning.[6]

Sound familiar? Those issues sum up the average modern teenager to a "t"!

> It is very important to understand that many of the behaviors adults identify as signals of maturity and development are less connected to the age of our teenagers and more connected with the time since the onset of puberty. So, when we say to a 21st-century teenager, "You are thirteen years old, you should know how to act!" For a teenager who just started the process of puberty, they are much further from how we believe a thirteen-year-old should act as opposed to a teen who started puberty at the age of eleven.7

As the logic and cognitive powers of a teen are slowly developing, the emotional regions of their brains are working overtime. Imagine an already hyperactive child who has just been given a two-foot-long Pixie Stix and is up long past their bedtime. The teenager is dealing with a battle raging within their brains of competition and malice between their emotional and cognitive regions that causes the inconsistency we often associate with teen behavior. The cognitive centers of the brain are functioning more slowly than emotions, which also leads teenagers to have difficulty understanding others' emotions and perspectives and recognizing facial expressions adults often take as social cues. This is not due to unwillingness but because they cannot. This is why when you give your teenager or student "the look," which is a very clear indication that they should stop a certain behavior, they often continue as if they did not notice or loudly—bringing to public attention the very behavior you are trying to quietly stop—asking, "What?... DAD! WHAT?!"

One example of this is that teenagers struggle to notice irony or sarcasm whereas adults activate their region of the brain focusing on facial expressions and meaning, being able to discern the statement as ironic or sarcastic by noticing the speaker's face.[8] A teen will look at the same face and have more prefrontal cortex activation, therefore missing the facial connection almost entirely. Teachers live this experience almost daily when teens miss statements that have levels of sarcasm. During my years in the classroom, I cannot count the number of times a student asked, "Will this be on the test?" I would sarcastically reply, "Oh no, none of this will be asked." Clearly a sarcastic statement as teachers do not have time with the high number of content standards to cover topics that will not be tested. Even if you add a slight grin after a sarcastic statement to signify that you are teasing, multiple students will still reply wide-eyed and hopeful, "Really, we don't have to do it?"

Of course, you have to do it! That's why you are in school.

I even one time told a class that since our content was based in Germany, our test would be written in German! Many complained and I doubled down (while wearing the slight grin I mentioned above), saying that I could not report they had mastered the content if they didn't know the language of the region. After some time, the class quieted, and I noticed one girl feverishly filling out notecards. I walked over and asked her what she was doing, she looked up, a little annoyed to be disturbed, and said that she was writing words in German so she could study for the test! I was shocked and told her that I was kidding earlier, and needless to say she was relieved but still didn't get that I was kidding or sarcastic.

The slow cooking of the PFC makes teens more worried about and sensitive to being excluded socially.[9] The emotion centers of the brain are working overtime, and being left out is seen as a painful affront and one that teens attempt to avoid at all costs. This is why your teen may "freak out" if they miss a series of texts in their friend group or are not able to meet up with their friends because of other family plans. They are not devaluing you and your family, they are terrified of not being around their peers and the events or gossip that may come out of those meetings, and they cannot help it. This fear of being socially excluded is also why teens worry so much about their appearance. They do not want to be left out of their social circles because of the way they look or because they are not meeting current fashion standards. You may be scratching your head right now thinking of your teen, student, or self and saying, "My teen always wears sweats and a hoodie." You are correct, but for a modern teen, that is the style and dress code for friend group activities. To adults, it may seem like they are "dressed like a slob," but that is the trend. They are also attempting to create their own identity and style, so the clothes the adult favors are just the worst outfit ever. Think of how that same teen, especially females, will change their leggings/sweats and hoodie to a crop top and booty shorts when they attend an event with teens outside their close social circle. They change to attire that will provide them with the opportunity to receive the most attention and acceptance from other teens, especially the opposite sex. It's all about the "fit" and "rizz."

Simply put, the modern teenager has an awful, developmentally caused, case of *FOMO,* or Fear of Missing Out. The development of the PFC representing the end of the teenage years in your mid-twenties is the reason people often change drastically from one who would not miss a social event for anything to a mid-to-late twenty-something adult who relishes a Friday night at home with a movie and a glass of wine. To teens, you—with your fully developed PFC and love of staying home—are now lame. Or as they would say, "mid."

The delay in development for the PFC also creates a period when teenagers lack the ability to cognitively assess what they are doing and to overthink situations where social involvement, sports interest and involvement, musicality, resourcefulness, and creativity are at their highest.[10] The teenage years are the time of life when teens are undeniably more idealistic, creative, and inventive than adults are. The reason? The brain areas that control these abilities are the last to be pruned or developed, so they are not subject to overthinking by the PFC. It is the reason a group of female teenagers are comfortable performing the latest TikTok dance in the middle of a crowded Walmart whereas I get self-conscious dancing in a dark karaoke bar.

Risky business: Dopamine and rewards

I mentioned TikTok above for girls dancing in public places to the newest dance trend, but there is a dark side to TikTok as well. We are all pretty well-versed in the idea of social media challenges as the news media loves to fill their airways and articles with stories of dangerous trends. These dangerous "challenges" are almost always aimed at and produced by teens. The pressure to have a presence on a site such as TikTok is an item in the second backpack of twenty-first-century teenagers. A recent risky trend on the popular social media app was to jump off speeding boats in lakes, often to the popular TikTok "Oh No" sound effect. This trend has been the cause of several injuries and at least four deaths in the summer of 2023. In one case in Alabama, four teens were killed while attempting a stunt such as this.[11] The Alabama Law Enforcement Agency's Marine Patrol Division released an update stating that the deaths were not related to the TikTok challenge from this past summer, but one does have to wonder if that may have been due to legal pressure from the social media site. The question is: why do teenagers attempt risky, dangerous, and sometimes lethal activities?

The Taylor Swift of the brain: dopamine

We must first start with the reward system in our brains and that pesky little chemical that we are all constantly trying to receive even a little bit of: dopamine. Dopamine is a neurotransmitter that is part of our brain's reward system and aids in helping us feel pleasure. For brain chemicals, due to its takeover of our mainstream understanding and discussion, dopamine is Taylor Swift; almost everyone knows what it is and that it is powerful, like it or not. This chemical also plays roles in learning, attention, mood, movement, heart rate, kidney function, sleep, pain processing, and many others.[12]

When you think of or experience something pleasurable, a dopamine release is triggered in our brains, often referred to as a "dopamine rush." This rush brings pleasurable feelings, and we all want pleasurable feelings as much as we can get them. Dopamine is also part of our brain's reinforcement system.

Have you ever been at a get-together and are making your plate at the table containing the multitude of potluck finger foods when you see something you think looks different but may be tasty? You put this new, odd-looking, hopefully tasty morsel on your plate and perform the circus-worthy task of balancing your plate while trying to eat, shoved in a corner while sitting on a shaky ottoman. Finally, as you have tried all the more familiar foods on your plate, you taste the novel little morsel you found earlier. As your teeth work their grinding magic and your taste buds extract the flavor data, an explosion of flavor happens, and you find this new food to be delicious. Many of us may rush right back up to grab more, but some of us may say that was the last thing on the plate and the plate is empty, so no more. Those who can say "no more" have some weird Vulcan discipline powers that I have never mastered.

Now for the fully human majority, we find ourselves, especially at a potluck, grabbing the most delicious item every time we walk by the buffet table, or in the moments we find ourselves disengaged and bored before we know it, we are standing next to the meatballs collecting little toothpicks like it's a new hobby. That is our dopamine reward and reinforcement center of our brain working. You found pleasure (and a bit of novelty since it was a new food in this example) in the food once you tried it. Your brain wanted to repeat that reaction, so it sends out dopamine, and you feel the excitement of thinking about it (craving) and then the satisfaction from getting another one.

Our brains want to allow dopamine to deliver us pleasurable feelings and experiences. It actually trains itself and physically changes neuropathways to make sure we can repeat the actions that produced that dopamine rush. It's the reason why when we post a photo on Instagram or Facebook, we check our phones every few minutes to see how many "likes" or positive comments we have received. Getting likes makes us feel good, and we keep trying to replicate that feeling until we cannot.

In contrast to the rush of dopamine, our brain, which is always seeking balance, has a little self-regulating process called homeostasis. Once we get our dopamine rush and the anticipation and result we were seeking are completed, we get a dopamine dip.[13] Our brain lives out the age-old adage of "for every rise, there is a fall." The dip in dopamine makes you feel disappointed after you have had the pizza you have been dreaming about all day. As awful as this is, it is the brain regulating itself and making us wonder if one more piece of pizza would cause that disappointment we are currently feeling to disappear and the pleasure return. People who struggle with addiction do not know how to reason through not needing another piece, and they continue to go back to the metaphorical buffet table because they are constantly seeking that pleasurable feeling.

Let's look at a teenager in the average classroom. Dopamine, and our ever-increasing knowledge of it, can guide our understanding of our teens in the classroom and some of their decisions at school. Since our brain wants the action or experiences that produce dopamine, it strengthens the pathways that lead to that reward. In class, if students are called upon, or dare I say even venture to volunteer, and they give the correct answer, then the brain naturally reinforces the pathways that led them to the correct answer and the praise that followed. They will now be more naturally motivated to persist through future learning challenges.

However, if the answer is wrong, the brain wants to avoid the uncomfortable feeling that comes from a decrease in dopamine, so it will search to find the proper way to answer the question. This is why teachers must give positive feedback that guides students even when they answer incorrectly because positive feedback will help guide our brains to make the correct connections the next time we attempt to answer.[14] The student that was wrong but received immediate positive feedback will listen to the next student's answer, and if they answer correctly, the brain will strengthen those pathways that lead to the correct answer. If a student gives an incorrect answer and is merely told, "incorrect," or, God forbid, receives a curt, cold, "Nope!", they will continue to receive a dopamine dip and may avoid answering future questions altogether. Too much exposure to wrong answers without positive feedback and reinforcement will train our brains to not attempt to answer questions because they want to avoid that feeling.

There is a real danger to this. As teachers and parents, we must ensure that we are careful to encourage and explain a proper route to the answer so our teenagers' brains can learn and they, neurologically at least, want to answer and think about questions.

Rewards

Our brains seek out the positive feeling of rewards and experiences that have previously brought us some amount of pleasure, but how exactly do modern teenagers and their developing brains view rewards? Due to their still-developing prefrontal cortexes, there is actually a very distinct difference in the way teenagers view rewards compared to both children and adults. Using brain scanning, children, teens, and adults were asked to perform a task with correct responses rewarded with monetary values of varying size.[15] During this experiment, scanning revealed that in both children and teens, the activation of their PFC was widespread and unfocused. These results were very different from the developed PFC of adults, which was streamlined and led to focused activation of the logic and reasoning section for the level of task and monetary rewards. Remember from previous sections that the child and teen brains have much more gray matter there because it is one of the last brain regions to prune (or lessen the amount of gray matter), resulting in more streamlined neuropathways. There was a distinct difference in the activation of the reward-motivation section of the brain (the nucleus accubens) between teenagers and children. In other words, teenagers were motivated in a different way than children.

As this experiment proceeded, it was found in adults that the size of the reward—be it small, medium, or large—produced small, medium, and large increases in dopamine secretion and motivation. Adults produced the appropriate expectation and dopamine-driven anticipation and pleasure feelings that came from the reward. Children produced the same amount of activity of motivation and dopamine-related feelings regardless of the size of the reward. Kids just liked that they were getting a reward and did not have a variation in how their brains saw the reward.

Shocker here, but teens were different. The scans of the reaction to a medium reward looked very similar to the scans of children and adults. A large reward created a gigantic increase in dopamine anticipation, pleasure, and motivation to continue or work for that reward. What happened when teens received the small award? Remember in this experiment the rewards varied. When given a small reward, the activity for dopamine and motivation in the brain declined! The teenage brain goes crazy for big rewards, far more than adults do, and has negative effects for small rewards for action.[16] Their brains actually make them feel sad and uncomfortable, the same way they do when they get a question wrong! For rewards, teens oscillate between huge anticipation and satisfaction and feeling uncomfortable and sad. They are a car swerving across the lanes, destined to lose control and flip at any time. With their immature PFC, teens stand no chance of allowing logic and reason to limit their expectations versus a hyperactive dopamine system.

We have all seen this played out in real life and probably thought our teenage children or students were just jerks at the moment. You tell your children that you are going to do a family chore session. At my house, we are constantly picking up sticks as our house is surrounded by trees. So, you tell them that if they work hard with minimal complaints, you will reward them. Your younger child immediately gets excited, and your teen, being a teen, seems unconvinced but goes along with the chore with as much fervor as a teen can muster. Once the task is completed, you happily tell the kids you are going to take them to ice cream. Your younger child excitedly says, "YES!" To him or her, a reward is a reward, and it is ice cream after all. Your teen rolls their eyes and says, "Ice cream? That's it?!" Their brain and heightened dopamine system had them thinking that maybe it would be concert tickets or a trip to the beach.

Unreasonable? Yes.

You ignore the groaning and slow movements and focus on the happiness of your younger child, wondering, "Where did my sweet baby go?" when thinking of your oldest. You may even say something very parent-y like, "You should be thankful, some kids do not even get ice cream!" Your teen most likely rolls their eyes again, but, if you are lucky, they stay quiet and finish their ice cream. The experiment from earlier showed us the reward, even though it is very reasonable for the task they performed, actually feels lousy to teenagers.

It is hard to motivate teenagers for this very reason at home and especially in the classroom. As parents to modern teenagers, it is important to understand why they seem so unmotivated. It's a waiting game until their PFC catches up to their dopamine system. The important task for us adults is to make sure we are not adding guilt to their already loaded second backpack for not being as happy as we would like with our rewards and gifts to them.

Risky behaviors

When I was a teenager, I would ride my candy-lime Schwinn BMX bike off of my roof, onto our family's trampoline, bouncing over the protective fence around the pool straight into the deep end, bike and all.. I would deftly retrieve the bike before it sank to the bottom and start the process all over again, thinking, in all my teenage wisdom, "Maybe this time I can add a flip before I hit the water." I even did it once while my friends shot paintballs at me. Genius. Every one of those steps was dangerous, and it never crossed my mind. I shudder to think what my parents would have thought if they would have seen me. This type of risky behavior, with little thought for harm or consequences, is a hallmark of the teenage years, but why? You guessed it, that pesky PFC being unpruned and undercooked at this stage in their development.

Brain scanning and experimentation have shown that teenagers activate their PFC less than adults do when considering a risky action. The PFC is the logic and reasoning center of the brain, so less activation of the PFC equals more risky decisions and behaviors. So, teenagers are god-awful at performing risk assessment due to their undercooked PFC. The issue is not that they are only lousy at-risk assessment but that they personally do not believe harm that may befall others could hurt them.

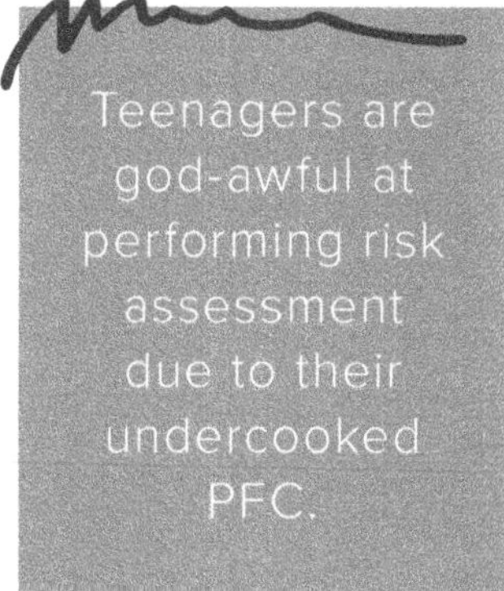

This phenomenon, especially in males, creates the idea that teenagers believe they are invincible. They know their bones can break, but their brains do not allow them to think that could happen to them. After all, bones break in freak accidents, such as during a football game, or freak accidents like wrecking a bike, not during something they actively decide to do. Does that line of thought make sense? Nope! That is how their minds work when considering risky behaviors. Interestingly, studies have shown that teenagers have the same reasoning skills as adults for normal activities, but when it comes to something risky, they have less cross-talk between their limbic region (emotions and actions) and their frontal region (PFC).[17]

An enlightening experiment was performed by Sarah-Jayne Blakemore of the University College of London.[18] She showed how teenagers' poor assessment skills actually form. Blakemore would have her subjects approximate how likely a specific event is to occur (getting hit by lightning, winning Super Bowl tickets): she would then tell them the actual odds of the event happening. Some of the odds given could be positive news, meaning that the possibility is greater than assumed, or negative, meaning the odds would be much higher (or lower if it could happen to the subject). The subjects were then asked to assess their probability again. Here is where the enlightening information showed itself. When asked again to assess their odds, adults internalized the odds and gave responses incorporating the new information. Teenagers, much like adults, incorporated the new data for positive news and gave a new estimate of their chances, but for negative news, the new information did not even make a scratch in their estimates. Dr. Robert Sapolsky gave an excellent example of this teenage phenomenon: Researcher: "How likely are you to have a car accident if you're driving while drunk?" Adolescent: "Once chance in a gazillion." Researcher: "Actually, the risk is about 50 percent; what do you think your own changes are now?" Adolescent: "Hey, we're talking about me; one chance in a gazillion."[19] This example explains why it is so dangerous for twenty-first century teenagers to branch out on social media (we will discuss social media in depth in Chapter 5) or to partake in online gambling. They cannot fathom that they may be victimized by an online stranger or lose all of their money on a bad bet. It must be an anomaly, and they will return to the behavior again assuming the negative outcome could not happen to them again.

In summation, teenagers take more risks because they often act on a gut feeling instead of rationalizing the negative effects or they will overthink and not act on a gut feeling as they should. Teenagers took longer in an experiment to answer questions over negative situations ("Should one catch their own hair on fire?") than their adult counterparts because it took longer for their frontal brain to find the correct thought.[20] They also are lousy at risk assessment. We cannot solely base this on the lack of a fully cooked PFC or frontal brain. There is also the previously mentioned and age-specific idea of novelty. Adults desire different sensations from our dopamine systems than teenagers do. Teenagers want to swing off a rope from a cliff into the chilly water below; adults want to stare at their car and feel the satisfaction after they have given it a good wash and wax. Novelty is craved by teens because experiencing new and different things is how we develop our tastes for later in life such as music, fashion, personalities, and food. So novelty and risk-taking are hallmarks of the teenage years, but there is still one more factor in why teens may leap off the cliff and onto the rope swing without looking below: peers.

We all know the powers of peer pressure and will examine that more closely in Chapter 4 when we discuss emotions, but the power of peer pressure and risk-taking can be shown experimentally. Adults and teens were asked to participate in a video driving game.[21] One session was performing the driving game alone, and a second session was done with two peers using headsets to comment on their performance and to persuade them to drive faster and make riskier driving moves. The adults in the test had little change when the two peers were added to their performance. The teens on the other hand showed greater activation in their dopamine reward system and started taking riskier actions while driving. Merely by knowing their peers were watching and hearing their voices, the teenage brain believed they would get greater rewards, peer acceptance, by driving riskier than adults. The teenage brain follows peer pressure because peer acceptance, or the thought that their peers may hold them in higher regard and tell others how "cool" they are, was worth the risk.

Story Time: Free falling

In Hendersonville Tennessee, Old Hickory Lake is a popular residential and boating area (Dolly Parton, Johnny Cash, and Conway Twitty all had homes on the lake). On one of the many coves, there is a high cliff that teenagers and adults often jump off of into the deeper water. They are seeking the thrill and novelty of plummeting into the lake.

One summer, there was a particularly long drought, and the water level of the lake was lower than usual. For most serious boaters, this was scary because their boat's prop is always at risk of hitting shallow parts of the lakebed or a log that was formerly submerged. Recreational boaters loved it because it gave them more areas to anchor their boats and walk around in the water while enjoying their favorite beverage without needing to float or tread water.

One this auspicious summer day, several hundred boaters were taking advantage of the shallower and were standing around their boats having a raucous nautical block party. One teen decided to climb up the back of the cliff through the wooded area to reach the top and look over the bay. Once other boaters noticed him on the summit of the cliff, they immediately attempted to get his attention and wave him off because even the deeper area was shallow to the point of concern when jumping from that height. The frantic boaters got his attention, and he sat down at the top and enjoyed the view. Relieved, the boaters below went back to their drinks, dancing, and conversations. Crisis averted, and the party can resume.

While the teen was thinking of jumping, several of his peers had also climbed to the top of the cliff and had now reached him. They started doing what teen males, and some females, do. They were teasing him about not jumping. They explained it was still probably deep enough in a certain spot and told him since he was first to the top that if he jumped, they would jump as well. Seeking novelty, the dopamine rush of flying through the air and plunging into the cool water, and the respect of his peers (and hopefully the attention of some of the girls in the group), he moved closer to the edge. Boaters noticed him back near the edge and looking like he was preparing to jump started to wave him off once again. He knew they were concerned, but with an undercooked frontal region of his brain and the influx of dopamine, the prospect of the new experience, and the influence of his peers behind him, his poor PFC stood no chance to infuse logic and reason so he would conclude that this was an awful, dangerous idea.

He took two steps back and bolted forward off the cliff toward the "deeper" spot his "expert" peers pointed out. His shirtless, Viper sunglasses-clad male friends threw their arms in the air to celebrate his bravery. The air rushed over him and the water rushed upwards toward him as he fell. Dopamine flooded his brain, and a wave of euphoria washed over his body... until he hit the water. In the moments of euphoria, he forgot all about the water being more shallow than usual and did not pull his legs up to the proper "cannonball" position. Foolishly, he stayed in the "pencil" position with his legs pointed straight down.

His legs pierced the water and went straight to the surface below, impacting at great speed and breaking his tibia and fibula in both legs. Under the water, he screamed in agony and reflexively kicked his mangled legs to bring his head above water; all he got for his effort was searing pain and no movement toward the surface. The pain brought panic, and he forgot to thrash and still tried to kick his legs, which brought shockwaves of pain until he passed out underwater. He was in shock and floating in stasis below the surface. Luckily some of the onlooking boaters saw him jump and headed toward him. He was pulled to the surface by responsive onlookers and pulled to safety. He could not get in a boat with his shattered legs, so he was slowly dragged behind a Waverunner to an area paramedics could get to.

The undercooked frontal region of this free-falling teen's brain, desire for the dopamine rush of the novel experience, and the pressure of his peers made his poor PFC useless and resulted in a very risky, dangerous decision.

Parents as de facto frontal lobes

We have covered and learned about the structure of our brains, rewards, and dopamine systems; undercooked PFCs and risky behavior; and peer pressure (covered deeper in Chapter 4), all using the latest scientific information from neuro-scanning and neuroscience, to better understand teens and what they may carry in their second backpack. Now, we will use our new understanding to discuss what parents and adults can do to help lessen the load in the second backpack in these areas. Parents, you very well may have to take on the role of actively being your teenager's frontal lobe while theirs is still cooking. You will have to act as a support system in a different way than you assuredly already do, helping to guide them through development. This is why this chapter and the previous chapters have been so crucial to make sure we understand that they are not just "acting out" or not thinking, but that they are caught in a hormone and dopamine-filled maelstrom all while having a frontal lobe that is not yet ready to aide in the crucial decisions they will make. Before we can do this and figure out exactly how you will be their frontal lobe, let's first make sure that we are not creating an expectation based on our biased perceptions and, therefore, propagating some of the least desirable behaviors of the modern teenager.

Making the monster: perceptions of development

Opening a new area of knowledge from scientific advancements always brings in changes that are heralded as "breakthroughs" and "revolutionary." The brain, and teenage brain, have been no exception, with the advancement and application of neuro-scanning and experimentation using said scanning in the field of neuroscience. Scientists understand that new methods, technologies, or techniques can provide new understanding and major breakthroughs, but realistically, using them often delivers several more questions than they do answers. That is the purpose and goal of science: to find the absolute truth through experimentation and testing and to have your findings possibly proved wrong by new advances. The public, and especially parents, hope new advances and findings bring concrete answers and solutions. For the newly discovered knowledge of the teenage brain from the 1990s to the present, parents and parenting professionals hoped neuroscience could explain "standard" teenage behavior. More importantly for parents it was hoped, and often assumed, it could provide answers on how they could be good parents for their teenagers.[22]

However, when researching such a topic with wide-ranging effects on our society and understanding of the teenage years, there was a chance that many of these findings could seep into the zeitgeist of society and confirm, rather than challenge, the current understandings of self, the development of others, and society. With such advancements, it is a realistic viewpoint that neuroimaging has been a large factor in the fundamental change in how we think of ourselves and others. This is often referred to as neuro-realism, where neuroscientific research is used to make a certain phenomenon "real" or proven.[23] In our case, teenage brain development and their behaviors.

We all breathe a sigh of relief when we find out that we are not the cause or to blame for an issue in our lives. It is very natural, and parents and parenting professionals breathed a very deep sigh when neuroscience revealed that the teenage years were unquestionably unique, and, therefore, many of the most alarming behaviors were because of teenagers' uncooked PFC.

The whole premise of this book is to better understand behaviors that teenagers struggle with while also learning the other issues they are working through that are filling their second backpack to make it heavier. Can the influx of neuroscience in the realm of common knowledge reinforce our beliefs of teenage behavior and therefore create a self-fulfilling prophecy of bad teenage behavior? This is a worry because we, as a society, should be using neuroscience much in the same way I hope for this book to be used: to help inform us and develop strategies to better the lives of our teenagers and ourselves. If we only refer to the teenage brain in negative terms concerning aspects such as impulsivity, risk-taking, moodiness, and immaturity, then we are laying the groundwork for teens to express these behaviors freely with little concern. Sadly, this is what we often see currently. I have seen so many parents shrug, frustratedly sigh, and soberly declare, "teenagers" when their child partakes in a stereotypical teenage brain behavior. Instead, like we have previously discussed, we should focus on understanding those behaviors and helping our teens make the best decisions based on that knowledge instead of the old tactic of demanding obedience based on autocratic parental control.

In 2019 a study was published covering the perceptions of the teenage brain from both parents and teens themselves.[24] It was first found that the idea of the teenage brain was mostly associated with the undesirable behaviors mentioned above. Parents also closely connected the teenage brain to increased risk-taking as well. It was also found that parents have more negative beliefs about the teenage brain and that teenagers correctly predicted that adults would think negatively when asked about the teenage brain. When teenagers agreed with the negative connotation about their development, they were more prone to show risky behavior than teenagers who did not believe their development had negative attributes. Teenagers had a stronger focus on the positive aspects about this time of development, but by being aware of the negatively held beliefs of their actions during this time, they were more likely to behave in line with those beliefs, especially with risk, impulsivity, and academic performance. Some parents and the majority of scientific literature agreed with the positive aspects of teenage brain development. So, the question is: if scientific literature, teens, and many parents believe this could be a positive and growth-driven period in our development, then why is there such a saturation of negative beliefs toward the teenage brain?

The findings showed that teens' views on their development affect their behavior. If they think our society and adults expect them to drive recklessly, experiment with drugs and alcohol, be moody, and struggle academically, then they will do those exact things. Why? Because there is a built-in excuse, and it's easier to lean on that excuse than to put in the work to avoid all of the above issues. Neuroscience proving that the teenage brain is, in fact, physically different was treated as a definitive breakthrough, showing there was a reason for typical negative teenage behavior. These topics that permeate our society must not be treated as simple scientific findings and casually put out into the world. Rather, they should be carefully explained to the public to ensure false narratives about the topic are not born. Otherwise, stereotypes will be created, and the true findings will not be used for the greater good. The findings concerning the teenage brain are still dealing with people's children and humans jump to conclusions about their children with little evidence to prove their assumptions. Case in point, how many future MLB players are declared by proud moms and dads while their child shows some prowess on the baseball diamond, but is still in elementary school? It is a lot in case you were wondering.

Our society and the media took the studies and created a self-fulfilling prophecy and many could argue a convenient scapegoat. The societal collective sigh of relief explained teens' brains are different and work differently; therefore, they act differently, and there is nothing we can do. Many who should have been working hard to use this knowledge and create better systems to accommodate teens and the scientific findings felt they were let off the hook. It is the equivalent of realizing your vehicles brakes went out and confidently declaring, "The brakes are out, so there is no point in steering!" We have helped create the monster that lives in our homes. Instead, we can use this knowledge of their brains being different to help them navigate this crucial period while also still allowing them autonomy and freedom to develop. The gifts of neuroscience should be used to confirm that as the adults in their lives, we **CAN** and **SHOULD** step in and lighten their second backpack. We have two clear options; help our teenagers develop to their fullest OR sit back, throw our hands up, and frustratedly declare, "teenagers".

I know which option all of you reading this will choose.

Two ways to be your teenager's frontal lobe

We know that we cannot sit by and rest on the stereotype of teenage behavior if we want to faithfully help our teens and students. How do we step in and help them without the conflict, screaming, and slamming doors we fear during this time? You may be asking yourself right now, "My teen won't even do my simple requests, like showering, without yelling or rolling their eyes at me. How can I step in and do even more without making everything worse?" Those are great questions and real fears. The first step in alleviating those fears is knowing you now are armed with the knowledge of how our brains work structurally and many of the reasons our teens express the behaviors we see during this period. The second step is realizing that since our teenagers have an under-cooked frontal lobe you will have to step in, becoming a type of external frontal lobe for them. Finally, you will have to decide which form of frontal lobe is best for you and your teenager.

There are two possible roles you can take as your teenager's external frontal lobe. As we have all most likely read parenting books, articles, and magazines, we know that parenting is a fluid job, requiring flexibility and situational reactions. The same understanding applies to the two following roles. Sometimes you will need to merge or switch between the two as the situation you are dealing with unfolds, but it is important to have one as your default style so you and your teens can come from a place of consistency.

The first role is that of guardian. In this role you are the teenager's guardian of stimulation. The guardian role uses the well-known levels of emotionality, risky behavior, and impulsivity of the teenage brain to identify and warn of possible dangerous behaviors. As the name implies, this role focuses on protection from risks. The main risks for the developing teenage brain in this role are any behaviors that could physically damage its natural development.[25] External addictive behaviors such as alcohol and drug usage, eating disorders, gambling, and newer digital behaviors (cyber bullying, gaming, porn, and social media). These possible damaging behaviors are all easy afflictions for the teenage brain because they prey on impulsiveness and the desire for short-term rewards (a.k.a. dopamine dump), which are basically the calling-card teenage behavior. Parents embodying this role are empowered to be more direct and protective with their teenagers. This role is achieved by establishing clear rules and expectations for these behaviors. Guardians have two main strategies to reach this goal: prohibition (in the case of alcohol and drugs) and motivation of your teenager through rewards (which may need to be novel because we must remember that even sensible rewards make teens feel lousy) or punishment.

Key to the guardian role is establishing rules and sticking to those rules for behaviors such as gaming, phone usage, and social media. That's right, if you make a rule where your teen must charge their phones at night in a different room so their phone is not a temptation to stay up late, then you must stay strong and continue that practice regardless of the myriad of excuses and possible confrontations this may cause. It is easy to hear well thought out reasoning our teenagers may give us coupled with their mature looks to loosen some of our rules, but since their brains are a "work in progress" and vulnerable, the guardian must stay strong. As Horsthuis explained, "For a long time, our expectations of teenagers were too high. We wanted to take them seriously because they look so mature and because they themselves want to be taken seriously. But the fact is that you cannot expect them to be all that reasonable."[26]

To embody the guardian role, you must have clear rules, clear prohibited activities, reasonable expectations, and established punishment and rewards for your teen. It is also important to not shy away from confrontation and to seek out possible difficult conversations. You are the guardian of their development, acting as a de facto external frontal lobe for your teen; be sure to be a beneficent, caring guardian.

Guardian parenting example—Cell phones and bedtime:

"Son, it's ten o'clock. You need to plug your phone up in the living room and start getting ready for bed."

"Dad it's only ten, I'll plug in at ten-thirty and go to bed."

"No sir! You need at least thirty minutes without a screen so your brain can settle down and you can get enough sleep," Dad says as he steps fully into the door to make sure his presence and meaning are not misunderstood. "Remember, sleep is so important at your age."

"None of my friends put their phones away this early!" the son says sitting up on his bed facing his dad to make sure his dad sees how serious he is. "You are going to make me look like a loser!"

"You can catch up on anything you missed in the morning and while your friends are tired and distracted in school you will be alert and learning!"

"Bruuuuuhhhhhh! You treat me like such a baby! I am fifteen years old, not five!" the son bemoans.

Taking a calming breath, lowering his voice, and sharpening his tone so his son knows the decision is final the father explains, "Be that as it may, son, you know the rules and if it isn't plugged in within the next five minutes you will lose the phone for the rest of the week!"

"Ugh!" the son angrily declares as he sluggishly gets up and heads to the living room to plug in his phone and get ready for bed.

> "Further, it's all too easy for teens to make dumb or destructive mistakes when they're up late and their neurological brakes are tired. Why allow

> conditions where your kid can make an impulsive, but lasting, error at one in the morning?"
>
> —Lisa Damour, *The Emotional Lives of Teenagers: Raising Connected, Capable, and Compassionate Adolescents*

The second role to become the external frontal lobe for your teen is the role of coach, which asks the adult in the teenager's life to coach them through the various stimuli they will face. The coaching role asks adults to find a way to get the best out of their teenagers, and its driving aim is to help the brain develop by giving teens the freedom to experiment and try the novelty of youth. The unique way the teenage brain works due to development is seen as an "opportunity." As Leef! Magazine stated about this parenting style, "A teenage brain not only fancies excitement, but by doing so it has an opportunity to learn to deal with problems and feelings of fear."[27] Parents should still set rules and expectations, but these are not for true prohibition or protection. The rules in this role are designed for teens to rebel against in a controlled manner. In stark contrast with the guardian role, coaches do not punish or reward with rules but rather wields them to focus on negotiation, intrinsic motivation, and collaborative decision making.[28]

The coach role requires adults to think along with the teenager, using the adult's experience to clarify consequences and then mutually discuss what effects the teenager's actions could have been. The guardian role saw teens as pseudo-adults who may look the role but are not mature enough to take on adult matters; whereas the coach role seeks to stimulate the teenage brain. Adults in this role should not fear their teens making adult decisions but should guide them through them with the understanding that adult situations help make them mature and guide their brains through this developmental stage. Risky behavior, social experimentation, creativity, idealism are all traits that are not closely watched and guarded but are beneficial and help to create the unique adult your teen will be one day. The *coach* embraces the parts of the modern teenager that make most adults cringe, only stepping in to ensure their decisions help them excel in the area it applies to.

For most adults, the guardian role seems much more familiar considering if you are a certain age, most adults were raised in that manner. We may add a bit more understanding and less, "Because I SAID SO!" to the role because most of us have evolved past that specific style of authoritarian parenting. Clear sets of rules, rewards, and punishments with slightly lowered expectations, and open communication are still logical for us, but teens may need more conversations and explanations as to why decisions are being made. The coach role provides this but may create feelings of dread while reading what is expected of the parent during that role. It ventures toward the "permissive" parenting style, which has limited rules and allows students to "figure things out themselves."[29] We have all seen parenting styles such as this and maybe thought, "Those parents just let their kid do whatever they want!" This is not entirely true because an important element of the coach's role is open discussion and not being afraid of possible confrontation. You absolutely must be a coach to your teen, NOT a spectator. Get the most out of your teen by coaching them through the teenage years, and do not be afraid if they love really intense scary movies, are experimenting with fashion trends that seem odd to you, or become highly interested in social justice or politics. The *coach* observes, discusses, and guides them through these "trends" so their brain can develop and mature.

Coach parenting example—cellphones and bedtime:

"Son, it's ten o'clock. You need to plug your phone up in the living room and start getting ready for bed."

"Okay Dad, I'm going to finish up this conversation real quick."

"Okay, I am going to go to bed. Make sure to plug your phone in so you can get some rest. Make sure to not stay up all night."

"I'll go to bed as soon as I am done. Goodnight Dad," the son says without looking up from his phone.

The next morning, Dad peeks into his son's room to find the light still on and his son lying on his bed on top of the covers with his phone next to him.

"Wake up son," the dad says while sitting on the bed. "You have to leave for school in about thirty minutes."

"Er, what?" his son says groggily. "Is it time to get up already?"

"It is." His dad says as he picks up his son's phone and shows it to him. "Looks like you never plugged in your phone and stayed up pretty late, huh?"

Sheepishly his son sat up saying, "Yeah, Jake was upset about a girl, so we snapchatted most of the night."

"I am glad you could help Jake out, but as a growing boy you need sleep. You will have a hard time focusing in school and won't be in top condition for practice after school," his dad said as he started to stand up.

"I know, tonight I am going to go to bed early so I am not tired tomorrow."

"Good son. Remember, it's good to help out friends, but how you do in school falls only on you, so you need to remember to put the phone up and sleep." He started out of the bedroom door but turned with one hand on the door frame. "Problems, especially girl problems, always wait, so they will be there for you to help with when you get up."

"Ok. Jake is on his way," the son said as he pulled on his favorite old hoodie and checked his phone.

We now know modern teens have an under-cooked prefrontal cortex, how their internal reward system works, why they take risks, and how adults may need to perform as a de facto external frontal lobe for them. While filling the role as an external frontal lobe for teens, it is important to select either the guardian or coaching roles based on what type of parenting may suit you and your teen the best. Do not try to be a parent that you are not or become something your teen will immediately rebel against. Know yourself and know your teenager. You may need to merge elements of the two forms to support your teen the best.

Research and parenting books suggest seamlessly switching between the two roles when the situation calls for it. You may need to be stricter at times while also letting go of some authority to allow your teen room to explore this life. You can do it if you know yourself and make supporting your child during this dopamine-fueled, emotionally centered, novelty-seeking time in their life your main goal.

The key is to not obsess about who is really in charge! Everyone knows you are, so just go with the flow, man.

Communicate clearly and set your expectations. We are taking the first arduous steps of this great adventure, transitioning from reacting and gossiping with our friends about how difficult or reckless our teenagers are, to better supporting and understanding them, how they function, and what is going on inside them.

The goal, as always, is to better understand the items teens may carry in their potentially bottomless second backpack. If we know what it currently contains, what may go in it, and how to hopefully lighten the load, we will better understand and support the teenagers in our life.

We are now one step closer to that goal.

Parents, take the wheel.

Batten Down the Hatches: The Emotional Hurricane

"I sit here locked inside my head, remembering everything you said."
— *Staind, "For You"*

Your teenager walks into your home carrying the awful comments making fun of his teeth and acne directed toward his latest Instagram post, the fight he had with his girlfriend over text, the suffocating feeling of doing great on his classwork yesterday but today was a whole new set of work he had to bend all of his energy toward to maintain his grades and basketball eligibility, the words his coach said during the awful practice he had today, and the argument you had with him before he left for school for leaving his plate in his room and forgetting to take the trash out. Heartbreakingly, several times today, dark thoughts, some even toying with the idea of suicide, have crept into his mind.

These moments and the words accompanying them swirl throughout his mind, cruelly coming to the forefront every time he starts to feel peace and settled while at school. A storm is brewing within him, and he has just stepped into your home. The same beautiful eyes that first stared up at you as he was placed in your arms are now staring you in the eye, loaded with the weight of teenage life.

What do you do?

Do you recognize the emotional pain he is carrying in his second backpack? Do you see him as a mini-adult because of his size and burgeoning facial hair—after all, you were part of the argument this morning with him, and you also had a rough day with a demanding, volatile boss as well and you are fine—or do you see your child who needs you to start fresh and just be there?

A storm is brewing, and the clouds on the horizon are dark, brooding, and moving toward you with the promise of imminent danger. All humans fear a storm. It is a deep and hidden part of our ancient psyche, from a time when a storm ushered in a myriad of ways to fall ill or die. Even with all of our modern technology, a powerful storm still gives us pause. It is an instinct buried deep in our amygdala from days before warning systems and strong shelters that whispers to our brain, "pay attention, smell the air; danger is fast approaching." Yet when it comes to our teenagers, we know the storm is inside, but we do not fear it; in fact, we often coax it out because how dare a child take out their emotions on us, their reason for life, shelter, safety, and care. You are not only caught up in the emotional storm of teenagers as their parent, teacher, guardian, or trusted friend, you are a strong part of it. The storm is a swirling wind, bashing together conflicting teenage and parental ideas such as safety, the teen need for belonging, discipline versus novelty, and finding oneself, new experiences, relationships, and structure.

Understanding what our teenagers are carrying emotionally, slumping their shoulders with a weight they do not fully comprehend will help weaken this storm. The question is, do we as their guardians understand their emotions and how those emotions actually affect them compared to us?

The answer, most often, is no.

We treat teenagers the same way we treat an adult who emotionally lashes out at us. With teens however, we add a bit of extra vitriol because we see these storms as defiance and disrespect. What do we do? We rage back at them with an extra shot of incredulity and personal hurt because our sweet little baby is now large, awkward, and talking to you like you were not the person who wiped their butt and kissed their boo-boos. Their emotions are a part of teen development, and they flow through every item stored away and weighing them down within their second backpack.

What exactly are emotions?

Every single person reading this has and knows what emotions are when feeling one, but do we know why they exist and where they emanate from? Emotions are based on our survival, surging to the front of our consciousness after an unconscious evaluation of a situation.[1] The feelings we experience from those emotions are a conscious manifestation of that unconscious assessment. Remember our discussion previously of the amygdala and how it protects us from Chapter 2. We found ourselves wandering through the woods looking for our wayward pup and heard viscerally, almost feeling, a stick snap. The emotion, fear—the oldest emotion we have—fills us consciously from our unconscious evaluation of possible danger. Darkness, the untamed woods, and animal noises equal danger and a constant gnawing of fear to our ancient amygdalae. Add in the sound of a stick snapping from the weight of a possible predator creeping within striking distance, and that gnawing emotion of fear becomes full-blown, terror-inducing fear.

Our other emotions, all which are present at birth, also have functions related to some form of survival, be it social situations to ensure comfort, entertainment, and protection or finding a mate and continuing the propagation of the human species. Much like our senses of sight, smell, hearing, and touch, emotions are important social survival tools. They can often be construed as some annoying human weakness that keeps us from reaching our full potential.

Wrong!

Emotions are the very thing that makes us human. We feel, and it truly is beautiful.

Emotions are what make us human. We feel, and it is beautiful.

The emotions of a teenager burn hotter than those of children or adults. This is clear to see if you spend more than fifteen minutes with any teenager. They experience the extremes of emotion more regularly than children or adults, and with changes happening to them both externally and internally, it is not hard to see why. Teens are shedding the skin of childhood and emerging (slowly) into the body, mind, and responsibilities of adulthood.

Watching the ease of childhood grow smaller in the rearview mirror of life is painful. Teens are insecure because of societal and physical changes happening to them, frustrated over wanting independence and new experiences while being told "you aren't old enough," and coping with the pain and excitement of peer and romantic relationships. Difficulty, frustration, pain, and excitement all combine to create the emotional storm of the twenty-first century teenager.

Story Time: Aren't you going to yell at me, man?

One quiet Thursday afternoon, I was sitting at my desk making lessons for the following day when I heard raised voices outside my classroom door. I perked up to listen and heard the voice of one of my senior boys, we will call him Kaden for this story, yelling at our principal. I opened the door to Kaden marching away from her while screaming, "Y'all just find stupid-ass ways to get me in trouble!" and the principal was scooting after him yelling back, "You know the rules and you better stop walking right this instant!"

Kaden was just beyond my door, and as our principal yelled. He spun around with a wild look in his eyes, pointing his finger at her and screamed, "You know what you stupid bi—. . ." At that moment, knowing both student and principal had reached a point near combustion—both operating solely from their limbic region—I stepped in front of Kaden and put my hands up to the side, palms up, to show I was not a threat. I then placed them on his shoulders to guide him to my room. He stopped mid-insult, fixed his gaze on me and growled, "Get out of my way Dr. Lauer!" I calmly informed him it would be best if he stepped into my room. He looked at me, then over my shoulder at our principal, dismissively huffed, and strode into my room, slamming the door behind him. Knowing my principal was also on edge, I told her that I would talk to him and get him to calm down, so things did not escalate. Through gritted teeth she instructed me to get him calm and send him to the office to see our assistant principal for discipline. I nodded and opened my door to head in.

When I entered my room Kaden was pacing back and forth, saying every curse word known to man—and a few I had never heard before—and had already kicked over a desk. I shut my door and walked right past him to my desk and resumed working. He barely noticed me but starting yelling about how no matter what he did, "they" would find a way to get him in trouble for something. He continued to call our principal several colorful names and rage at how he hates school and everyone in it.

Kaden had a wonderful heart and natural intelligence, combined with a smile and charm that could get anyone to do anything for him… when he was calm. He had a temper and emotional swings, being a bit of a wild child and getting involved with the wrong side of the law for several after-school activities. He also possessed old-school southern manners, always answering with a "yes sir" or "yes ma'am." I honestly enjoyed him as a person, but school, its structure and rules, were not his thing.

As I sat and typed away on an email, he started to calm and really noticed that I wasn't paying attention to him. He stopped pacing, still breathing heavily, and exasperatedly said, "Are you not going to yell at me man?! I just cussed out the principal and kicked over one of your desks!" With that, he sheepishly walked over and picked up the desk and put it back where it belonged. I leaned back in my chair, appearing as nonthreatening as possible, and said, "No sir, I am not. You were upset, and as a senior you know that cussing at the principal is wrong." He stared and me and visibly relaxed. I asked him what had caused the blow-up and he informed me.

His offense was a minor rule violation. Rules of its type often irked older students who feel responsible enough to not need them and did not want the slew of consequences that may arise from violating said rule. His anger, therefore, was not without merit, to a point, and I explained that to him. He eventually put his hands in his pockets, looked down, and said, "I'm sorry Dr. Lauer. She just always tries to get me in trouble!" I told him I understood, but how he reacted only proved any point being made against him. He ended up saying that he should apologize and that he was sorry again. I held him in my room for a few more minutes, talking to him about how we respond to anger, and eventually, he went to the office to receive his punishment but had a successful remainder of the day.

Kaden was caught in the emotional storm of being a teenager. He had strong emotions but could not regulate them and properly think through the moment. Once he was provided some time to cool down and apply reason, his good heart and pleasant nature returned.

It is up to us to not shrug off our very complex emotions but to understand and support them. Let's start that process by examining how emotions are formed during our development.

Who am I? Creating the inner-self and identity

Who am I?
Why do I feel what I feel?

These are questions every human being has asked themselves in some form since the dawn of our species. The phrasing may have reached higher levels of sophistication over the millennia, but the feelings the questions stem from are as old as our species. The emotional journey of every human being has two major periods—on top of the millions of emotional events in between these two events—that shape us emotionally.

The first stage of emotional construction occurs from birth to the age of three. The brain is new and fresh, and most of our neural pathways are created during this period. When you make a silly face and your baby lets loose that adorable giggle, they actually are creating the neural pathway for happiness and associating it with you. Very cool, huh!

The second explosion of emotional construction happens during the teenage years where, as we have previously discussed, the brain reorganizes and starts to prune neural networks to seek efficiency. During these principal eras of development, we begin the process of "self-construction."

Self-construction is the blueprint for our beliefs, values, feelings toward daily life events and people, behaviors that shape our individual view of the world, and how we construct meaning from events. Our brains, once the "self" is constructed, bring in millions of data points from the world and apply those data points with personal meaning, all in alignment with how we construct our blueprint of "self."[2]

Let me explain in plainer terms. It is pretty dang important! Okay, maybe I won't go that simple in my explanation.

Have you ever observed two teenagers who are the same age, from the same area, and have very similar families and upbringing but act and look at events completely differently? I am sure you have. Many of you may be shouting into the pages right now, "Those are my teens who live in my own house!" You are not alone in misunderstanding the reason for those differences. One teenager is outgoing with a smile that lights up a room and loves any new opportunity to be social and involved. The other teen loathes the idea of meeting people and large public gatherings… or speaking to other humans… or sunlight… or smiling. The reason for this difference was some developmental, environmental, emotional, or social event(s) that occurred during these two periods of self-construction explosion.

Like I said, pretty dang important!

Self-construction uses its blueprint to create the inner self. Our inner self takes all of the billions of data points we interact with and funnels those to create a worldview that follows the blueprint created during self-construction. The inner self is critical for two main reasons.

First, it is the very center of our identity; it is "who" we are.

Second, since our inner self is a subconscious construction, we cannot control it, and that fact can cause anxiety, stress, and emotional struggles.[3] Our inner self helps us create the following parts of our personalities and thinking processes:

- **Self-esteem:** the basic personal opinion about yourself and your abilities, how we appear to others, and our skills and talents we possess.
- **Self-consciousness:** The understanding and feeling that you and your behaviors are being observed by others. This often results in anxiety about the impression you are making.
- **Sense of humor:** Interactions you do or do not find humorous and how we deal with stressful situations and painful emotions by finding humor in them and laughing at them as opposed to becoming upset… at least we hope we can do this.
- **Constructive emotionality:** The power to use your emotions in a controlled manner for each situation much like one uses their senses.

You walk in the door of your home and smell an enticing scent. After a few more deep pulls of the air through your nose, you come to the happy conclusion the source of the smell is delicious bacon. Constructive emotionality aids in assessing the emotional situation and matches the needed emotions. This keeps you from giggling while your boss informs the staff that they are all being laid off.

- **Emotional intelligence:** the capacity to know and understand your inner self, your feelings, and navigate the emotions and needs of those around you. This is a very "grown-up" skill. Modern teenagers are learning how to know themselves during this stage of development but struggle to come out of that narcissistic mold until their mid-to-late teenage years.

The inner self does not come from a specific region of the brain unlike many of the topics we have covered. As a subconscious structure of our minds, the inner self is a neuro-social structure that is a product of the environment and social relationships we encounter as we venture through main periods of self-construction: birth to age three and the teenage years.[4] It consists of body, mind, and environment and is a unique aspect of social cognitive beings. Put another way: because we are social animals, we created the inner self with the goal of possessing the ability to present ourselves to others and interpret our environment through a social lens.

All humans yearn to be accepted by others. If we didn't, eccentric mountain man would be a much more sought-after life option!

Identity

Innovative developmental psychologist Erik Erikson created the universally accepted theory of human psychological development using different stages of development and how the inner self is created and refined during those stages. The stages of development are prescribed age ranges, but it is important to note that a person may develop outside of those descriptive age markers. This may especially happen if some traumatic or environmental event occurs that delays development. In each stage a continuum of development is presented where the subject could fall anywhere along that continuum.

For example, in the "Puberty to Year Eighteen" stage, the continuum is identity to role confusion.[5] Erikson explained that during the teenage years, teens are searching for their identity (self-construction/inner self), which is a very healthy aspect of ourselves to find and nurture during this stage of development. Otherwise, teens can become confused with who they are causing internal and developmental conflict. Your teenager or student falling on the "identity" end of the spectrum has recognition of their peers, are beginning to know who they are, and they are developing a sense of who they may become and the values they hold. This is cause for celebration if your child falls on this end of the spectrum.

If your teenager or student falls on the "role confusion" end of the spectrum they: are not sure who they are, tend to be bullied at a higher rate, and struggle to develop a future vision of themselves since they currently do not know who they are.[6] Where our teenagers fall on this continuum affects many of their attitudes and behaviors long into the future. We will come back to this when we discuss attachments.

Since we are on a journey to understand the modern teenager, we need to also understand how creating an identity looks and affects them. Teenagers are developing themselves to fit into the world and find their place within it. These factors make teenagers consumed with how others think of them.

Sound familiar?

The opinion of others is a constant litmus test (or formative assessment for my teacher friends) on who and what they are as people. Constantly worrying about how they are seen by others creates a type of teenage egocentrism, which fascinatingly is universal throughout all races, ethnicities, and cultures.[7] Teen egocentrism generates a very unique world for our teenagers. They view themselves as different than everyone else. In the history of the world, no one has ever had the problems that they have. Sure, you yourself were a teenager dealing with many of the same issues, but "That was like a ZILLION years ago, Mom!"

They will change the world (because only they know how) AND they are facing a unique set of trials that no one could fathom in their wildest dreams.

How many times have you sat down with a teenager to share how they could react more appropriately in a situation because you have already lived a very similar situation, and they acted as if you were speaking a different language and shrugged off your advice? By understanding their development, we can start to realize they are not just being "hard-headed little jerks," but cognitively they are forced to think that you could not understand their specific situation. As odd as teenage egocentrism is—and maddening for every parent—it is an important developmental tactic. It ensures their painfully crafted identity is wholly their own, providing the tools to work through complex situations later in life and not just carbon copying someone else's identity.

Within this unique egocentric world our teens live in, David Elkind, author of *Child Development*, found teenagers create two internal belief systems that allow them to continue to develop their identity.[8] The first belief system is the *personal fable*. The personal fable creates the internal belief that the teenager in question will unequivocally be famous and a legend during their lifetime, loved and adored by people for their talents. Is it starting to be clear why your sophomore son who plays basketball on the junior varsity team went two for eight at the free-throw line last game but still declares with utter confidence that he is "going to the NBA and will be the G.O.A.T!"?

I cannot tell you how many famous rappers I have had in my classes over the years… at least in my students' own belief in their talents. This level of internal confidence generates the teenage ability to try new things and put themselves out in the world to develop their own identity.

The second personal belief system teenagers create during this period is the *invincibility fable*. Remember in Chapter 3 how we discussed the risky behavior of teenagers? Well, the *invincibility fable* is the pesky personal narrative, mixed with the desire for novelty, peer pressure, need for acceptance, and impulsive behavior, forming the perfect mixture to create the mentality for teens to jump off cliffs into shallow water. Teens positively believe they cannot, or will not be harmed, whatever it is that they are doing. How could someone with their talents (*personal fable*) not land perfectly when riding their bike off of the roof onto the trampoline (*invincibility fable*)? Suggesting otherwise to them absolutely makes no sense.

During this period of development, teenage egocentrism also creates an "imaginary audience" whose main task is to observe, critique, and monitor every single thing the teenager does. Imagine the famous iteration of the human conscience in the form of Jiminy Cricket, who acts as a sentient version of your conscience and tells you if what you are planning on doing is right or wrong. The imaginary audience for teenagers is much like that, but instead of a well-spoken, sharply dressed cricket, the teenage version would be a very snarky judgmental version. I like to imagine the character Envy from the Pixar film *Inside Out.*

A typical interaction with the imaginary audience may sound a little something like the following. "You really said, 'You too!' to the cashier at McDonald's when he said, 'Enjoy your meal' in front of all of our friends. OMG! You are so embarrassing!" This mental construction judges modern teenagers and makes them more self-conscious. Honestly, it is the only voice they listen to. It also creates some form of meaning for every situation the teen experiences—"He touched my hand when he passed me the worksheet!" (imaginary audience: *Because you are super-hot, and he must love you!*) or "He saw my outfit and his eyes got big and he looked away like he wanted to laugh!" (imaginary audience: *Your outfit is hideous, and you look like a clown!*). Modern teenagers, as all teenagers of the past have, barrel through their day responding to and interacting with this imaginary audience.

The search for self-identity is the impetus behind the most frustrating and maddening element of living with or teaching teenagers: arguing. It is such a visceral segment of parenting or teaching teenagers that I could clearly picture the physical response most of you had reading that single word, "arguing." Even arguing with adults has a purpose during teenage development. Remember, during this time teens are attempting to find their own identity and reach "identity achievement" where they figure out their beliefs, values, talents, and culture that will become who they are as a person. How do we often find out what we honestly believe in? When we have to defend or clearly explain our position on issues. Now add in a cup of impulsivity, a dash of immaturity, a tablespoon of underdeveloped sophistication and vocabulary, and a prefrontal cortex that needs to be cooked at 350 degrees until they are in their mid-twenties, and voila! A perfect recipe for arguments is born!

Teens use negotiating and arguing to test who they are at the current moment. They push against the adults in their lives to test those beliefs and strive for independence. You may also notice teens switching their viewpoints on topics as they work through their own beliefs, or teens may attempt to say something incendiary to observe how people react. This is a dual tactic as it first fills their need for attention, and second, checks their own beliefs on the topic against how others react. As hard as it is to see in the moment, the fact that your teenager verbally spars with you is a sign of trust; not that they would admit that. They know that you care for them completely, therefore, subconsciously, they make you the anvil that they forge who they are against. And their attitude is the hammer.

Due to their lower sophistication and vocabulary, many discussions about topics such as politics, religion, social issues, and relationships are stymied by criticism, finger-pointing, accusation, hurt, and broken trust. Teens struggle to understand they may hold beliefs and still thoughtfully listen and challenge opposing beliefs with facts or logic. Instead, they often become heated, lacking the proper skills to have a civil discussion. This can be ridiculously frustrating, but now that we are aware there is a purpose to their arguing… over everything… we as adults can attempt to stop falling for the trap and guide them through their thinking.

Armed with the knowledge that teens are attempting to find their identity, the adults in their lives can transform those moments from screaming matches into learning opportunities by staying calm and modeling proper discussion and arguing techniques. The real trick is knowing this in the moment and not losing your cool on them. Again, with all you have on your plate, this can be very difficult, but one that can produce the best results for all involved.

We as adults have the power to transform a formerly hair-pulling situation into one of growth.

Discovering your identity can be exhausting, even more so for someone with an undeveloped logic center of their brain. As teens navigate these turbulent waters, they often fall into four different identity styles: diffusion, foreclosure, moratorium, and achievement.[9]

Starting from the bottom up, achievement and moratorium are the least affected by adults in the identity discovery cycle. Moratorium, as the name describes, is when teens take a bit of a break from constant identity creation and experiment with different experiences, beliefs, and ideas without needing to make a long-term decision about them. This style occurs when teens go off to college or are out of their parent's house as members of the workforce if they do not attend college.

Achievement is the final stage where a lasting understanding of "self" and their identity is reached. Typically occurring after college, once a career is determined as they are starting off on their own. Moratorium and achievement both flourish when our children are out from under the influencing umbrella of their family and friends.

Foreclosure occurs when a teen completely steps out of the whirlwind of identity creation and starts to accept the traditional values and beliefs of the family without questioning or exploring those beliefs. This style sounds fantastic as a parent. You mean my child will simply do and believe as I have? Hallelujah! Beware though, foreclosure is dangerous because your teenager is not preparing themselves for the challenges they will face as adults. They are running plays from a playbook designed for a different era for a different team. The end result may be the teen living at home evolving, over the years, into a directionless adult with few long-term goals living in your basement.

Diffusion is the development style most often observed with modern teenagers still living at home. Diffusion occurs at the moment the confusion of determining their own identity is the highest. The day-to-day process is intense and emotionally draining. Couple this with the fact that the modern teenager has thousands of options to "zone out" of the process. Their brain actively seeks mindless activity to take a break from the swirling, stressful, and evolving thoughts they must conquer to understand who they are. During most of their waking lives, teens are passionate and intense about their beliefs. At times though, they become utterly overwhelmed.

To step away from this intense thought process, teens partake in avoidance activities such as spending hours on social media, playing video games, streaming TV shows, or sleeping. You and everyone else are immediately thinking, "That is all my kid does!" There is a reason you think and feel that. Teens are acutely involved and influenced by peer interaction and relationships (more on this in Chapter 7).

Therefore, they spend most of their passionate identity creating activities during school hours or when they are around friends. Sadly, this means that when they are in our homes, parents and guardians get to experience the time when they are disconnecting from those thoughts and morph into food-consuming screen zombies. Teachers will easily attest how the teens they teach are passionate about fairness in schools—just ask your teen their thoughts concerning their school's dress code if it has one—a social situation that may be discussed during lessons, or the drama of their friend group and burgeoning relationships.

Diffusion is also the reason educators often struggle with trying to reach and create engagement with teens because they are figuring out who they are and cultivating peer and romantic relationships. At the same time, we expect them to care about the French Revolution, algebraic expressions, and the cultural impact of The Crucible. "Old dead guys," - as I refer to them to my students - and static equations can barely hold a candle to the more pressing matters of getting to sit at the "cool kids table," or "Mackenzie thinks I'm hot!"

Sadly, when thinking of school the fact is that a teen can work their tail off completing their assignments in all seven classes, coupled with navigating the social and identity stress of the day, and then upon returning the next day they have to do it all again. That is… exhausting! Especially to reward-motivated teenagers! Is that not the exact reason most adults become burnt out with their careers? Continuous tasks with very little reward other than a paycheck. And our children don't get a paycheck; they get grades and the promise that after twelve to sixteen years they MIGHT be able to make a decent salary. By around fifth grade, most children begin to feel the methodical nature of school, and the lack of tangible reward is pointless and exhausting.

Finding worth in school and the work it necessitates is a common battle for both teachers and students. Many teenagers start to use diffusion even during the school day because they start to become overwhelmed. The current media and public opinion on education is also a factor to consider here. If parents are telling their teens that public schools are bad, teachers do not know anything, or you don't learn anything in school; why would a teenager choose to work hard? Recent political issues in the media have also gone a long way to aid student apathy as well. If a teenager observes politicians, members of the media, and their parents constantly attacking education, then it is easy calculus for them to decide it is not something they value.

A question to consider: are adults actively muddying the waters concerning the importance of education and the opportunities it provides for teenagers?

With that question in mind, now imagine the anger and confusion one must feel after experiencing the demeaning of education and teachers by their family, media, and public opinion when the same teen gets punished when they bring home grades their parents do not find adequate. As adults in the same situation, we would boldly declare the goalposts of our expectations are being moved so we cannot hope to be successful. The thought of disconnecting and taking on mindless tasks when finally at home seems pretty enticing after all of that, does it not?

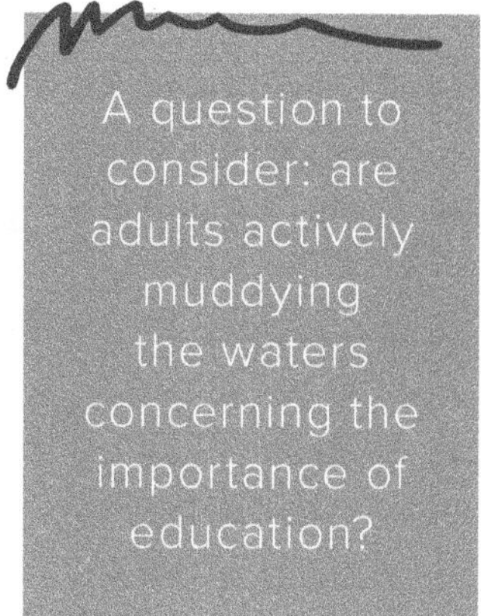

If you are thinking of a teenager in your life right now and are feeling queasy because you are not exactly a fan of who you feel that teen's inner self may be, I have good news for you. Our inner self can change and may always be changing. It is a representation of the totality of our thoughts, feelings, behavior, and beliefs. Our teenagers are molding those aspects of who they are as they develop.

To ease the queasy feeling you may have, understand the inner self can change by evolving our values based on the people we find the most important to us—for teenagers, that consists of their peers by a large margin. More on this and how we learn and choose to react to the people in our circle later. Although you may feel that you are being a real drag on your teens when you harp on them about certain friend choices they make, you are helping them develop a strong and positive inner self by curtailing the personalities they draw their values from. Keep up the good work because even though you receive many exasperated "UGHs" and eye rolls from your teen, you are helping.

The key to that delicate dance is balance and understanding; walking the tightrope of positive guidance or heavy-handed dominance, which could very well create a self-fulfilling prophecy and drive your teen into the waiting arms of the very people you pray they do not associate with. If you avoid that balance and start to veer into controlling your teen not just behaviorally (which is good for an adult to make sure you have established boundaries, expectations, and consequences or behaviors for your teenager), but also psychologically, the results can be an apathetic and passive-aggressive teenager.[10] When psychological control is exerted on a teenager, you are imposing your ideal identity on them. During the teenage years, as we have seen, creating their inner self/identity is paramount to teen development. If that process is hindered or dictated identity and relationship crises may occur during adulthood. If psychological control is applied, the result is the oft-apathetic teenager we fear. Teens in this situation feel they cannot affect their own lives, therefore, apathy grows as they wait for what they need, like, and value, to be dictated by their parents. Much like a plant that has been neglected, psychologically they begin to wither.

Story Time: Sisyphus—rolling the stone of teenage life

In Greek mythology, Sisyphus reigned as the king of Corinth.[11] He was brave, clever, lustful, and deceitful. He found his way into several conflicts during his life where he was able to trick his way to victory. Sisyphus even tricked Death into showing him how the shackles that were meant for him worked and bound the god in his home, temporarily removing death from the world.

Death was eventually freed by the god of war, Ares, and death returned to Greece. Sisyphus knew that deceiving the gods would bring him torment, so he created a plan with the help of his wife to be allowed to return to the living world once he died. The plan worked, and he returned to the living world for several more years until Zeus discovered Sisyphus still lived and sent Hermes to seize and deliver him to Tartarus, the deepest and darkest level of the Greek underworld.

In Tartarus, the legendary punishment was revealed to Sisyphus. Zeus informed Sisyphus that he was charged with rolling a massive boulder up a steep hill. If he was able to push the boulder to the top of the hill and keep it there, Sisyphus would be permitted to leave the underworld. The clever king of the gods added a devious catch to the bargain with Sisyphus. Every time Sisyphus was able to move the massive boulder, with great effort, to the crown of the hill, cruelly, it would shatter into rubble and appear whole at the bottom of the hill, or it would roll back to the starting point of his torment. This was the plight of Sisyphus for all of eternity. Constantly compelled to push this massive boulder up a large hill only to watch it shatter or roll back to the base. Doomed to begin the arduous task again and again.

A former student of mine, Jack, had trouble all year long completing and turning in work when it was due. No matter how many times he was goaded into working on it or helped, he, somehow, managed to not finish it. After several days of doing every assignment and turning them in on time, the encouraging change in behavior suddenly stopped. Assignments were not being turned in or completed. I asked Jack to stay after class and talk to me about the negative turn of events. As he slowly gathered his materials, allowing the other students to filter out of the room, he came up to my desk, and I asked him why he had reverted to his old ways. Jack dropped his eyes to the floor and muttered, "It's just too hard." I asked him if he was referring to the current unit and he flatly said, "No, all of it." I gently nudged him to elaborate further. After a deep breath, he explained to me that he wanted to do well, but it was all so daunting to him. Jack explained that if he did all of his work—a considerable task for him mentally—and turned it in, he felt great. He would go home confidently and feel like he had earned his XBOX or arguing about politics and movies online free time. Sadly though, he would return to school and have to do it all over again. After several days of working on seven different class assignments, trying to stay connected to his friends, and do the chores his parents had for him at home, he was mentally and emotionally exhausted.

Jack did not see the point. If he did just enough work not to fail, then he would have more time for everything he wanted to do.

Jack was a teenage Sisyphus. He was smart and clever but felt he was contently pushing a boulder up a hill only to have it shatter and reappear. I told him the story of Sisyphus and that the top of the hill for him was either the end of each year or in a more macro view, graduation. Looking that far ahead seemed to make his eyes glaze over as if I was mentioning a theoretical place. His brain plainly could not imagine something that far away. Remember the constant need for novel rewards we discussed previously that teens have? My attempts to advise Jack to take life and his schoolwork one day at a time sounded hollow even to me. I knew how difficult that was to navigate even as an adult, and it still did not lessen the exhaustion from all that teenagers are facing.

Jack was facing something many teens face: the lack of understanding that school, careers, and love are all a part of a continuum. We never stop working and adding to those parts of life. Teenagers have a very hard time conceptualizing life as a continuum. Life to teens is transactional. I do something and I get something. We know that is not the case in most aspects of life.

Could this be the main cause of teenagers being disconnected at higher rates from their education? The very nature of the continuum combined with all the other developmental factors they are going through exhausts them and produces a "just do the minimum" mindset. How can we as adults keep their boulder at the top of the hill? What can we do to help to make sure our teenagers are not tormented as Sisyphus was?

Attachments: Setting the stage for our lens of the world

Humans, as emotional and social beings, are born with a natural need to forge meaningful bonds with their caregivers.[12] These bonds are our very first connections to the outside world, and they influence our attachments throughout the rest of our lives. To clarify, attachments are an emotional bond created with another person possessing true emotional meaning and weight. These are far from the superficial attachments we are familiar with later in life. They are ancient and evolutionary, securing our survival when we are infants and informing much of our behavior from our early days to our death.

Attachment theory, first created by British psychologist John Bowlby, assesses our relationships and bonds between people, focusing on the parent and child dynamic as well as romantic partners. Bowlby defined attachment as a "lasting psychological connectedness between human beings."[13]As strange as it may seem currently to any parent that attachment required defining, we must understand the belief previously was caregiver/infant attachment was originally a learned behavior based on ensuring the infant would continue to receive food to survive. Bowlby theorized differently. Children not only desired food for survival but also desired and derived a sense of security from caregivers who are available and responsive to their needs. This sense of security becomes the basis their trust and behavior are erected upon as they explore their world.

Attachment and Bowlby's work were expanded in the 1970s by psychologist Mary Ainsworth. Ainsworth created the "Strange Situation," a groundbreaking study that became the most prominent method for measuring attachment in infants. Children between the ages of twelve and eighteen months were placed in a room filled with toys and their mother. After some time, a stranger would enter the room as well, and shortly after, their mother briefly left the room. Researchers observed the child's reaction as she left and then upon their reunion. The Strange Situation and subsequent studies helped to create four styles of bonding and attachment that explained the driving questions of Attachment theory: "Is there a bond with a caregiver? Is that bond secure or insecure? And from that secure or insecure bond, what form of self did you develop?"[14]The four bonding and attachment styles were: secure, ambivalent, avoidant, and safe and dangerous (disorganized).[15]

- **Secure attachment:** Children in this attachment style can rely upon their caregivers and show distress when separated and joy when reunited with them. Mom leaves the room and the baby cries and looks around but smiles as she returns and resumes normal play. These children also seek reassurance from their caregivers when frightened. Most common attachment style.

- **Ambivalent attachment:** These children become distraught when a parent leaves. Due to inconsistent parent availability, the child cannot rely upon the caregiver to be there when they need them. Considered an uncommon style, 7–15 percent of US children.
- **Avoidant attachment:** Children avoid parents and caregivers, displaying no partiality between parents and a complete stranger. Stems from abusive or neglectful caregivers. If a child is punished for depending on a caregiver, they will learn to resist seeking help as they grow and in adulthood.
- **Safe and dangerous (disorganized) attachment:** These children present themselves with a perplexing mix of behavior seeming dazed, confused, or disorientated. This is a baby you notice wants away when the parent picks them up or resists coming toward the parent. The safe and dangerous style stems from inconsistent parental behavior in which the child may find both comfort and fear with them, creating disorganized behavior. The child grows up and is a "wild card" as an adult.

Attachment styles we develop in infancy mold our view of the world and how we trust as we age. Both are factors adding to the creation of our identity. As children reach their teens, the bonding and attachment styles can produce different personality traits. Secure attachment teens exhibit traits such as the ability to resist peer pressure more successfully, better academic performance, development of healthy relationships, the success of traditional discipline techniques, and better emotional regulation.[16]

Teens with ambivalent attachment can be more easily bullied, are anxious socially, possess difficulty with boundaries in relationships, fear attempting tasks in fear of "getting it wrong," often blame themselves for relationship issues, and need repeated assurances.

Avoidant attachment teens are often loners, which create issues for them forming relationships. They also are emotionally closed-off, avoid tasks that require emotional vulnerability, are disliked or distrusted by peers, and do not respond to standard teenage discipline because they are emotionally detached from anything you could keep them from or take away.

Finally, safe and dangerous teens have the following traits: they live in a state of fear and anger, have difficulty naming the emotions they are feeling at a given moment, have little attachment and fewer boundaries in relationships, need their inner selves developed and regulated, and fail to respond to traditional discipline tactics, often responding with anger or violence.

With the throng of changes occurring in their lives, once they enter the teenage years, the emotional storm also depends on how one deals with stress and emotional regulation.

Teens with secure attachment styles possess a form of self-efficacy when dealing with stressful situations and are also more comfortable asking for help in stressful situations.[17]Ambivalent attachment teenagers tend to be hyper-attuned to their emotions, which causes them to overreact to perceived threats or chance of abandonment. Avoidant attachment teens, just as the moniker states, avoid dealing with anything that causes them distress and will also not seek out others for help. Lastly, safe and dangerous attachment teens present a lack of coherent strategy when dealing with their distress or finding comfort. They figuratively are all over the place emotionally and behaviorally.

Kaden from the *Storytime: Aren't you going to yell at me man?* is an example of safe and dangerous. He could be a charming, lovable, fun person to be around, but he could also fly off the handle, lose his temper, and do something impulsive that could endanger himself or the people around him.

The behavior you are seeing now in twenty-first century teens, be it your child, student, friend, or self, are not random changes from your previously sweet child or student that recently occurred. They are, in part, crafted from the teen's earliest days.

There is hope, though, if any doubt is had about the attachment style created during infancy. A recent study, focusing on displaying teens comforting or upsetting stimuli (pictures, sounds, video clips) and assessing natural physical responses, revealed parenting behavior during the teenage years can change how they deal with emotional regulation. It was found that teens who had recent parent interactions labeled secure were more open to the full range of emotional experiences, both positive and negative.[18]The ability to be open to experiencing, as well as expressing, both positive and emotional feelings creates personal confidence in the ability to face distress and assuage it.

In contrast, teens with avoidant styles physically reacted with a heightened response to negative pictures but focused less on (or avoided) both positive and negative pictures.[19] Safe and dangerous teens, much like previously observed infant behavior, had no recognizable pattern with physical or length of gaze on both positive and negative pictures. Safe and dangerous teens were, again, all over the place emotionally.

The hope I mentioned above to change how modern teens react and assuage emotional stress based on their original attachment style stems from how adults, and caregivers specifically, interact with teens while they are going through the emotional storm of teenage development.

As children leave infancy and march toward adulthood, the established attachment style relationship naturally evolves into a goal establishment and correction partnership. Children and teens need adults to have goals and expectations and correct their behaviors, misconceptions, and emotional reactions. Trust is still the driving factor during the teenage years, but trust now focuses on the confidence the teen has in the caregiver's ability to create security. This trust can be nurtured by embodying open and balanced communication and showing sensitivity concerning the perception of themselves, their beliefs, and their positions during disagreements on fundamental issues. An openness to the teen exploring independence in both thought and speech without immediately being forced to adopt an adult's view or beliefs is vital in creating the needed trust to foster secure attachments.

In summary, to create a secure attachment and allow your teen to be more successful in regulating their emotional responses, adults must work at creating open and collaborative communication while also understanding your teen is changing and exploring independence. That is great news because understanding is exactly what this work is aiming at, and we are well along the way!

You may be saying, "OK, but my teen was super lovable when they were younger and now seems to fall along the safe and dangerous style, and I don't know why. I am terrified." It is important to note that many of these development theories are generalizations and because humans are complex beings. The answer could be that your teen is acting that way because they are just acting that way. Maddening? Yes. However, random behavior is still a part of the human condition. With that caveat aside, teens may become safe and dangerous—barreling out of control—as a reaction to those close to them. Parents become safe and dangerous to teens through sexual, verbal, emotional, physical, or psychological behaviors.

It is very possible for parents to be safe (secure) for the child when they are an infant but devolve into being safe and dangerous when the child enters their teen years. If a father jokes and spends time with their teen but becomes abusive (emotionally, physically, or psychologically) when the teen forgets to complete a chore or performs poorly in sports or school, that parent has become safe and dangerous. When a mother leaves the teen home alone so she can party with friends, or marches aggressively into the school to defend her child from even the most trivial discipline issue; threatening to "have people fired," but also allows an abusive significant other to harass both her and her child, that mother is safe and dangerous. It is almost assured that teens who experience safe and dangerous relationships will have a shattered inner self and identity. Bound to replicate the same safe and dangerous behavior in future relationships and with their children.

Strive, with all your might, to **NOT** be safe and dangerous.

Shelter from the storm: What parents can do

Parenting is hard and exhausting.

Teaching is hard and exhausting.

Adults constantly have tasks needing completion to make our personal world go round, our own emotional victories and trials, and added to all of that is an emotional storm wrapped in a teenage body living in your home or sitting in your classroom. No one wants to add more to the parental plate, but the fact that our own attachment styles and personal emotional issues can undoubtedly affect our teens, has just been thrown onto said plate.

It is too much, and it is very easy to be resentful of life and the teenager in your life. Many choose to attempt to bend their will against their teens, forcing them through the simple parent or teacher-child dynamic to do as they are told and to be respectful about it. Sadly, as well, many decide to give in to their teen's constant emotional barrage and pray that their teen emerges from this stage and becomes their respectful child once more. This is much like many videos circulating on social media sites where a heated exchange is happening between two people and in the background, you see onlookers sitting, reading their newspaper, or scrolling their phone, acting as if nothing is happening until the exchange becomes too extreme. Finally, at that moment, they make the often too-late decision to intercede.

Let's not do that to our children or students. They are the most important endeavors we will ever take on. Knowing that and now possessing a working knowledge of the teenage brain, as well as many of the items they carry in their second backpack, let's continue this journey of knowledgeable assistance in their growth. To continue our journey we will add a few tools adults can implement to take shelter from and manage the emotional storm.

Beware the tyranny of "NOW!"

"NOW!"

Every adult has bellowed this word to a teenager they have in their lives. It is a complete sentence, final and definitive. Using this command clearly expresses that you are done hearing any arguments, excuses, or backtalk and expect the reasonable task you requested to be started or the behavior you wish to end to actually end. Below the surface, it has a much deeper meaning, and as adults with modern teenagers, we must be aware of the tyranny of now.

When using this term and dealing with the emotional storm of the teenage years, there is much more at stake than your frustration that bubbled to the surface necessitating its use. Due to the under-cooked frontal lobe, teens often have two forms of complaints concerning "now." The first is an issue of urgency, "I can't wait." Their version of now has to happen or else they will explode. The second is a form of reluctance, "I'll do it later," or "as long as I get it done at some point." Modern teenagers wanting the "now" and obsessing over that urgency slows their already under-cooked frontal lobe and allows their impulses (desire for reward/dopamine) to reign over them. Put simply, their lack of logic sounds the alarm in the adult brain as a defiant threat to adult authority.

Both of these can cause issues for the adults in their lives because it causes stress. For adults, you are wrestling for and demanding compliance to some task or instruction you have given value to. For teenagers, they are flexing their deep desire for independence and testing the waters of what they can and cannot do.[20] For both parties those are important goals, so you get a good ol' stalemate. Each is unwilling to give up that power they are seeking. The teen is getting a delay in the gratification they desperately seek from this scenario, and the adult is getting a delay of cooperation that, to them, borders on defiance. Frustration for both, leading to conflict.

Teenagers procrastinate as a way of reining in time. They are more aware of "their" time as opposed to the time others have demands for them. Gaining independence, their natural impulsivity, and that gnawing feeling of urgency lead to increased conflicts.

"It's my life! I should be able to control when I do things, and I am old enough to know when to do them!" the teenager would shout.

Parents feeling the loss of control respond, "Under my roof and as my child, I will decide when you need to do something!"

On the parental end, the feeling that you are constantly nagging them becomes even more stressful, which teens also feel but put the blame solely on the parent. They gamble that you will give up, and remember from previously, arguing is a way that they hone their beliefs, so an argument over delaying the task you asked them to do is worth it for that growth. I asked a student once when discussing this issue with a psychology class why something they thought through enough to ask permission for (such as going to a friend's house or staying up late) and knew they very well could be told "no" would then turn into an argument with their parent(s) if they were told no. Their answer: if I wanted it enough to make sure I asked permission, so I didn't get in trouble doing it, then it is important enough to argue with my mom over." That answer encapsulates the change from childhood to the teenage years. A child may sulk or even throw a tantrum but often accepts the answer or is easily distracted by a maybe. Teens are willing to fight for the activities that they believe they should be allowed to do.

Procrastination, or *delay*, is not always a negative part of their developing thought. *Delay* is important as teens develop because every situation is new to them. Therefore, delaying an action or decision is often exactly what we hope they do; take a moment to slow down and "think it through," but when *delay* affects something we as adults want, we naturally do not value it.

How do we stop the tyranny of "NOW!"? As with most aspects we have discussed thus far, the answer is first, understanding the "why" of their actions, and second, using patience with them. "Now" will take longer than it did when your child or student was a ten-year-old. Understand why it may be taking longer. You should remain persistent in the things you are asking because you still are the parent, but do not be shocked by the response. Talk it through with them and explain your urgency in the issue and how said task will not delay what they want to do by much. It's not wasted time to explain why it's important to you (you would waste that time anyway arguing), which also trains and awakens their empathy skills, a vital element in adulthood. Be aware when you are asking them to do something as well. If your son is in the middle of an intense game of *Fortnite* or is tied in the fourth quarter of Madden, plainly tell him as soon as that game is over, he needs to begin the task you requested. This avoids a feeling of tyranny for them, and subsequently an argument, and still gets what you want completed in short order.

Presence, not presents

Our sweet little children's faces lit up when they opened that new toy on Christmas morning, hugging it and jumping up and down. We felt amazing as parents to be able to provide them with so much joy, and Christmas felt magical. Now, with video games being able to be downloaded, toys being "for babies," the thought of you picking out their clothes makes them gag, or the item they asked for is so exorbitantly priced there is no way you could get it for them, you struggle to even think of what you could get them for Christmas. Even with all of those factors, you still get them something they desperately wanted because you are a good parent, and within a week, or month they do not use it anymore or are "bored" with it. That is teenage impulsivity and the constant want for novelty.

Let's avoid all of the above and focus on something that can give them the excitement of novelty and grow them as a person: experiences. Ditch the multiple presents at Christmas or birthdays if they are struggling to think of something they want and create an experience with them. Take them to a concert of the band they adore, or take them to an NFL, NHL, NBA, WNBA or MLB game. Plan a family trip near Christmas for a cruise or somewhere other than grandma's house. These experiences are also expensive, but they create memories that will last much longer than Lululemon leggings. An added benefit of travel is sharing and showing your teen different parts of our country or world helps to grow them culturally. This plan also aids in keeping your closets free from discarded toys, tech, or clothing they are bored with or now deem as lame. Everyone wins!

Very few people remember what you received for Christmas or a birthday five years ago, but I guarantee we all remember a trip we went on to an interesting place or seeing our favorite band for the first time. As an extra little bonus, as your teen's friends are all talking about the new game, makeup, or sneakers they got, your teen can brag about how they went on a three-day cruise to the Bahamas. They will still tell their friends they *had* to go with their *lame* parents, but the experience will matter.

Provide your teen with your presence and experiences that grow them, and they will become more mature, possessing a richer understanding of the world. These are both items that provide shelter from the emotional storm.

Beware how you (the adult) may change

Psychologist Dr. Carl Pickhardt once asked a thirteen-year-old how he knew his teenage years had actually begun. Dr. Pickhardt explained the teen responded instantaneously with "Because of how my parents have changed!" When asked to elaborate, the teen continued to explain how his parents used to be fun-loving, carefree, and relaxed when he was younger, but they had changed to become more serious, worried, and tense.[21]

Teenagers can be tough to deal with, and all of us notice when we are somewhere public and there is a group of unsupervised teenagers. We steer clear of the horde of teens because they will either be loud and annoying or causing trouble, we do not want to be a part of. As those years approach with our own children, that same worry and fear creeps into us, and we may begin changing how we treat our children, either subconsciously or consciously. You may be asking, "How did I change? They are the ones who changed!" They did change, but you may have as well, and that is something to be aware of. What are some of the changes adults often go through as their child enters the teenage years? Parents can often become more irritable, critical, suspicious, impatient (the tyranny of "NOW!"), sad, resentful, strict, and uncommunicative. Those are just a few.

We change because we sense and witness the changes in our children, and we react in a hopeful and vain attempt to return things how they used to be. Your teen used to stay in the family room with you and watch shows and laugh; now they lock themselves in their rooms and only come out after bellowing their name several times. You may react by barging through their door, asking what they are doing and why they are so detached now. The teen is obviously shocked—you did just barge through their door—and defensive because of your actions and the depth of the question you just asked. Your son may ask to go over to his friend's house, and when he was younger, the biggest question was contacting the friend's parent and making sure the date and time would work with them. Now as a teenager, you barrage them with questions about what they will do there, who else will be there, will the parents be there, etc. These are all natural for a caring parent, but your teen notices these changes, and the outcome could be strong emotions from them and conflict for the both of you.

Please attempt to not take these shifts in behavior personally. Your son or daughter is not sequestered in their room because they hate you; they just want their own space and time. Part of being a teen is becoming extremely self-absorbed. It is how they mold their inner self and identity. They truly cannot help it. If you have a request or task for them that you know will upset you if it is done poorly or you are not provided the respect you feel you deserve, remember back to Chapter 3 and be a good external frontal lobe for your teen. When you request something, explain the steps to complete it or how you would like to see them act and then supervise them to ensure the steps are getting done correctly. If your son is messy, do not just tell him to pick up his room. Walk into his room with him and explain to pick up all of his dirty clothes and put them in the laundry room, and then to neatly and in the correct place, put up the clean laundry sitting on his bed. Once those steps are complete, you then can tell him to organize his video games or make his bed.

It seems like a lot, but as parents we were more than happy to walk our children through the steps of tying their shoes or dressing them. They are still our children, so is this step so different?

Notice how and if you are changing toward your teenager. Do not assume that this change you are noticing is completely one-sided, which puts all of the pressure of adjusting to this time squarely on the shoulders of your teen, who is already adjusting to an avalanche of personal change. The change is difficult for you, and your potential change can be difficult for them as well.

The emotional storm of being a modern teenager will happen. Internalize the fact that the accompanying changes befalling your teenager are an evolutionary force that cannot be halted. Through your efforts and understanding it's a time that can either go smoothly - or spiral into a raging dumpster fire that engulfs your home, relationships, and maybe even your neighbor's cat.

Understand the changes they are experiencing, talk, explain, and guide your teen to calmer waters. Most of all, require zero conditions for your support. If they made you so angry earlier in the day that you actually contemplated the pros and cons of prison but later they come to you in tears or you notice they have a lost helpless look in their eyes, begging without words for the safety and comfort of simple hug, then for God's sake squeeze the bejesus out of them and let the past be.

That moment could be the most important thing both of you say or do the entire day.

5

I Feel Like I'm Going to Explode: Anger and You

"Holding onto anger is like grasping a hot coal with the intent of throwing it at someone else; you are the one who gets burned."
— *Buddha*

Let us be vulnerable with each other for just a second.

All of us have been afraid of someone at some point in our lives. I am not referring to some nightmarish boogieman we have cultivated in our imagination, the bully from your past haunting your dreams, nor a random stranger expressing a legitimate outburst in a public place or displaying open aggression or violence. I am referring to someone close, constantly near you whose anger was either so malevolent or unpredictable you feared being the cause of said anger. Someone who you are around often, and therefore, to avoid their anger, you may say or do things differently than you normally would. You find yourself constantly "walking on eggshells" in their presence.

We can all close our eyes and picture that person. It is not weak to fear the level of anger someone in your life may display. It is part of being human and having social or emotional relationships. If it is too uncomfortable or dangerous, hopefully you are able to evade that chaos in your life, but at the very least you learn what triggers their anger, and you work to lessen those explosive moments.

What makes us uncomfortable though is admitting that some of us may feel this same way about a teenager in our lives. Not a fear based on the possibility of violence toward us—at least hopefully not—but fear based on the unpredictability of their mood and anger.

Will they lash out at us for the simplest request or critique?

Will their anger arouse my anger, creating a rage maelstrom, temporarily dragging the whole ecosystem of our homes into its depths?

Adults do not want to admit that we may fear a child. It takes our power. Makes us seem and feel weak. If you are a parent, teacher, adult, or teen yourself, we have all been in this place before with at least someone. Perhaps your fear turned to anger so you felt you were always in control around a troublesome teen, but fear was present, and fear of how they may have acted if left "unchecked" still aroused your rage. It could be that you do not fear teens in your life, fearing instead what is awoken in yourself when they express anger toward you. You fear what you may say, or even more terrifying, what you may do. You fear, after the last door has been slammed, the shame you may feel sitting in the gloom of the post-argument moment for what you said and did while getting pulled into the rage maelstrom.

Good!

Fear means you are alert, you care, you do not want, nor are you comfortable with, anger reigning supreme in your life. That is a good place to continue our journey of opening, peering into, and understanding the items our teens carry in their second backpack.

Teenagers are unpredictable as John Townsend expressed to open this chapter. One moment they are lovable, showing you that sweet child whom you raised or who makes your classroom a joy. The next moment they are a back-talking, over-dramatic, Tasmanian devil screaming, "IT'S NOT FAIR!" after being asked to do a simple task or denied a personal request.

Teenage anger causes many problems and much stress within our families and homes. It is important, however, to understand that anger expressed by teenagers is not just another annoyance from dealing with teenagers. It can pollute the parent-teen, teacher-teen, or teenage friendships, creating a fertile breeding ground for more anger to grow. Anger and how they process and regulate it can also harm future socialization skills and relationships.

Our task is to dig deeper to understand anger itself, why teens feel it so acutely, the positive and negative ways we as adults react to it, and ways that we can calm and work with our teens to lessen the strife within our homes.

Anger: What is it and why does it matter?

Every single human being on the planet has experienced anger. Often, it is righteous. Sometimes, it is spontaneous and surprising. Occasionally, it can be a major source of embarrassment and shame.

What is anger's purpose though?

Why, even with our advanced intelligence, do we have the capability to become as feral as our ancient, nomadic forebearers? Understanding the purpose of the emotion itself, along with both its positive—yes, it does have positive purposes—and negative aspects will help us understand why twenty-first-century teenagers feel anger so intensely, and often, so randomly.

In its most basic and evolutionary terms, anger is based on fear and is a natural response to feeling loss, pain, separation, and grief.[1] Anger is an "action" emotion. It propels us to move forward, keeping us from being drug down into ourselves by the anchor of loss and grief.

Imagine yourself watching a movie: the hero loses a close companion while fighting the evil forces of the antagonist. Our hero witnesses their comrade fall in battle from afar. They release a primal scream as the killing blow falls and begins to cut their way to their fallen comrade, destroying any henchman in their path.

Our hero scoops their fallen friend into their arms and succumbs to their grief with heartbreaking intensity. In the theater, there is not a dry eye in the house. After sobbing into the nape of their fallen friend's neck, the switch happens. Their sobs slow into sniffles, slowly their head rises, and red tear-rimmed eyes peer at the antagonist who struck the killing blow. Those eyes brim with fury and burn with hatred. Patrons in the theater grip the arms of their chairs tightly as a slight gasp escapes their lips and their bodies stiffen. The switch from grief to rage was so quick, so intense, that the violence to follow is not hard to imagine. Anyone with loved ones can easily place themselves in the hero's psyche.

We can feel the rage and imagine wiping the tears from our eyes as we prepare to avenge the fallen. Our hero gently lays their fallen friend in a comfortable position, not ready to accept that for them comfort no longer matters, and stands, fists clenched. The antagonist grins, excited he/she will finally get their battle, and they rush at each other.

We have all seen this movie before.

It works because the anger stemming from grief and loss is buried deep within our primal brains. Anger also emerges when accomplishing an important goal is impeded due to some external factor. Anger begins when a negative experience can be ascribed to someone or something.[2] Once we establish the source of our goal being impeded, anger's function is to motivate us to create a response or action to resolve the issue. In this sense anger not only aids keeping us alive in an evolutionary fashion but also has crucial social elements. Anger allows us to communicate to others that a boundary has been crossed or a socially accepted norm has been befouled. Therefore, anger allows us to have social cooperation and fairness as our society has progressed. Anger has been one of the tools for establishing both our norms and personal and societal boundaries.[3]

Imagine the standard social norm—in most of the Western world at least—of meeting and introducing yourself to someone. You approach them, or they you, look them in the eye, extend your dominant hand, pronounce your name, and clasp hands in a firm handshake while they inform you of their name. A simple greeting, originating in the age of armor-clad knights, who extended their sword-arm and clasped each other's forearm to prove they were unarmed and willing to be close enough to facilitate mutual trust.

Now, imagine a stranger entering the room. They approach you to introduce themselves, and instead of extending their hand to shake yours they jump into your arms, wrap their legs around you, and plant a sloppy wet kiss on your forehead. Your anger, and every witness's shock, clearly allows everyone in the vicinity to understand a greeting of that nature is not acceptable.

Is being mad also being bad?

Being mad and experiencing the emotion of anger is not also "being bad" in every situation. We previously explained many of the important social functions that anger helps us carry out. Boundary setting is paramount in any human interaction, and anger aids us in identifying which boundaries we have broken, and how far we can push the established boundaries. Although I previously defined anger as having someone or something to blame for impeding a goal or creating an obstacle to our other desires, it has also been found that 50 percent of self-reported anger episodes had no real external agent[4] Anger can be coaxed out of us by physical discomforts such as chronic pain or a simple headache. It can also come from environmental factors such as repulsive odors, tastes, or sights and extreme temperatures. Ever find yourself in tight quarters with a group of people when it is extremely hot outside? Typically, the tempers get about as hot as the temperature does.

Anger can also come from within ourselves. This form of anger is derived from personal frustration with the other emotions we may feel at a given moment. We become angry with ourselves for feeling anxious in a situation, becoming sad, or having thoughts or impulses the logic within us screamed to not have. How angry do you become with yourself when you grab that second doughnut from the box, knowing that you are attempting to lose weight, but they were fresh hot Krispy Kreme doughnuts, and the impulse overpowered you? You ate the doughnut in all its glazed opulence but felt shame and guilt, followed by anger at your weakness. Modern teenagers are constantly learning about their new world of increased independence and social and romantic stressors, which provide many pathways for self-imposed anger. Maybe when your teen snapped at you or lost his cool—for no apparent reason—he was actually imprisoned in his cage of anger because he blurted something impulsive and awkward to his crush or sent a text to his best friend that could cause a rift between them. Sadly, as the parent or teacher, you just happened to be in the wrong place at the wrong time to run face-first into the buzzsaw that is teenage anger.

Our eldest son, being a freshman in high school at the time, was just "off" one week. He would sulk through the house—when he ventured out of his room—and every response to any questions asked of him was a half-muttered grumble, made worse by his newly deepening voice, making every time he answered us seem like a really bad Rocky Balboa impersonation. Mopey and grumbling he went through the week, but around bedtime one evening, my wife asked him to brush his teeth and get ready for bed. The quiet brooding teen vanished, and attitude incarnate became the main character. He questioned everything around the bedtime routine: why does he have to brush his teeth at night, why does he have to get ready for bed if we, the adults, were going to stay up longer, why does he need a good night's sleep since—and both my wife and I being teachers loved the following often used, and always wrong, teen trope: "we don't do anything at school anyway!" It should be shared that at the time I, myself, was his world history teacher! This mini-midweek mutiny was an attempt to work through his anger by throwing out anything he could to make an argument.

Teens, right?!

My wife, at first, stayed calm but pushed back as the snarky retorts became worse, the anger increased, and the arguments he made became more random and sillier. By the end, we all were using raised voices, and our eldest went to his room, slammed his door, and threw something against his wall. Not being parents who suffer destructive outbursts from any of our children, we both burst into his room expecting the final round of the heavy-weight fight. What we did get was the exact opposite.

Instead of a prize fighter glistening with the exertion of a fifteen-round slobber-knocker, our eldest looked worn and haggard. If he had been able to grow a beard, I am confident he would have had a full five o'clock shadow. Seeing him in distress immediately put both of us into "parent mode," setting aside any anger or pride to find the root of the issue. Upon sitting calmly and talking with him, we discovered that our son and his best friend had been going through a bit of a tough time. Being in panic mode our son had sent an accusatory text about their growing divide. He was embarrassed by the text and was trying to wait up to see if his friend would reply, hoping they could continue talking via text message.

We informed him that all friends, as does any meaningful relationship, go through turbulent patches such as this. Sleeping on it and letting cooler heads prevail may be good for both of them. As with most things in life, the situation was never as simple as we often think it is. His anger was not in truth aimed at us, or bedtime, but instead at the teenage craving for independence and at his own actions; blended with visceral and real concern for the friendship.

Shame and fear are powerful motivators of anger in all of us.

Shame and fear are powerful motivators of anger in all of us.

His anger revealed to him his values of how and what we say to our friends, and the fear of not being able to resolve the issue. Even though it surprised us and blew up my wife and I's evening—it is very difficult to gleefully watch an episode of Master Chef before bed after getting in a row with your fifteen-year-old—our eldest's anger was at first a negative event, but after investigating further, showed itself as a positive for his journey into adulthood. His anger, although unfocused and ill-aimed, was protecting him, crippling his own values while also revealing to him the true value of their friendship.

I posed the question in the title of this sub-section, "Is being mad also being bad?" The question is another way of asking that if we are mad, is it always a negative event? The word "being" in the midst of that question is not something that can be overlooked either.

Often, when we are angry, we tend to become the anger we are feeling. It overtakes much of our personality and behaviors, much like our English phrase "in pain" where the person experiencing the pain can only be described as being "in," or part of the pain. If any of you reading this have ever experienced true severe pain, you are nodding along with this. You are the pain. It is not something to the side that can be forgotten while another task is being attempted. It pervades our thoughts, emotions, and actions. You are in it, merely attempting to keep your head above the waters of its agony, hoping not to be drug under. Anger is very much the same when it comes on in full force. You are, in reality, "being" anger incarnate. Does that imply we are also the sentient form of bad behavior because we are expressing anger?

The answer to this question is no.

Anger is neither good nor bad, healthy nor unhealthy.[5] It is not a malevolent living force, it is purely just an emotion. What matters concerning anger is what you do with the emotion, and how that anger is ultimately expressed. If your friend has been treating you differently and your sadness predictably gives way to anger, prompting you (it's an action emotion, remember?) to confront them, how do you wield that anger? If you ask, non-accusingly, why they have been acting differently, your anger was wielded positively to resolve an issue and protect yourself. If you become angry at the same situation, approach your newly estranged friend, and scream in their face while pushing them, your being mad just became you being bad.

When coping with the devastating disease of alcoholism, it is a common occurrence for victims of the disease to blame alcohol itself as the main culprit. And why not? It is the most visible and blame-worthy malefactor of their ruination. When finally admitting they have a drinking problem and seeking professional help, or legally mandated help, the counselors at Alcoholics Anonymous (A.A.) often combat the blame of alcohol with the same retort; alcohol is neither good nor evil. Reminiscent of anger, it depends solely on how you use it.

Millions can have an alcoholic beverage or two and maintain their composure. Sadly, millions of others have a drink or single sip, and that cascades into a full-on bender, either due to the disease, personal disposition, repressed anger or trauma, or dozens of other reasons. Alcohol does not care. It has no plans or evil machinations in store for you. It dispassionately waits, is used, and how we play our cards after that determines how the cards may fall.

Anger is paired with the same process. It may be the same offender for all of the negative elements in your life. It very well may be the singular external cause of your downfall, but anger did not "do" anything. It existed, as an evolutionarily-required emotion. And YOU chose how to use it!

That statement is not meant to be callous, but to wield anger properly for a given situation is no easy charge. Uniqueness dominates the situations of our lives. One could dedicate a lifetime to never using anger aggressively, and depending on the unique context, emotional weight, and personal importance of the situation in tandem with minute-by-minute physical and emotional fluctuations such as mood, health, sleep, finances, relationships, and previous trauma, one could fail just as easily as someone who has never attempted to control their anger.

Do not give up though! The positive changes from being aware of yourself and anger are well worth that depressing possibility.

Anger, being an emotion, possesses the potential to be the boulder from the myth of Sisyphus mentioned in Chapter 4. We may arduously shoulder its preponderance of mass high upon the hill only for it to shatter, and with it, our will shatters as well. We find ourselves back at the foot of the hill with a fresh boulder, distressed that our meticulous efforts to reach the peak have shattered, causing us to have to start anew. We are filled with shame, embarrassment, and even more anger. Is that not how we feel when we lash out negatively? Shattered, hurt, embarrassed, and dreading looking up at our hill and renewing our ascent. The hill is so much more than a hill though.

It is everything in life that holds us back; in most cases, the hill is ourselves. We make our own lives more difficult at times; especially the lives of those who love us. Sisyphus's boulder represents life and all the tasks—mundane, monotonous, and monumental—living entails, and in this case, the hill, our anger, keeps us from reaching the summit.[6]Happily, since the hill is anger, we have the agency to affect its gradient and size. Unchecked and negative anger ensures a massive hill to push our boulder upon. To keep it from becoming impossible to ascend, we have to undertake the brave thing and walk up to the mirror, look ourselves in the eyes, and recognize what makes us angry and how we as individuals respond once there.

Anger is neither good nor evil.

It is a part of every human being from infancy until death. How we use it determines its position on the spectrum of good and evil. To ensure our hills do not become unbearably steep like Sisyphus's, acknowledging our triggers, removing ourselves from people and situations consistently causing anger, and controlling those situations to avoid triggers once identified are an ongoing battle we must all put energy into to ensure victory over destructive anger. We now know a little more about anger, its origin, and its effects.

Knowledge is half of any battle.

The light side or the dark side of anger

The global phenomenon of George Lucas's and Disney's *Star Wars* saga, and the expanded universe, has been dominating the box office, television, merchandise, toys, and popular culture since the original movie's premiere on May 25, 1977.[77] A franchise that absolutely is a wonder for its enduring success, especially considering at the time of its premiere the genre of science fiction was often relegated to B-movies or children's cartoons. But why has the *Star Wars* story and brand endured since that May evening in 1977, and even more so, how has it managed to evolve to reach new generations?

The magic of its longevity is not merely nostalgia or a cult following of fans. *Star Wars* did not attain global phenomenon status by accident, nor did it create legions of fans because of the various star ships, exotic planets, or lightsabers. Full disclosure though, if lightsabers are ever invented, I will be the first in line, regardless of my age.

Star Wars remains one of the most recognizable stories and brands in the world on the merits of its deep connection to the human psyche, life, and the choices we make. It has, for many of us, entered the mythos of our culture. Some enduring characters and archetypes have been found in stories dating back to the *Epic of Gilgamesh.* Classic archetypes create a familiarity in structure that permits our minds to find the meaning behind those characters instead of surmising where they fit within the story. There is the Warrior/Hero in the form of Luke Skywalker. The Shadow/Villain is found in the menacing figure of Darth Vader. The Outlaw/Rogue archetype is in Han Solo, and the Companion in Princess Leia.[8]

The other character, some have argued the true "main character," was the Force: a living entity that surrounds and binds all life forms and grants special abilities to those with a special connection and the discipline to study its workings. The Jedi, keepers of peace and justice for over a thousand generations, choose the light side of the force, severing all connections and possessions. Jedi wield the Force for knowledge, guidance, and defense. The Sith choose to follow the dark side of the Force, giving into their fear, anger, hate, and passion in pursuit of power, personal gain, and aggression.

The decision of what "side" to follow is one all of us must face! Light or darkness, knowledge and calm or passion and aggression. The enduring popularity of the *Star Wars* universe stems from our connection and deep understanding of these beloved characters. We share and understand their elation and agony when they find themselves face-to-face with the fundamental decision that affects even the smallest of actions.

Do we embrace the light, or do we venture into the dark?

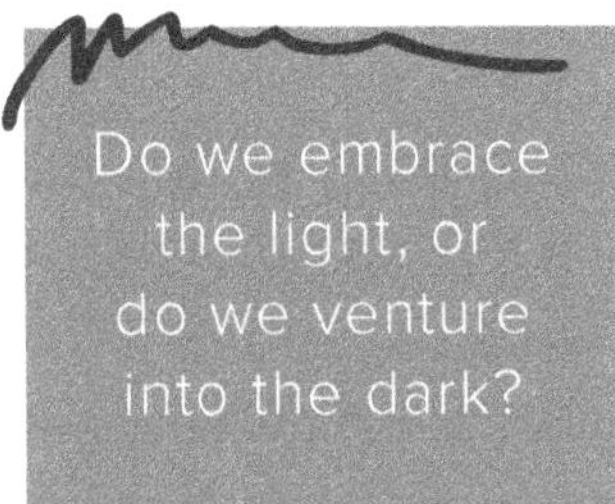

We have all been Luke, longing for adventure, praying for an end to our monotonous life, and desperately craving to be the shining knight. Luke, like us all, has also been tempted by darkness. During moments of extreme pressure or stress, his anger crept in, risking a plummet into the darkness. We have also all been Darth Vader: wounded and tortured, caring only about the power we can hoard for ourselves and use against those who may wound us further. Vader, as all of us have, believed he was beyond hope and unworthy of love, only to find something in his life that pulled him back to the light and redeemed his soul.

We connect with these characters because they are us and we are them. Anger, more specifically how to use it, comes down to a choice or a series of micro choices. Life, as reflected in the movies, teaches us that these choices are never made in a vacuum. There are trials, tests, and temptations that produce ripples expanding deep into our lives, affecting every situation and person within our wake. Because we are human, we dance upon, over, and back across the line between light and darkness, hoping we don't become mired in the darkness of anger.

Anger itself does have a light and dark side. It simply is, and it possesses positives and negatives that are vital to be aware of for both you and the teenagers in your life. Because anger is so hurtful to experience, we often look right through the positives and focus on the intensity of the event. A mistake far too many of us make, far too often.

The light side: positives of anger

One of the most curious aspects of anger is when we do become angry, we *decide* to become angry.[9] Other emotions spring upon us based on situations we find ourselves in. I have never thought about being happy, I just became happy and appreciated the situation that caused my happiness. Even our descriptive terms for our emotions show they are spontaneous: we *fall* in love, *burst* into tears, and are *frozen* by fear. All spontaneous terms, but for anger it is described as "becoming angry." A slower—in terms of emotion selection—methodical process.

We decide to become angry by evaluating what was done or said and then declare that action as an affront to a goal we aimed to accomplish (and yes, the goal can be as simple as getting the last piece of pizza), our well-being, or that a complaint we made was justified and should not be ignored.[10]

According to the recalibration theory of anger, the emotion is multifaceted and adaptive, allowing humans to identify injustices, coercion, and violation of norms.[11] The theory explains that anger is not simply a negative destructive force in our lives, but more so an emotion that should be deployed to help combat events our frontal lobes determine as injustices. So if you were to just hear the functions of anger according to the recalibration theory, the average person would declare, "Anger is a pretty helpful emotion!" Most of us do not think of it that way because we focus on the often-explosive conclusion of unchecked anger. Anger has a bad reputation and an even worse PR agent, but the emotion in its purest form is positive and protects us from the more invasive parts of our lives.

Some of the positive aspects of anger are:

- It *helps to right wrongs* (Perceived or actual by forcing us to confront situations we have assessed as a wrongful action or word and state our position on the situation. This can be awkward and painful, especially for teens, but this skill provides more healing than harm.)
- It *voices grievances* (Ever see someone who would never say anything if they were being taken advantage of and then one day they explode emotionally? That was anger forcing them to confront the grievance.)
- It *protects us from danger and harm* (Anger makes us aware a situation may be dangerous. It is also an action emotion as we previously discussed, so it is the "fight" emotion in fight, flight, freeze, or flop.)
- It *opposes mistreatment* (Anger, even in its subtle, slow-burn form, forces us to speak up or act if we perceive mistreatment to us or others we care for.)
- It *recognizes and opposes violations* (Ever been in a room when someone cheats while playing cards or a board game? Your family/friends quickly call out the alleged cheat because a set of norms and rules had been established and someone attempted to subvert them. This key skill of anger allows us to stay a civil—most of the time—society.)[12]

There are many more positive aspects of anger that may be overlooked by the more overt and dangerous aspects of the emotion. Anger as a positive is a key emotion in creating a socialized society.[13] It allows us as a species to create cooperation (rules, values), collaboration, and fairness by giving each of us a personal and societal pathway to discourage exploitation, manipulation, and injustice. Popular television shows create drama and anxiety for the viewer by presenting an alternative to this way of life, such as in post-apocalyptic shows like *The Walking Dead* where societal rules and norms have been destroyed, and our society breaks down to one of survival and violence.

Recognizing the positive elements of anger is key to helping teenagers adjust and grow because, as we have previously discussed, socialization is one of the areas of life that teenagers desperately desire to branch into. If they have not learned how to use anger positively, our teens will struggle to feel accepted and create positive relationships later as they transition to adulthood.

The dark side: negatives of anger

This one is easy!

We've all witnessed the dark side of anger at some point in our lives. In fact, all of us have ventured down that path before and exploded at some point in our lives. Most of you reading this most likely only remember times of anger expressed personally or by someone close that would fall into this category. Do not worry, you are not some negative person who only remembers bad things; the amygdala and frontal lobe work together to remember potentially dangerous situations for our fight or flight responses. But you are now aware of the light side of anger, so we can all work on identifying and remembering those aspects to create a more positive image of the emotion.

I abhor losing my temper. It makes me feel ashamed, weak, and unintelligent as I assure myself that there could have been a way to avoid the blowup. It is natural though, and as discussed previously, at some level subconsciously, the emotion was defending us over some violation. If it is such a useful emotion, then why do we have to feel so shameful after expressing it? I do not have the answer to that question, but we can put a positive spin on the feeling you have after expressing intense anger. If you feel shameful, then that means you are empathetic, understand social situations, and are not a sociopath.

Good for you! That is great news for everyone in your life! The answer is unequivocally to avoid saying to yourself or others, "Just don't get angry." (And gentlemen reading this; please, for the love of all that is holy and sacred, do not tell the female in your life to "Calm down!" when they are upset! It's for your safety.) None of us are saints; therefore, avoiding anger completely is not feasible. Walk into a situation with the knowledge you now have, know yourself (which does not mean deluding yourself like many do), realize what is happening, connect with what you are feeling, and then begin reflecting on what specifically is making you angry.

These steps open up a whole new emotional world where each of us can strive to correct the violation our brain is alerting us to. Once that is achieved, you can move forward positively with your head held high. You will soon find that much of what you allowed to sneak in and activate your anger was not worth the stress, shame, and shattered relationships.

The dark side of anger has two main branches from which our anger can follow. The first is aggression. Aggression, operationally defined as some act resulting in harming or hurting someone emotionally or physically.[14] There are so many variables for each situation and person involved, it can be difficult to categorize aggression. Broadly speaking, aggression is typically viewed as being either proactive or reactive, with overt (assault) or covert (theft or lying), or physical, verbal, or relational. Someone who makes use of proactive aggression uses that aggression to accomplish a goal in a quiet, calculated method—we often call this simmering anger—such as showing strength or controlling the situation without "making a scene."

Conversely, a reactive aggressive person is easily irritated and provoked by others, reacting poorly to any slight against their person, actual or perceived. This person is loud and quickly allows everyone near them to surmise they are "big" mad. Once a reactive aggression individual lets their anger take hold, they no longer care about social goals or norms. Visually, reactive aggression displays clear acts of anger (shouting, throwing things, physical violence, slamming doors) and is what we would call "hot-blooded." Proactive aggression may display few outward signs of anger and is more calculating, being referred to as "cold-blooded."[15] Proactively aggressive individuals are terrifying! They can smile directly at you and then behind the scenes work to undermine something important to you.

I would much rather deal with a reactively aggressive person because, other than the volume and potentially destroyed possessions, you are immediately aware of what they are angry with and may begin to remediate the situation. My mind immediately goes to the popular show *Game of Thrones.* Most of the characters were openly reactive in their aggression, drawing their swords at a perceived or actual threat but willing to fight and die over the affront. The most terrifying characters—I'm looking at you Cersei—take the threat and work covertly to destroy the other character politically, socially, or financially.

The second branch of anger is manipulation. Following the same pathway as proactive aggression, this branch works to weaponize our anger into bringing guilt toward those who have caused the apparent affront. Instead of acting outwardly aggressive (reactive aggression) when using manipulation, we place blame and fully play the victim. Aggression makes us say things such as, "Don't ever do that to me again!"

Meanwhile, manipulation has us turn the tables on our antagonist and declare statements such as, "How could you do this to me?" and "I thought you cared and I could trust you!" These tactics follow the proactive path because we are not simply explaining our hurt but using that hurt to bring similar pain to the antagonist in our situation. Spending my career either in a middle school or high school, this is often the most implemented form of anger, especially from teenage girls. Teens are so empathetic to each other, and their developing brains crave the knowledge and novel experience from feeling someone else's pain that when experiencing anger, teen girls often attempt to make their friends internalize what they are feeling. The danger from manipulation is, of course, causing mental harm to whomever your anger is aimed at, and as we will discuss in the next chapter, a cycle of anger, arguments, aggression, and manipulation can be created. Once the victim of manipulation processes the initial guilt or negative feelings oppressed upon them, they can often become angry themselves and start the process anew. There is no healing in this scenario, and the longer that we stay within our anger without expressing or dealing with it the closer to the surface the anger resides in us, and therefore is easier to lash out with.

Much like how teens can be pulled into the maelstrom of their new and intense emotions, we all can be pulled into the chasm of anger, watching the light above us fade, and realizing the darkness within us is more present and active than we ever imagined. The cycle of aggression or manipulation is the reason you often see adults in relationships, or parents and their teens, seem to be unable to have a simple conversation without some form of snark, disrespect, or outright aggression. They have been pulled into the chasm, and their anger is so close to the surface it is easily brought out into the open and they no longer know how to not be offended by the other person.

Story Time: Choosing the light over the dark

A few years back there was one of those model students that all parents and teachers hope their child or their students become or emulate. Eric was the best athlete in the school, being a member of the football, basketball, track, and baseball teams. He was also a high-achieving student with mostly A's and the Vice President of the Student Council. He was charming and handsome to boot and always behaved and was respectful in the classroom. One day in my class, I even overheard another student exasperatedly say to him, "Man you are HIM, why do you try so hard in class because you already have offers to play ball?" Eric looked at him bewildered and said, "I'm a student-athlete, and 'STUDENT comes first! I need to make sure I am able to have any job I want if ball doesn't work out." As a teacher overhearing this, I wanted to fist pump and say, "YES! That's it right there!" This is the mindset we all dream our children and students to have because we all too often see students believe that everything will be given to them and they are guaranteed to be a great rapper, athlete, influencer, etc. just because that is what they want to do. But Eric was still a twenty-first-century teenager and had peer pressure and that infamous under-cooked frontal lobe.

As much of as a leader Eric was, he still was a teenage boy and believed his friend group was the only place he was safe and accepted. His friends, who were mostly athletes as well, and more the stereotypical teenage athletes, believed most of the rules did not apply to them and struggled to get by in their classes. A favorite pastime of athletes—as shown in basically every movie and show that centers around high school—is to pick on non-athletes, students with eccentric tastes and dress, or intelligent introverted students. Eric's group was no different in this tired high school trope. He was not an overt bully, tending to stay quiet when events such as that were taking place, but again, being a teenage boy, he would laugh at the antics of his friends.

The group began picking on a male student who was shorter and much skinnier than most of the boys in their grade around October. For the purpose of this story, we will call him Derek. The antics never became threatening or overly physical, they just loved to bug people with little annoying actions, such as throwing mini-paper wads, giggling whenever he spoke in class, and teasing them as they passed in the hallway and lunchroom. The faculty were frustrated because when you saw or heard any of this, the behavior would be corrected, but it was never an egregious enough offense to earn a more severe punishment that would help put some fear in them. Or when one was put in serious trouble, their parents would show up at school—after the student broke the rules to text them after getting in trouble—and raise so much hell that they were given a slap on the wrist to re-establish the peace and tranquility of the school. The irony here being that if another student did what they had been doing to others to their innocent little cherub, you better believe they would be in the office raising hell to ensure the offending student was punished. As educators, it is very easy to see even in younger students this entitled "rules for thee, but not for me" mentality many parents tend to display when their child finds themselves in the principal's office.

One afternoon, after being picked on by Eric's friend group in the lunchroom, Derek had reached his breaking point. And who could blame him? Students were streaming into my class, and Eric was the only one of his group who was in that particular class. As Eric entered the room Derek marched up to him with a determined look in his eye and shoved his finger firmly into his chest.

"Why are you and your friends picking on me, I never did anything to you!" he said angrily, with his voice cracking on the word "friends."

A shocked Eric looked Derek up and down, then around at the other students who were now staring in anticipation and fear at what could happen—some slid their hands into their pockets to have their phones ready in case a fight broke out—and then with an unsure voice said to him, "It's nothing personal, man, they are just having fun." Wrong answer.

"Fun? Fun!?! Do you think I am having fun when you all throw stuff at me and make me look and feel stupid?"

Eric looked ashamed and said nothing.

"I am just the same as you!" Derrick bellowed, looking around, realizing for the first time that they were not alone in the room. "I love sports, and I come to all of your games and cheer you all on! Going to games is fun and gets me out of the house!"

"You really come to all of our games?" Eric said sheepishly.

"Yes, I do! I can tell you exactly how many receiving yards and touchdowns you had last season," Derek proclaimed confidently. "The only reason I don't play sports is because I'm small, and my mom is annoying and thinks I'll die or something stupid like that." Hearing this the other students had gone from anxiously waiting for Eric to obliterate this smaller upstart, to judgmentally leering at him for what he had put Derek through.

Eric looked down at his shoes and without looking up murmured, "I didn't know you like sports and wished you could play."

"Well, even if I didn't, that doesn't give you and your goons any reason to be jerks to me!" he said loudly, gaining more confidence every minute. "Everyone thinks you are so perfect, but what do you think I would say if people asked me about you?"

"You probably wouldn't have much good to say," Eric said, barely above a whisper.

"You got that right!" Derrick said as he stared him straight in the eye and walked to his desk as the bell rang.

Students poured into the cafeteria the next afternoon and went through the lunch line with the unique duality of high school, half of the crowd emitted the buzzing activity and energy of hungry teens barely able to stay in line, which stood in stark contrast to the meandering zombie-like movement from those who could care less and were just waiting to sit and pick at their food to pass the time. Eric's friends found the spot at "their" table and shortly resumed their childish picking on Derek and his friend group.

There was a subtle change though. On this day, Eric was not chuckling along as he consumed his standard two full lunches. He ate quietly, looking down at his tray. Anyone not just merely looking at him, but actually seeing him, would notice the blank stare painted on his face was not one of boredom or brain-drain from a tough academic day but one that concealed simmering anger and conflict.

Eric's friends oscillated between cutting up with themselves and picking on Derek's friend group. As with most teen groups though, once the reaction to their bullying wasn't found to be extreme or funny enough, their behavior escalated to attempt to get that response.

"Eric, watch this," one of his burly linemen said as he put a line of ketchup onto a tater tot.

"Dude, don't!" Eric said with annoyance and anger in his voice.

Chuckling, as he continued to put a growing mound of ketchup on his tot, his burly friend said, "C'mon man, it's just to get their attention." As he finished piling on his ketchup mound, he glanced at the lunchroom supervisors to make sure their attention was elsewhere, turned, and let loose the ketchup-loaded tot. It found its mark squarely on the side of Derek's head; ketchup exploded and instantly matted his long black hair. Eric saw Derek's face shift and phase through confusion, rage, and then defeated embarrassment as he worked the numbers in his head, realizing he would be turned into a pile of goo if he retaliated. Laughter then began to erupt from the students nearby and Eric witnessed Derek's defeated embarrassment shift one last time into abject misery. He had seen enough.

Eric slammed his empty lunch tray on the table, stood up with his second tray, and walked over to the cart containing silverware, condiments, and napkins. He grabbed a handful of napkins, walked over to Derek and offered the napkins as he apologized for his friends. The lunchroom was suddenly silent, and Derek looked around, half expecting this to be some clever ruse to make this awful day even worse. Studying Eric, looking for any sign of deception or retribution for scolding him yesterday, and finding nothing alarming, Derek slowly accepted the crumpled wad of napkins and began wiping his ketchup-matted hair. Eric placed his remaining lunch tray next to Derek and slid into a seat without comment, letting him continue to wipe off the ketchup. The lunchroom now hissed with the whispers from groups wondering what would happen next and why Eric had sat there.

"Are they friends?"

"What is Eric doing sitting with… him?"

"Just wait, I bet Eric is going to punch him or do something worse!"

"I heard that Derek has done all of his homework since kindergarten."

"Why is he sitting with the weird kids?"

As Derek finished wiping his head, Eric resumed eating and Derek could only stare at him wondering, in the same fashion the whispering student body had been, what would happen next? In between bites, now once again emanating his usual casual and relaxed manner, as if he belonged at this table and nothing was out of sorts, Eric asked, "So, who's your favorite NFL team?"

Derek, speechless at first, feeling as if he had missed some part of a joke or zoned out of an active conversation, started to answer, but over Eric's shoulder, he noticed that the big burly tot-tosser and a few others from Eric's former table were being escorted out of by one of the principals. A smile crept to the corners of his thin-lipped mouth as he continued to answer.

"Honestly," Derek said as he took a bite of his burger and quickly chewed it, still smelling ketchup in his hair, but smiling as he chewed, "I like them all."

"Hell yeah!" Eric replied while shoving half of a burger into his mouth, quickly chewing and swallowing the mouthful. "I can get down with that."

Anger and you

Eric listened to the anger he felt and chose the light side. He could have easily punched his big burly tot-tossing friend, or, worse still, chose to lean into the bullying mystique Derek had placed upon him the day before. He could have easily turned the embarrassment from the tongue-lashing into reactive anger and punished Derek for calling him out. Instead, watching his friends continue to pick on Derek and his table after Derek showed him exactly how much the teasing affected him, he realized he was angry at making Derek feel "less than."

Early in this chapter, I explained one of the positive functions of anger is to inform us that our values have been violated. The simmering anger as he stared at his lunch trays was signaling to Eric his value set had been violated by some action. As he sat at the lunch table, he assessed his anger and realized it was not the embarrassment of being called out, it was that he and his friends had made Derek feel different. Deep down, Eric knew that was wrong, and he did something more people should do, especially teens, and followed his values and beliefs even if it meant risking his current friendships.

Now that we have a better understanding of anger, what it is for, and the pathways it can take within us, we now have to put this understanding to work. It is vital for us to not exclusively identify anger as a negative emotion but more so as an alert and action emotion. It helps us keep our place in society by identifying affronts and keeps us in line with our values, so anger arises when we become aware of an action that runs askew of those values. Anger is so incredibly hard to navigate because it is such a powerful emotion. You feel it, and at times want to lash out. Sadly, we often lash out the most at the people closest to us: our spouses and children. Even though it is difficult to navigate, we must start to recognize first, that we are angry, and second, what is the reason for our anger?

You are most likely saying to yourself right now, "Shew, this sounds really difficult." It is, and I am about to make it more difficult still. While you are learning about your own anger and what it is informing you, your teenager is attempting to do the same thing with less life experience, an under-cooked frontal lobe, and a Costco-sized mayonnaise jar of hormonal chemicals flowing through their brains. Oh, and they are navigating through those barricades to their development on top of managing their other emotions, yearning for more independence and autonomy, experiencing the emotional roller coaster of their first romantic entanglements, and creating and managing their social status, friendships, and life which are of the utmost importance to them at this time.

Yikes.

I hope you did not drop this book and run after realizing what you are contending with. Don't panic, we will untie that Gordian Knot together.

I laid out what anger is and its functions so you can understand what the twenty-first-century teenager living in your home, in your classroom, or looking back at you in the mirror is feeling, as well as what you the adult are also feeling. Next, we will continue to unpack the second backpack of your teenager and see why they are feeling so much anger, how parents and adults can make it worse, how screaming to prove you are in charge does NOT work, and how teen and adult brains view conflict and anger differently, which makes every argument worse for one of the combatants over the other. If we can understand why modern teens are angry and how we can avoid feeding that beast until it consumes us as well, then we will be able to extract a colossal weight from that second backpack.

Let's dive into the War at Home and begin the process of manifesting peace and understanding with our teens, for everyone's sake.

The War at Home: Anger and Family

"Teens are impulsive, self-centered, and irrational. They have outbursts of anger and disrespect, then in a few minutes, they swing back to love and compliance."

—*John Townsend*

Diamonds are coveted the world over for their lustrous sparkle, indestructible nature, and rarity. But their value precisely emanates from the primordial process in which they are created.

Coal, deep within the Earth, is beset by extreme heat and pressure. These two factors begin to reconstruct the atoms within the coal into the crystalline construction that creates the coveted diamond appearance. The carbon that provides the natural composition of coal is also hardened to its maximum level, producing the hardest of all natural substances. The final step in creating these little treasures is the crystalline structure becoming mirror-like, allowing diamonds to reflect light. The coal has now transformed into a glittering, near-indestructible, natural entity, and from those qualities, its status symbol and value are derived. Intense heat, pressure, and time transform an ugly lump of earth with moderate value into something dazzling, expensive, and highly coveted globally.

I struggle to think of a more fitting parallel to raising children than that of the process of creating a diamond. There is pressure, there is heat—in the form of the emotional ups and downs of parenthood and the intensity of the teenage years—the process changes us at an atomic level, and if it is done correctly, something of unmistakable beauty and value forms.

Make your relationship with your teenager a diamond.

In the previous chapter, I laid out what anger is, what functions it performs for us (both positive and negative), the different forms anger embodies, and what that means for each of us as individuals. Now let's apply that information to our teenagers and their lives at home or in the classroom. The pressure of the situation—one of the key ingredients to the formation of diamonds—is that this process is extremely difficult. To lighten the load of the second backpack our teenagers carry, we must take that difficulty head-on. Your task is to balance the stressors of your career, the demands at home, your responsibilities of being an adult, your marriage or relationships, and now this.

Did you hope your life with your teenager would maintain the same sweetness as when they were a small child? You know the time I am referring to. A sweet time, where upon returning home from work, they would run to you, arms outstretched, almost preternaturally understanding that their little arms around your neck, as you squeeze them close, is the only stress relief you need. I sadly need to inform you those moments will happen, but with a nostalgia-inducing rarity that renders them bittersweet. But, as the great Stephen King poignantly shared in his novel *The Wind Through the Keyhole*, "If the sweetness of our lives did not depart, there would be no sweetness at all."[1] We do not stop seeking the sweetness once it departs, though. This chapter does not end with King's quote; we will continue to work and find the pathway to that sweetness, even if it is naturally rarer as the years march by.

Some may read this and think, "My parents argued and got angry with me, and if I talked back, I would learn REAL quick not to do that! And I turned out fine!" Or "Why should I be the one to try and change the dynamic that people have been doing forever? They will grow out of it."

Those are both valid thoughts to have. It is very difficult to attempt change and to enact the mountain of work necessitated by bringing about change. They are your children or students, and you have the right to treat them any way you see fit under the guidance of decency and law. Consider this though: if your treatment and dynamic with someone you have committed to, either by choice or parenthood, is negative or does not work over and over again, then you have entered a degenerative cycle that will only continue to degenerate further.[2] All parties will suffer terribly and continue to suffer. As author and clinical psychologist, Jordan B. Peterson, expressed in his book *Beyond Order*, "Your life becomes meaningful in precise proportion to the depths of the responsibility you are willing to shoulder. That is because you are now genuinely involved in making things better."[3]

The time we spend with our teens does not need to be constantly bitter; it can be one of love and the guidance all modern teenagers crave, deep inside, past their undercooked frontal lobe and over-active limbic system. We have the knowledge and ability to create a personal dynamic with our teens where we will not pine for our sweet children of the past but come to appreciate the young adult our child has developed into.

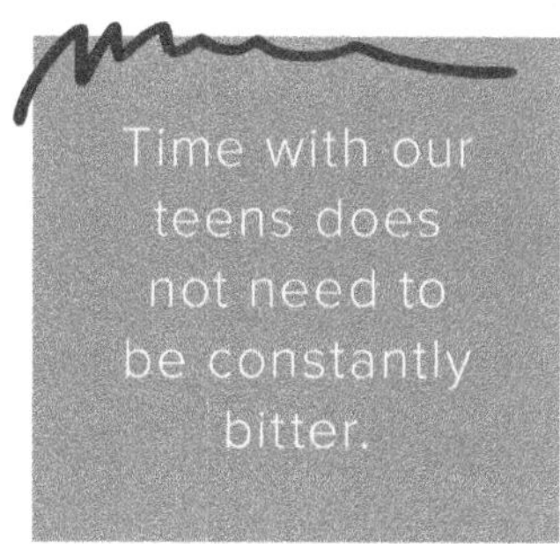

Finding Neverland... and leaving it: Who our teens are becoming

As a youth, I adored Peter Pan in all of his iterations. And what young boy would not? A magical boy who could fly lived in a tree house community with his friends, had little structure or rules other than those self imposed, and fought pirates… for fun! That is the dream of every young boy.

There is a fallacy with the magic that Peter Pan provides though.[4] Pan is magical but lives in Neverland and only ventures out on rare occurrences to find friends he wants to bring back, and then quickly returns. Due to Neverland's mystical properties, he does not age or mature in body and mind while he remains there. He is both childhood incarnate, with its magical view of the world and carefree lifestyle, and what teenagers desire; the enchanted novel-seeking exuberance of childhood with the autonomy and activities of adulthood.

Pan's greatest foe, the menacing adult pirate with a hook for one of his appendages, Captain James Hook, endlessly chases Pan and his Lost Boys, hoping to eradicate them and usurp control of the island. Hook is not solely a hook-handed maniacal pirate, he is at the opposite end of the spectrum than Pan: he is adulthood in pirate form. Hook has been damaged by life—his hand was devoured by an oversized crocodile—as have all adults with some form of loss or trauma in our lives. The trials, losses, and trauma of living real life can leave us bitter and angry at anyone who has not faced the same losses, as it has done with Captain Hook. The very same crocodile who took his hand found the taste of human flesh delicious and is constantly pursuing Hook, but there is a catch to this game of cat and mouse. Along with Hook's hand, the crocodile carries a ticking clock in his belly; therefore, his stealthy approach upon stalking Captain Hook is betrayed by the subtle ticking of that clock. A constant, personal reminder to Hook, that even in this land that time forgot, his time is coming.

The meaning woven into the fabric of the story here is that life will take a bite out of you, and time as well as death will never stop searching for you. Time is literally ticking away until we all are ultimately caught by our own crocodiles seeking to devour us. The enduring struggle of the youthful magical hero versus the aging evil pirate villain is more accurately described as Peter Pan battling *life* itself, and subsequently his very own mortality.

When the story of Peter Pan is viewed through the lens of Pan versus life itself, his fearlessness and bravery cease to be understood as noble attributes and take the form of fear and unwillingness to face uncertainty.

That is not bravery at all.

The true embodiment of bravery manifests in the character of Wendy, Pan's great love. Wendy is introduced to Pan and falls for this wild swashbuckling boy, who smells like the wind and freedom. She traveled to Neverland and immediately assumed the role of "mother" for Pan and the Lost Boys, organizing their homes and darning their socks, perhaps a bit of foreshadowing for her later decisions. After brief periods in Neverland, Pan would return her to her home, but each time he returned she was a bit older until one evening he returned to find her married and with a child.

Wendy sacrificed the magic and adventure of life with Pan for the unsure pathway of adulthood and embracing life in all of its ups and downs. Pan could not fathom why she would sacrifice feeling the wind in your hair while flying, or the mix of fear and exhilaration one feels while crossing swords with one Hook's pirate henchmen. To Wendy though, those things were not life. They were fun distractions, but maturing, accepting responsibility, and having a family were the true adventures in life.

In Steven Spielberg's *Hook,* while crossing swords with Captain Hook in the climatic final battle, Pan retorts to a deadly promise hurled by Hook declaring, "To die will be an awfully big adventure."[5] Later, once safely back with his family, an Elderly Wendy proclaims to Pan, "So, your adventures are over." Pan quickly responds, "Oh no. To live. To live would be an awfully big adventure."

In this version of Pan, he accepts life and all of the risks and has made the mature decision to age and experience the ups and downs much as Wendy did in the original story. Twenty-first-century teenagers live a life much like Peter Pan. They want the carefree lifestyle of Pan and his Lost Boys but also desire the adult aspects of life congruently to their freedom.

Having a foot in both worlds, though, is to live a life like Pan, where the adventure of real life is partially stalled, and although they may feel free and grown enough to mortally fight pirates, they may never develop and learn the joys and lessons of love, loss, success, and failure. It is our job as the adults in their lives to guide them from being Lost Boys to healthy, happy adults.

Lost boys

Our teenagers are unknowingly Peter Pan and the Lost Boys. The transition to the maturity and changes of the teenage years comes quickly, dragging with it the freedom and carefree desires of childhood but demanding the autonomy of adulthood. It unquestionably is a fascinating time in all of our lives. With their desires both pulling in opposite directions—much like Peter Pan's shadow attempts to pull away from his physical body—and the hormonal chemicals of puberty, frustration and anger naturally begin to build within our teens.

The first response to their growing frustration is the desire to be left alone. This desire for solitude is natural and provides the opportunity for teens to experiment with their autonomy. While they are locked in their rooms or dedicated spaces—which you may have noticed has slowly become more lair-like with closed doors, darkness, and all the amenities they need to emerge from their self-imposed family exile as little as possible—teens regulate their moods from the stimuli they are experiencing, practice introspection on their actions, behaviors, values, and beliefs, and develop their new teenage identities.

This can be difficult to understand as a parent because the shift happens in slow increments until they are lair-dwelling creatures. When our children are younger, parents pray for a few moments where their child will entertain themselves and allow them to do what they need to without someone clinging to them every second. Suddenly, they are sequestered away in their lair and seemingly uninterested in anything happening at home. I vividly remember an evening at home when my wife and I came home from school after securing our three children from their various schools and practices. After a few minutes of everyone in the kitchen talking, grabbing a snack, and putting away lunchboxes and backpacks, our kids snuck away to their lairs, and my wife and I were sitting at our kitchen island looking around at the now quiet living area. My wife looked at me and stated flatly "I guess they are done with us until dinner." For both of us, this was a stark change from previous evenings, when there was always at least one of our children needing something from us or just wanting to be around us. Now… crickets.

As the teenage push away from their parents increases, so does the possibility of teenage anger and aggression, especially in boys.[6] Girls get plenty angry too, but they tend to be more open to expressing and discussing their emotions, which at least gives parents a pathway to resolution. Boys express themselves with loud words and actions, choosing physical outbursts over discussion coupled with the surge of puberty-related testosterone, which edentulates fear, making dangerous behaviors during periods of anger and aggression far more likely.

As parents you may find yourselves the recipients of much of their frustration, often having very little to do with you or anything you did. Your crime to receive this punishment: your proximity and familiarity. Not fair at all, is it! As disheartening as it may be, this tension between teens and parents is not an accident; it is wired into our brains to start the subtle process of preparing your child to leave your home and find their people.

Sad? Yes. But also, very important!

Reflect on your own thoughts whenever you find a grown adult still living with their parents—barring a major personal disaster forcing them into that situation—well into their late thirties or forties. An adult living at home with their parents and working jobs (or not) similar to teenage jobs makes the negative thoughts of "loser," "weirdo," or "dropout" dance through your mind. We naturally start to feel there may be some issue with that person or that they have little motivation to branch out on their own and create a life.

This happens most often to males in America, with over seven million males aged twenty-five to thirty-four living with their parents and not working or looking to work.[7] The best part? One of the commonly used nicknames for failure-to-launch syndrome is "Peter Pan syndrome!" These patients, like Pan, refuse to grow up and leave Neverland. Imagine if we all stayed home and did not leave our mommy, allowing her to clean our rooms, make our breakfasts, and pick out our outfits. We, especially men, would be a sniveling society of man-children with *SpagettiO's* stains on our adult-sized Osh Kosh B'gosh overalls.

Our species would quickly end as there would be little motivation to leave our homes other than pure physical desires. Nature created the teenage desire to separate and express anger and frustration with parents to ensure we step away from our parents and siblings and create our groups. Eventually, these new groups become families, allowing our species to propagate and spread… and also save our sanity from living with our kids or parents until we die.

Allow your teens to have their alone time, but set expectations for dinner, family time, visiting friends and relatives, and other social situations. Let them grow while also making sure they have both the skills and desire to leave Neverland. Do not let your teens become Peter Pan or his Lost Boys.

Loading the cannons for battle

The stage is set for the "war at home" to begin. Teenagers try to separate themselves from their parents, boys being primed for angry explosions that potentially could become physical while girls are ready to scream and burst into tears. Let's not pretend that females cannot, or will not, become physical as well, though. I know many females who, if their ire were raised to the appropriate level, could put Dwayne "The Rock" Johnson through a concrete wall.

The two sides of the conflict have created a palpable tension within the home. On one side, parents desiring to keep their connection to their children constantly battling insidious thoughts that push them toward that gentle knock on their teen's door that could begin a fresh battle in the war. The knock is justified to parents because they "just want to know what is going on in that room they won't come out of!" On the other side, teens hungering for freedom and autonomy to create their own groups and find out who they are. Feeling they have zero space anywhere in the world—especially if parents either burst through their door or lurk near it—and little purpose or value other than that prescribed to them by their peers and romantic interests. To them, as the parent or teacher, you are incessantly keeping them from interacting as much as they would like to. . . with everything and everyone. UGH!

Can you feel the tension? These two opposing factions fabricate a battlefield where the opening salvos are often from two simple scenarios.

Teenagers, possessing the aforementioned craving for novelty, freedom, and autonomy, combined with the impulsivity of their under-cooked prefrontal cortex, produce the "why not" scenario.[8] A well-placed "why not?" statement, seemingly innocent, can be the inaugural declaration in an epic teen versus parent argument. Much like a body shot in boxing, "why not?" statements may seem like they do not have much of an effect, but they add up to serious damage. Teenagers, feeling their new autonomy, looking like and believing they think like adults, do not understand why they would be told "no" for a request they have already deemed appropriate. They cease to understand that life has multiple layers, and a "no" is not intended to be punitive.

To parents or teachers, the ask either does not make sense or cannot be done due to all the other events or constraints on the family/classroom timeline. Or teens refuse to accept that their parents are saying "no" to protect them. After all, how could their parents be worried about them being hurt or finding themselves in trouble when they have already assessed the situation and surmised they will be fine? They are invincible after all… if you remember, bruh.

The "why not?" scenario is the gateway to an argument; one that is balancing on the edge of a knife. If teens accept the initial response to the "why not?" life carries on as normal. If they retort negatively to the explanation of the "no" or are given a, "because I said so!" then their attitude-laden comeback will launch a similar statement from the parent or teacher. Now you are playing a game of ping pong with negative comments, all while the anger and the tension in the house is rising.

Dig your trenches; the war has begun.

Every facet of teenage life also begets fresh and more numerous expectations of them. I believe we have all blocked the memories of the transition from childhood into the teenage years concerning the changes our lives at home underwent. I do not remember when I started putting my laundry away once washed, picking out my outfits, or any discussion of new chores expected of me; it just happened, and that was that. It may be an evolutionary trait or the passage of years, but I have no memories of those changes. Upon reflection though, it is a drastic change in our lives. One day you are a carefree child, waking up to folded laundry and a hot plate of waffles waiting for you. Then, seemingly instantaneously, you are a teenager, and your morning consists of a laundry basket of crumpled clothes waiting on your bed and the hollow ringing of Cheerios hitting the empty bowl.

This is not a bad thing for our teenagers, though. They need expectations. They need to learn these things and how to help around the house. But when researching the causes of anger at home, it is an interesting and striking change. New expectations from friends, school, parents, romantic interests, athletics, and themselves provide the first feelings in their life of being overwhelmed, and since you are Mom and Dad or a teacher they are close to, they allow themselves to release that pressure on you. This all adds up to create the "why do I have to?" scenario.

The "why do I have to?" scenario stems from the natural teenage desire for more autonomy and freedom. Even seemingly small requests to lighten your load at home, such as taking out the trash, are seen by teens as a chance to 1) express their desires to have autonomy and 2) have a say in the things that take their time from them.

It is easy to see how this scenario leads to conflict if we do not filter these mini rebellions through this understanding. As the parent you just want something done quickly so you don't have to do it and can work on something else, while your teen wants to know why they have to leave their lair and do something that you have been doing for them most of their lives. It's easy to snap at them when they ask "why?" to these scenarios. They are both testing how you will respond, so they can remember and catalog it, and attempting to solidify their personal time. It is also easy to not respect teenage time since, as adults, we have stressful jobs and responsibilities, and we have also already attended school and most likely had chores at home.

We must remember all of this is new to our teenagers, and to them, it can seem that we are adding more to their already full emotional plate for no other reason other than that we can. Restrictions to their freedom in the form of rules on who they can see and socialize with and when they are allowed to flex their new social wings can also bring about conflict from this scenario.

Each side in this conflict is fighting the same battle. For both teens and adults, there are issues of teenage independence, with teens feeling oppression, declaring, "You always say no!" or "You won't let me." Parents, in the teenage independence battle, envision a fledgling revolt on the horizon declaring, "You challenge who is in charge and our rules!"

There is also a battle over the new self-identity and becoming their own unique and autonomous person. Teens feel unaccepted or unwanted. These feelings are due to constant correction, being told no, and conflict. Parents, sensing this new person their child is becoming, fear their child has steered away from the values and beliefs they have spent years instilling. They feel they have failed, their lessons and values falling on deaf ears, while teens feel they have just awakened into true personhood, but are slowly being suffocated by rules and restrictions.

Pirates

We have discussed what teenagers desire as they develop and how those changes can create conflict in our homes and classrooms. Now, let us analyze the actions parents and teachers take, adding to the potential conflict in our homes, as well as what those actions could mean, if not changed, to the overall development of the teenagers in our lives.

If teens are Peter Pan in their longing of both childhood freedom and adult behaviors and actions, then parents naturally are the pirates of Neverland. We are the adults on the island, and it is absurd that children control it. Therefore, a war must be waged in order to wrestle power back into the hands of adults. As any good warrior entering a battle is, the adults are all equipped with armor.

As we become parents, we also don emotional armor forged from love, closeness, and compatibility to protect our children in the battle for their safety and happiness. It is first worn when our children are born, and we use it to protect against the possibility of illness or tragedy. Hopefully, this period is conquered with our armor unscathed, but the stress alone from worrying about the health of your new beautiful baby naturally weakens our emotional armor.

The second use of our armor is to protect our children from both the elements of their infancy and the probability of physical harm during their rambunctious toddler stage. Every parent knows the toddler years are a time of bumps and bruises. Once, when our youngest child was around two and a half years old, my wife and I had Easter photos taken. Shortly after the session, the photographer called and informed us that she had digitally removed the bruises from his legs because he was a little spider monkey and always running, rolling, and jumping off of things. To say we were embarrassed is an understatement because we did not want the photographer to believe we were bad parents, or, even more terrifying, that we were the cause of the bruises. She quickly informed us that she removes bumps and bruises so often from photos of toddlers that she typically removes them without saying anything to parents.

The third battle we enter with our parental armor is when our children are of school age. In this battle, we use our armor to be their knight in shining armor. We must protect them from themselves as they struggle to adapt to the new demands of being in school as well as from emotional harm other children at school may inflict. This age starts to wear on the armor of closeness and compatibility as it is important to protect them but to also make sure what the situation was and if they were fully or partially at fault. The silliness and immature acts of the pre-teen years also wear this armor due to the constant corrections, redirections, and changes our children go through during this stage. It is difficult to keep that armor strong when your eleven-year-old runs through the house thinking they can jump off all of the furniture like Michael Scott and Dwight Schrute in *The Office*, belting out, "PARKOUR!" as they do!

As we enter the teenage years, our armor is cracked and worn. The same child we loved and protected has changed. There is an unwanted abrasion in the relationship. This is coupled with the fact teenagers experience negative emotions at a far greater intensity and display extreme mood shifts, creating natural tension with every interaction.[9] As our teens become more assertive with their demands for autonomy and opinions, our now-battered armor breaks further, and we end up battling the very person we have spent years protecting. That is not easy to deal with on any level. Not to venture into the overtly cliche, but knowledge here absolutely is power, and in this case, a pathway to relief.

As much as parents feel like you are now more akin to an annoying boss than a parent, research shows parents still play a crucial role in your teen's understanding and regulation of their emotions.[10] Let me say that as plainly as possible. As parents or adults raising or guiding a teenager, you matter to the teenager in your life! Internalize that fact and move forward with the power and confidence I hope it provides. This also means that you are not a victim of your teenager's moods or anger. With this knowledge let us view anger in its positive form in that it incorporates important signaling of unaccomplished goals or affronts to our person or values. Knowing your teen is presenting anger because of that positive function we can use anger as a unique opportunity to create intimacy and closeness to your child. To accomplish this connection, it starts with more work for you as the parent or teacher. I am sorry.

Mental work needs to be done on the part of adults to shift your teenager's need for freedom and autonomy with emotional guidance and support. This begins by adjusting our response to teenage emotions.[11] If you react negatively, reject their emotions, and carry out inconsistent discipline when emotional situations arise, issues concerning both coping with their emotions internally and expressing their emotions to others begin to cement as personality traits.[12] If as parents we display discouraging reactions to teenage anger and emotions such as dismissing, ignoring, minimizing, or especially immediately punishing their display of emotions, then a slew of negative life challenges may arise.[13]

Teenagers who have not learned to internally cope and appropriately express their emotions and anger outwardly have increased issues with social skills. They may develop poor personal relationships, peer rejection, and possibly enter into toxic romantic relationships. Candidly put, aggressive teens develop into troubled adults. I have never met a parent or teacher who wants their own behaviors to be the reason their teenager has issues with emotions and relationships as adults.

Life in the trenches: The stalemate of family conflict

World War One was unique in the annals of history for the trenches used to avoid the deadly rapidity of the newly invented machine gun. Over 35,000 miles of trenches were dug during WWI. Those trenches created an unforeseen new problem: a stalemate that the tactics and technology of the time could not break.[14] Conflict in the home between parents and teenagers has developed the same problem. We have entered a stalemate, where victories are short-lived and the territory gained by such victories is often quickly lost, sending both combatants back to where they started. To end this stalemate, we must change our tactics, but first, we must understand what causes the stalemate of parent/teen conflict and develop new tactics.

To understand the conflict, we may face with our teenagers, recognizing the day-to-day process that breeds conflict is paramount. The stalemate of anger with our teenagers is a circular cycle. Conflict causes anger leading to further conflict, or anger causing conflict, which in turn causes a slow simmering anger within one of the parties leading to future conflict.[15] The anger yesterday may predict and cause the argument today while an argument yesterday may also predict and cause the anger today. And around and around we go.

Are you dizzy yet?

Circular Cycle of Parent–Teen Conflict

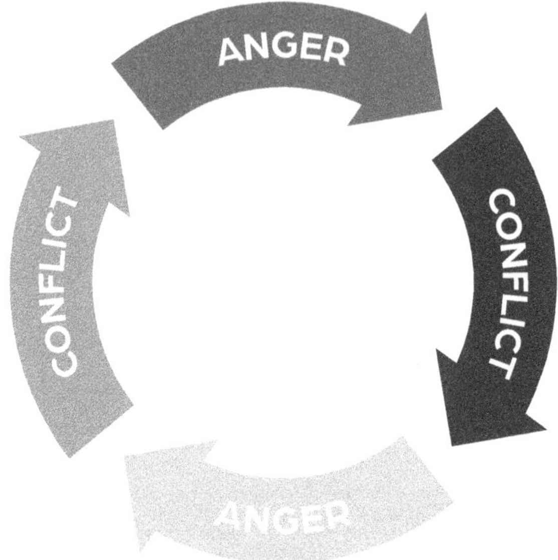

figure 3

Within the cycle of conflict, four elements feed into the loop of insanity you may be feeling: anger residue, anger preservation, anger persistence, and anger transmission.[16] Each element feeds into the cycle, and each can be the reason the cycle continues to advance. Anger residue occurs when either you or your teenager carries anger from a previous conflict into the next day. This is the slow burn of rage where you may have confronted your teenager about a poor grade on a test or forgetting to do a task. It may also originate when they say or do something that creates a brief conflict but is then quickly moved on from. Your teen may have smarted off, and instinctively you quickly let them know that their behavior will not stand. The feeling is tense and a bit awkward, but the issue subsides. But for you, the anger simmers—you dwell on how and why they smarted off, having several mental arguments throughout the day—and then the next day when they do something you disagree with, your anger is compounded with the emotions from yesterday, and the seeds for a large destructive battle are set.

Sound familiar?

Many of you may be realizing how often we are all guilty of this. Anger residue can be detrimental to both parents and teens for long-term connection as it severely damages each person's basic understanding of the relationship. It can also be negative for your physical health, causing constant stress and continued anger. Research has shown parents experience less anger than teens following a conflict as adults perceive the issue as resolved following a conversation once each party has had time to calm down.[17] In a beautiful example of teenage egocentrism, based on their under-cooked PFCs, teens showed little anger residue or attention to their parents' feelings and lingering anger. If you have ever felt not "seen" by your teenager when they have angered or hurt your feelings, it's okay, you are not crazy. Teenagers literally fail to see that you are hurt or that they could have been the source of your anger and emotional pain.

The very natural dynamic of parent-teen relationships can create the element of anger preservation in the constant loop of hostility. Anger preservation occurs when anger felt today may grow instead of subsiding, priming either member for conflict the next day. The actions of either you or the teen one-day lead to a reaction from the other party that causes a conflict in the future. You yell at your child for taking forever to get ready before school, and they proceed to give you the silent treatment. As the parent, you notice their not-so-sly attempt to avoid you and confront them the next day, leading to a full-blown argument based on a situation you barely remember. You just stepped right into their trap. Your teen is not a diabolical genius, though, they did all of this subconsciously. But alas, you are now fighting.

Teens experience anger preservation when parents set rules or ascribe punishments based on situations that they naturally push against such as cellphone usage, curfew, bedtime, and access to their friends. Teens also view punishments based on previous issues as a parent-created conflict and may carry that anger over to a future conflict. You catch your fifteen-year-old daughter on her phone well past her bedtime and when her phone was supposed to be put up for the evening. You are angry, so you tell her to plug it in somewhere outside of her bedroom and go to bed, now. The next day you sit her down and tell her from now on, her phone must be given to you at bedtime, and it will be charged in your room. She perceives this new rule, and your carried-over anger from last night, as conflict aimed at her and blows up the moment she has to give you her phone. Interestingly, most teenagers tend to react quickly in the moment and often do not notice their parent's angry actions the next day, again showing the natural teenage egocentrism.

Conversely, adults build their anger over time and tend to look for the slightest change in their teenager as a signal the embers from the previous conflict are still burning. Therefore, whenever they see this signal, they reignite the flame and do something that causes a new conflict based on the old issue. Adults, being more attuned to their teen's moods, may act to avoid conflict if they notice displays of anger or frustration.[18] Every adult hates admitting they may avoid their teenager if they sense a conflict possibly happening, but we must remember that the experience of adulthood has taught us to pick our battles. Do not be ashamed, you are being judicious with the stress you choose to interact with and accept. That's good.

The final two elements that create the cycle of conflict are anger persistence and transmission. Anger persistence is when the emotion persists for several days and just will not go away. Less reactionary than the previous elements of the cycle, anger persistence could be a sign that the parent-teen relationship is already breaking down much like a romantic relationship that is on the verge of collapsing. Every little thing the other person does seems like nails on a chalkboard to other members of the relationship. This is a very stressful and dangerous situation as conflict lingers around every corner. Adults tend to be more at fault here than teens because adults apply much more meaning to micro-conflicts than teens do. We tend to believe a deep meaning exists behind every action and feeling our teenagers have. Due to their natural impulsivity, this just is not true. Parents are also haunted by the memory of that sweet little child who believed Mom and Dad hung the moon. Will asking your teen to put away their laundry cause a major argument? Maybe. Will being two minutes late at curfew cause a tongue-lashing, lecture, and eventually grounding? Again, maybe. Anger persistence transforms both parents and teens into the character Anger from the Pixar movie *Inside Out*: a ball of rage that will quite literally, at least in the case of Anger, blow their top once they reach their boiling point.

The final element of the cycle is anger transmission. This lovely little evolutionary mimicry trick is born when the emotions or behaviors of one family member are adopted by another family member. They are still your children, so transmission typically travels from parents to children.[19] They watch us; every rookie parent is quickly told by other seasoned parents that children are similar to sponges, and since they are still learning how to be an adult—though if you asked them they would quickly let you know "I'm grown, man!"—they often emulate how we react to situations. If you get flustered easily and start cussing that stubborn lid on the pickle jar, do not be surprised to hear your thirteen-year-old curse when he cannot get the cereal box open.

Fathers transmit their anger and emotions to their teenagers the most. Fathers are less perceptive to their teenager's moods and feelings unless those moods are either extreme anger, sadness, or physical injury. Therefore, their transmission is typically a one-way street. Unsurprisingly, boys detect and embody their father's emotions the most often. Mothers, on the other hand, "obtain" their emotions from their children when transmission is present instead of "sending" them as fathers do.[20] As a way to understand and protect their children, mothers naturally mimic their children's feelings to empathize with what they are experiencing.

Moms really are the best in every way possible, are they not? Let's all take a moment and call our mom and tell her we love her. It's the right thing to do!

Ceasefire: What can we do?

The stage has been set, and the battle has been raging: Pirates vs. Lost Boys, Teenagers vs. Parents. How can we find a way to a tentative peace and lasting understanding? Like anything personal, creating true change in our homes or classrooms comes first with a heavy load of personal work on ourselves and our understanding. My hope is that the information shared in current, former, and future chapters will provide you with the information to begin self-awareness, change, and understanding. But, there are some concrete tactics that may begin the peace process.

To start, assess your interactions with your teenager. Has your tone, body language, or patience changed with them since they became teenagers? We have discussed, upon anticipation of our teens becoming defiant or snarky, that parents can change toward them first. I asked several teenagers about this very topic, and one boy around the age of fifteen anxiously stated, "I used to like coming home where my dad would say 'hey buddy!' and ask how my day was, but when I hit high school, it changed to, 'do you have any homework or chores that need to be finished?' " Throwing his hands in the air he continued, "And there was no reason to change, I didn't do anything bad! I was just older!" With our knowledge of the elements of the Circular Conflict Cycle, we now know that changing preemptively toward our teenagers can potentially create a self-fulfilling prophecy. There is a chance, if we are not careful, that we can create the very conflict that we fear.

> If we're not careful, we can create the conflict we fear.

Why are we yelling?

What are your interactions with your teen when the potential for conflict arises? Do you quickly snap and yell? Does any mistake or pushback—"lip" as older generations may dub it—cause you to get heated toward them?

Understanding how often we raise our voices at our teenagers in anger can be another tactic to begin a lasting peace. This is often a sensitive subject because all parents, yes, even the most perfect, patient parents who seem to have it together at all moments, lose it from time to time. Discipline and even yelling can be important when properly used as a parent. Telling parents to refrain from yelling at their children assumes the guise of "being soft on kids," but this is not being soft on kids. If they have done something to deserve a raised voice have at it, but with any anger, be sure that your ire does not become insulting or demeaning. Concerns arise when the yelling becomes constant and chronic, evolving into a major element of your interactions, even to the point where screaming and conflict are all that you know with them.[21] Staying calm does not show weakness as long as you address the issues; in fact, it can teach your children how to react in those situations and aid in developing their emotional intelligence and confidence.

Teenagers, especially those whose standard interaction with the adults in their life is yelling and degradation, are far more likely to develop behavioral problems, lowered self-esteem, and depression, which is a poison every parent fears entering their children[22] Yelling affects their connection with the very humans they should be the most connected to. Once again, we may have created the very thing we fear happening to our teens; they may pull closer to friends, attempt experimentation with drugs, or seek out overly early romantic and sexual encounters to create some form of caring connection. If we can do anything to stop our teens from feeling they need to attempt those dangerous teenage activities, then I believe we all would agree that we should make the effort. This makes even more sense considering yelling, honestly, does not even really work.

When we yell most of what we are saying is not being stored or learned because of our good old friend from Chapter 2, the limbic system. Yelling triggers our stress response system, fight or flight, which brings about either fear, anxiety, or aggression.[23] Remember, humans cannot learn when we are stressed, we react to the threat and then assess after the threat. Sadly, especially when yelling is extreme, the only thing our teens will learn is to be fearful when the adult in their life seems angry.

We have to ask ourselves then, other than making us feel better in the moment, what is the point? Teens can assess if we are angry in other ways than us needing to yell at them. Please do not feel you are being lectured to some "holier than thou" sophist who never yells. Previously, I stated that every parent loses it at times, and I am no different.

The day before writing this section my youngest son and I were rushing out for school, and he left the gate cracked open. The crack that the ajar gate provided was just enough for our five-month-old puppy to bolt out and run wildly through the yard and street. I, in true "busy-parent fashion," pushed our departure time to the exact minute where I could drop him off and get to my job on time. I was angry that he left the gate cracked, and chasing our pup added ten minutes to our leaving time, obliterating my perfectly-planned work arrival time. Watching the time slip away and seeing the exuberance of this new game on our puppy's face added to my anger. So, despite all of my research and personal journey to implement the tenets of this book, I yelled at my son to catch our puppy and yelled at the dog for running around wildly. So basically, I yelled at my puppy for… being a puppy.

To use a youthful term from a few years back: total fail. I was still angry by the time we loaded into the car and continued the angry lecture toward my son. It was my fault I did not leave early, but I placed the blame on the gate being opened and lost my cool a bit. It happens, but shortly into the drive to his school, I felt awful. It happens to us all, so don't feel ashamed or that you are a bad parent. You are not. Don't fall into the trap that social media creates showing every one of your friends as perfect families or perfect parents. You may feel that you must hold yourself to that standard, but social media is not intended to show the real version of anything. It consists of glamorized recreations of the very real moments of our lives. In the filter-obsessed world of ours, don't forget that social media invented those very same filters. Real life, even the sweetest moments, has blemishes, bumps, freckles, and warts. Why? Because it is real, and beauty is found in the merging of perfection and flaws.

If you do find yourself in a similar situation to the one where I lost my cool, there are steps to help your teenager grow and use your outburst as a teachable moment. Being a parent is very, very hard. Add to that the responsibilities of work, household duties, and family responsibilities, and it becomes a variable pressure cooker. When you do lose your temper, remember to apologize. Show your children that adults take the blame and apologize for their mistakes.

Sit your teenager down, once you have cooled off, and explain why you were angry. Look them in the eye—we are modeling that too—and say that you are sorry for yelling at them. Ask them what feelings they experienced when you were yelling at them. These simple steps identify proper behavior after an outburst and teaches them to assess their feelings as well. It also conveys vulnerability on your end, makes you more human and therefore authentic to them, and reveals that parents can apologize too and don't always think of themselves as lords of their little fiefdom. (I promise you some part of your teenager believes this is how you view yourself, my lord or lady.) Modern teenagers have a unique ability to sniff out a lack of authenticity and sense when people are being fake. Small steps such as these begin molding them for the rest of their lives and the relationships they will enter.

Remember, big things have small beginnings.

Stopping the conflict before it starts

Both boys and girls feel anger toward their parents and teachers for the many reasons we have previously discussed. Boys, due to high levels of fear-blunting testosterone making their aggression and already poor decisions worse thanks to their undercooked PFC, show anger more easily and outwardly than females. Angry teenage boys can become terrifying due to their increasing size and overt aggression. When your teenage son or daughter starts to show aggression, it is important to start early expectations to mitigate potential anger.

Set the expectation that you will know where your teens are at all times and what they are doing. Setting this expectation early can help limit many of the undercooked PFC and testosterone issues in teenagers. If they know that you know where they are, who they are with, and what they should be doing, they will edit some of their behaviors to avoid consequences. This is a good thing!

Do not fall for the teenage tried and true "you don't trust me" trap.[24] You already are allowing them to participate in many events they want to do with their friends, so inherently you trust them. You are doing your job and protecting them from a dangerous world. Teenagers use guilt to attempt to get their way. Do not fall for it. If they are mad you care about them and want them to be safe, then so be it.

You can sit an angry girl down and talk to them, and most of the time they will internalize what you are attempting to share. Boys are naturally poor auditory learners—they understand what is being said but do not interpret and internalize those lessons well, hence the reason they often fall behind females academically in late middle school—so they often need multiple sensory inputs tapped when learning. Make sure when talking to an angry teenage boy to make eye contact, and to touch them as certain points are being made. A hand on the shoulder or pat on the knee helps them connect importance with what you are saying. Physical contact, as the kids say, helps them "lock in." Ask them to repeat what you just told them when covering important details. You may get some pushback and moodiness on this, but for boys, repeating helps to limit the "in one ear, out the other" problem you most likely notice with your teenage boys. Finally, use shorter sentences and make sure you give them a chance to respond if they are trying to or ask them questions to ensure clarity.[25]

Do NOT attempt to lecture boys.

Why? Because about two minutes into it they will be playing the next level of *Call of Duty* in their head or daydreaming about being an NFL star. If you notice these steps are not working, for boys especially, you may need to get a different but trusted voice to tell them the exact thing you have been saying to them. A coach, preacher, uncle, or family friend may work for them. It is frustrating your teenage boys may not seem to listen to you, but again, it is an evolutionary strategy to begin the process of them leaving your "tribe" and creating their own. Most importantly, do not give up. You have the love and the tools; you can do this.

Calming techniques

In the moment of anger, or directly after it, there are simple techniques that may help calm both you and your teenager. These methods can be performed individually by your teen or together, allowing you to model gaining control of your emotions.[24]

- **Drink water**—Downing a glass of water first allows the one who is upset to take a second to remove themselves from the situation, providing needed time to calm themselves. Second, water helps to metabolize the chemical cortisol, which is a key chemical that produces physical anger.
- **Look up**—When your eyes are focused upward, your brain begins to process visual information and sends the blood from the limbic system (raw emotional reaction) back to the PFC (logic and reason). If you notice your teen or a student becoming angry, especially when crying, have them look up and you will now be contending with their thinking brain instead of their emotional brain. This is a safe technique that anyone can do when they notice they are beginning to feel emotional and angry.
- **Deep Breathing**—When we become angry, we tend to breathe very shallowly and from our upper chest. These shallow quick breaths provide just enough oxygen for our muscles to react since, at that

moment, we are living in our fight-or-flight mode. Have your teenager or student stand up and breathe deeply from their diaphragm, holding that breath for several seconds before exhaling. More oxygen entering the brain allows it to calm down. If you are breathing deeply and are relaxed, your brain and body notice the cue that the threat must be over and begin to end the fight-or-flight response.

- **Heart and Stomach Pat**—When angry, our brain lowers the present level of the natural calming chemical serotonin. Our stomachs have more serotonin receptors than any other part of our bodies. When our teens become angry they should stand up, put their left hand over their heart, and their right hand on their stomach, and begin to rub both simultaneously. Rubbing both will activate those serotonin receptors allowing the brain to begin to calm itself.

Some of these techniques may seem silly or too simple to actually work, but all science and anecdotal evidence reveal they do have calming capabilities. As an educator, trust me, many times silly and simple works miracles. If you match these techniques with identifying your own triggers, utilizing the information covered thus far, attempting not to constantly yell, and understanding the changes happening within your teenager, you will be light years beyond where you would be if you were just "dealing with it".

Let's make our homes and classrooms sanctuaries of peace and growth for everyone who enters them. Through knowledge and understanding, we can work to bring permanent peace to the age-old "war at home" between teenagers and adults. Let's empty their second backpack of that stress and worry, allowing them to focus on the less controllable items weighing their shoulders down.

There will be ups and downs.

Your teen may be chugging a glass of water (or straight from the gallon of milk if they are like my boys), see you enter the room and stop, slamming the glass on the counter and marching to their room to dramatically slam their door because they are still angry with you. It happens. Keep moving forward, and if you find yourself chasing a puppy at 6:15 a.m. and yelling at your helpless son because he is the nearest to you, make sure to apologize and to model addressing and owning your negative emotions. Every step backward is an opportunity to stop and assess what needs to be done and then to move forward.

There is nothing more important than taking the turbulent teenage years and turning them into an era of learning, molding our children into the emotionally healthy and capable adults we pray they will become when we first gaze upon their chubby faces at birth.

Take the steps to bring an end to the war at home.

7

You've Got a Friend in Me: The Importance of Peers

"I think there's a time in your life where you don't feel like you fit in. I think everyone has that when you're a teenager, especially, and especially in the society we live in."

—*Matthew Vaughn*

Every sports fan fears the moment when your hero, the star of your team, begins to decline, and the question of their continued career and relevance starts to be discussed. It seems silly, but it is an immense time of fear for the fans. A hero of yours who has provided so many memories and joy over the years is now being discussed as someone who may need to be traded or put out to pasture (metaphorically speaking of course), ushering in change, and more intrinsically, a reminder that we are ALL aging, and no accomplishment, skill, or effort is permanent.

Is this not a perfect analogy for parents when their child enters the teenage years? You used to be the star of your team—"team" here meaning the relationship with your child before the teenage years—and now you find yourself "riding the pine" more frequently as your playing time is given to an exciting young rookie: their friends.

As with athletes, this transition is handled differently by each individual. Will you be the sage-like veteran who will guide and help the rookie gain success, or will you be the cantankerous old vet who refuses to give up your time in the spotlight until the decision must be made for you? The former option is clearly the best route for parenting. Unlike the old cantankerous vet, you most likely will not rediscover your swing and how to hit the curve ball, creating a resurgent season and providing one last taste of the glory of old. And why will you not have one last moment of glory during the teenage years of your child?

Because they will not let you.

The young rookie, a.k.a. your teen's friends, to the modern teenager's brain, are everything. Their friends are an untapped treasure trove of knowledge, opinions, and shared experiences, and you, a remnant of the past filled with happy memories but reminiscent of a style of play that simply will not work in the modern "game". Do not become too upset though; every experienced parent will tell you that your child will become very close to you in their twenties. During that period, your role switches from aging former star to former player turned front office consultant. Able to help, give advice, share laughs, and be their go-to for everything from a car maintenance question to being that safe voice they need to hear after a hard day. You read that right, your teenager will actually call you to just talk in the near future. Mind blown. Be patient, they will come back to you, armed with all the lessons you have guided them through.

Friends, to modern teenagers, are everything. They are confidants, sounding boards, partners in crime, fashion advisors, tutors, and someone to vent to. Teenage friends often possess similar thoughts, hopes, dreams, and regrets. Their driving need is to attach to a specific person or a group to share the whirlwind of changes with someone who is experiencing the exact same things at the exact same moments. Your teenager subconsciously is aiming to create a second family group anchored in social experiences.

It is easy as a parent to slide into a cycle of hurt and heightened frustration or anger (remember the cycle of anger from Chapter 6?) when facing this monumental change within your home and family dynamic. The feeling makes you feel disposable or used. It is easy to feel this way when your teenager is treating you like Joe Pesci in *My Cousin Vinny,* when he finishes cross-examining witnesses during the climactic court case and flippantly informs the judge, "I'm done with this guy."

After all you have done for them, it seems, painfully so, they are completely done with you. Please remember, no one, including your teen, doubts you love them. You simply do not understand all the social connections their teenage brain is craving. Your brain has moved past that season of life and now speaks a different language than its teenage scion. Their peers are the only people who can deliver that innate understanding of the current season of their lives.

The need to belong

The need to belong to a different group other than close family members is not a unique personality trait of modern teenagers, or the teenager currently doing God knows what in the dark, dirty, plate-and-cup-filled lair that formerly—in some murky half-forgotten dream world where this lair was bright, filled with laughter and bedtime stories—served as their room. The desire is old; older than speech, written words, and even the wheel, hidden in the amygdala and PFC, waiting for it to mature enough to express the desire. Viola!

See? Teens, choosing friends over family is not a deficiency in your love or parenting, but an age-old need to help our species continue to grow in numbers.

Take a look at our cousins, primates, specifically chimpanzees and baboons. Chimpanzees and baboons are two of the most intelligent large primates, with baboons believed to have the intelligence of a human toddler, and chimpanzees possessing intelligence similar to a six or seven-year-old human.[1] When two separate troops encounter each other near an established territorial boundary—let's say, a watering hole—the leaders of each troop, adult males, threaten each other with symbolic gestures, such as charging the other troop and stopping abruptly, screaming, and jumping up and down.

Honestly, after years in the classroom, this behavior is eerily similar to how young teenagers act before a fight breaks out in middle school. The peons of the group jump around, throwing insults and riling up the other peons, while the leader sits back and only becomes involved once he/she believes their troops are pumped up enough and the other side is appropriately intimidated. And as with most school fights, the teens or troops of primates in our example, eventually become bored with each side not willing to cross the imaginary line separating idle threats and bravado, from actual conflict.

As all of this is happening with the adult males, there is a teen chimpanzee watching at the edge of that imaginary line, spellbound. These are new chimpanzees, and a lot of them! No more same old routine, same leader treating you how they want, same old females to try and impress. New and different! His brain floods with emotions of excitement, and the only thought he can focus on is the feeling that if he has to spend one more day with the same old group, he may walk into the watering hole and let himself sink to the bottom.

He acts.

Like a spring uncoiling our primate friend runs toward the line right to its edge but stops as if there was a forcefield. He retreats a few steps, eyeing the other troop to see their reaction, and then excitedly rushes back toward the line. He does this dance of nervousness and excitement until he eventually crosses the line into the new troop's territory. Now, he sits, very still, not looking up to avoid any potential violence of the new group for his brash invasion of their territory. He is also ready to retreat to his side if any of the males pay a bit too much attention to this new teenage male.[2]

He will continue this behavior daily, slowly working further and further into the new troop's territory until, eventually, he spends the night with that group. He cuts ties with his lifelong troop—his family—and is accepted into this new troop. Now, there is new blood to mix with their group to ensure incestual deficiencies don't cause unwanted weaknesses in their offspring. The teenage chimp felt the ancient desire to leave his family and branch out. His teenage brain desired the novelty of the new group, which, as we have previously covered, is a leading reason human teens are the way they are. Human teenagers seek the same novelty of leaving their parents for social awakenings and new experiences, crossing the boundary into a new troop comprised of peers, and limitless potential.

Joining a peer group allows teenagers to move further toward completing two important goals of teenage development. First, their friends provide a pathway for them to unmoor themselves from their childhood and family becoming more independent. Second, their friends provide a sphere where they can practice and experiment with the thoughts and actions that create the schism separating childhood and their family from the development of their unique individualism.[3]

Peers share thoughts, values, beliefs, romantic practices, biases, and prejudices that allow them to assess how well they fit in and what changes need to be made to function well with the age group they will grow into adulthood with. Parents will always see their children as children, often, regardless of their age or accomplishments. I am 39 years old, and my parents still ask questions about my handling of, or give advice on, big decisions I have to make as an adult; as if I have not had years of self-reliance or experience. We never cease being "children" to our parents.

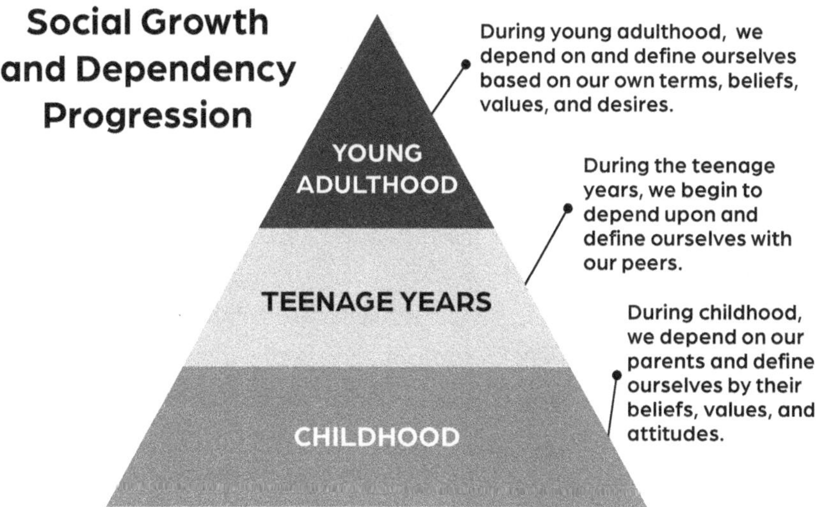

fig. 4 — Adapted from Carl E. Pickhardt's Social Growth Progression. 2024

Peer acceptance

We raise our children to know right from wrong, have morals and values aligned with our beliefs, and hope what we have instilled guides them to make the right decisions when they are on their own. As they become teenagers, they feel the primal need for independence and to transition into a group of peers to guide them into adulthood. This need causes them to move further away from the safety of their families at home and seek out people their age as much as possible. They have seen the mysterious new troop of primates across the watering hole and are charging that imaginary line in hopes of joining.

All that time we as parents spent impressing values and beliefs to be their own person, happy with themselves, gets lost, like tears in the rain. Their developing brain pushes against those teachings. It spins a web of doubt, ensnaring everything you've previously taught and currently tell them. Your years of guidance and confidence-building get pushed deep into the dusty attic of their mind. Instead, it chooses to amplify one pervasive line of thought: how do my peers think of me, and do they accept me?

When the modern teenage brain has been scanned, it reveals a startling susceptivity to their peers' perceptions of them. As adults, when asked to imagine what others think about them and then about their perceptions of themselves, two separate areas of the prefrontal cortex and limbic areas activate for the two separate questions. This shows that adults have a separate brain space for how they see themselves versus a separate space for how others see them. Don't get me wrong, adults still care about how some other people may think of them, but they also have a personal well of feelings toward themselves to draw upon. This is why a grown man can walk into a party in a crazy suit and not mind that some may be sneering. If you are confident, then your brain knows who you really are and draws from that.

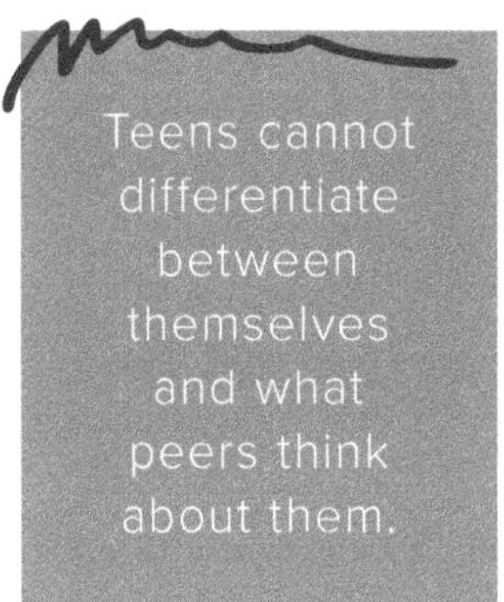

Teenagers are strikingly different. When scanned, their brains activate the same region for the two different questions.[4] Teens cannot differentiate between their own perceptions of themselves and what their peers think about them. In their developing minds the question, "What do you think about yourself?" is answered with, "Whatever everyone else thinks about me."[5] So, if a teen perceives that they are seen as a weirdo or loser, then they see themselves as a weirdo or loser. Basically, the exact opposite of what you have been teaching and hoping for as a parent. Facepalm.

The lessons and values you have provided your teenager are still present, locked within the dusty attic of their brain, but due to both their physical and emotional changes and higher levels of independence, they have now entered a period where social situations and hierarchy are the most important elements in their lives now. Friends are no longer someone to play a game with or hang out with. Friends are now the key to acceptance, popularity, and romantic opportunities. They know the beliefs and values you have drilled into them, but you are old and lame, so now they venture out to test, match, and alter your instilled beliefs to those of their peer group to gain social status.

The mission to gain peer acceptance will reveal itself to parents and loved ones as changes in the teen's behavior, dress, interests, and romantic choices. Your daughter used to love riding in the car with you blaring country music; now she rolls her eyes when you crank up a formerly shared favorite song while she asks to listen to Ice Spice and Lil Baby.

The shift in musical tastes allows her to fit into the friend group she has joined. You definitely notice the change in her dress. Gone are the sweet unicorn and girl-power shirts, replaced with crop tops and short shorts. This, again, is to match and gain acceptance with her friend group, and due to the increase in the reward system of the brain, getting a compliment on her outfit or body from another female, or especially a boy she is crushing on, creates a feeling adults would equate to chugging three *5 Hour Energy* shots. Teens crave that feeling and the acceptance that comes with it, so their dress and behaviors may become increasingly extreme. As a teacher of this age group, it can be shocking to see students outside of the school setting—where there is a dress code on the style of shirts allowed and length of shorts and dresses—and the clothing choices they make in social situations.

To gain acceptance, boys will make similar changes in their tastes as well but will often also engage in extreme behaviors to gain acceptance. They may push against authority or partake in destructive behavior to show they are worthy of acceptance. This is especially true for males attempting to jump into a social group they may not have been a part of previously, such as the popular boys or athletes. Girls can join different groups by matching the clothing tastes, and—unfairly so—the beauty standards of the group. Boys often have the same requirements but also have the added element of earning their spot in the group by proving they are "one of the guys."

I, personally, have been taped to a goalpost in little clothing and smeared with honey with the goal of attracting every bug in the vicinity to prove to "the guys" I was man enough to be a member of the high school football clique. Once my dedication was proven by this hazing, I then had to continue to prove I was worthy by stealing all the uniforms from the boys' basketball locker room and bringing them to the seniors on the football team. All of this was dumb and risky, but to a freshman who the seniors were allowing to join their group, I would have done anything. To my fourteen-year-old brain, the looks of fellow underclassmen as I was dapped-up by seniors as a member of their clique was the best achievement of my life.

I had admiration, clout, acceptance, and influence in school now. It was intoxicating. I threw away the values my parents instilled and that I lived by up until that moment for the taste of acceptance by the leading social group in my high school. And I did not feel bad about it in the slightest. This is the push for social acceptance the teenage brain craves.

Story Time: Break glass in case of emergency... or to prove you're cool

At my small rural high school, the varsity basketball team often struggled to have the same number of athletes as other schools in the area. As a result, there was an easier path for freshmen and sophomores to make the varsity team and earn actual playing time than larger schools in the area. The seniors on the varsity team this particular year were one of those special groups all teachers have every couple of years where they—for no particular reason—were a difficult group. Some years, each grade can be filled with wonderful leaders who want the best for others and the school, and other years, they want to "dog" each other, only do the bare minimum in class, and tease the members of lower grades. This particular year, the seniors were the latter.

They were difficult to have in class and very prone to making fun of their own classmates and hazing the underclassmen. It is always heartbreaking to teachers when you do not particularly like a class as a whole, and this was one of those classes. One of the freshman players on the basketball team, Brian, had been an awkward middle-schooler. In his sixth and seventh-grade years, he was taller than everyone but clumsy, gangly, and socially immature. We have all witnessed this type of teen, one who when they attempt to speak to a group of other teens, they all look at each other and either roll their eyes or make a face that looks as if they smelled something rancid. Brian desperately wanted to be "cool" but had struggled during his early teen years to make the often difficult, and for parents and teachers, confusing and at times heartbreaking, jump from his elementary friend group to one he believed would give him a higher social status. During his eighth-grade year, Brian grew even more, making him an impressive 6'3" by the start of his freshman year. Making the basketball team was his chance to make the social jump.

Brian made the team—remember, at this small school almost everyone who tried out made the team—and due to his height started to get a little playing time. He was even more gangly now and still had to learn how to function athletically in his long-legged body. Teens who grow so quickly often resemble a baby giraffe trying to learn how to run shortly after birth. Puberty was beginning to help him fill out and learn how to work his new legs, but there was still evidence of the clumsiness from his middle school years. And the seniors remembered his awkwardness. Even though he was helping the team—height is a valuable resource in rural high school basketball—he still was not "one of the guys," and the seniors let him know it as often as they could.

After a loss one evening, the team was changing in the visiting locker room and goofing around—they often didn't take losses very hard and had become accustomed to losing—by playing with some weights that were in the locker room and trying to go through the lockers. There was also a five-foot mirror bolted to the wall that the boys were posing in front of. They all knew this was wrong, but if you put several teenage boys into a room together, their reasoning goes out the window. Brian was laughing as they slung the small flat five-pound weights around like a Frisbee and tossed any locker they could open. One of the senior boys suddenly declared to the group, "Someone should throw the weight at the mirror!" Everyone laughed, looking around to see if anyone would actually do it.

This was it! Brian had his chance to show the team and the older boys that he was "cool" and not some goody-two-shoes freshman. He excitedly told them that he would do it and picked up the weight.

The team was shocked but quickly buzzed and stared with anticipation and excitement. Would he chicken out? Would he do it? They all inhaled sharply and waited. Brian stepped back approximately 10 feet from the mirror, held the flat 8" diameter five-pound weight between his thumb and fingers, turned his back to the mirror, and waited. Brian was awkward, but not stupid, he understood the moment and the suspense he created. As he waited, he dreamed of the mythical legend of awesomeness he was about to create for himself. The other players nervously chuckled, their eyes wide, waiting.

Suddenly, Brian spun, snapped his wrist, and sent the weight spinning toward the mirror like Captain America's shield! His aim was true, and the mirror shattered. The team erupted in excitement and incredulity, showering Brian with praise. Some of the more level-headed members slipped out the door back to the gym floor to avoid being linked to the act.

The shattering of the mirror, and the noise that followed, caused the coach to burst into the room as his post-game administrative duties were finished, signaling an abrupt end to Brian's triumphant moment. In line with what teenagers do upon being caught in a deviant act, the team immediately clammed up and moved away from Brian as the coach entered the locker room, acting as if they were just getting dressed. The immediate excuse was that it was an accident, but after pressing some members of the team harder, the very same seniors who egged Brian on eventually ratted him out. His parents were called, and he was disciplined by the school administration the next day.

Brian was unconcerned with getting in trouble because he knew the handful of days sequestered away in the dungeons of "In School Alternative Setting" (ISAS) would only grow his legend. Brian, sadly, was wrong. His father was angry and embarrassed, and after meeting with the coaches and school administration, he opted to pull Brian from the team as punishment. To the student body, Brian was just the awkward tall freshman who stupidly threw a weight at a mirror in another team's locker room. "Who even does that!?" was often heard during discussions about the incident by other students. Brian had also lost the friend group he coveted so intensely now being off the team. He would have to work to find a new friend group and erase the stigma of destructive, deviant behavior.

Brian's story, sadly, is one played out often with teenagers attempting to find acceptance from their peers. Girls may drastically change their dress and engage in gossip and negative talk about fellow students while boys will engage in silly, disrespectful, deviant, and often inexplicable behaviors, creating a convenient pathway for the age-old phrase "Boys will be boys." Boys and girls though have the same goal of gaining and maintaining acceptance of their peers which drives them forward. There is something else driving them, though, lurking in the back of their brain with the rest of their fears: the possibility of flat-out rejection by their peers.

Peer rejection

Rejection from anything is just the worst.

We can all remember a time when we were rejected. It was embarrassing, even emotionally crippling. In the moment you are being rejected, the world and all our hopes and dreams seem to be ending. This is one area where cell phones have helped; now rejection can be more discreet. Walking up to a girl's locker to ask her out while your friends watch and jeer at you is a thing of the past. Thank goodness! There is just nothing like being rejected AND having a paper ball bounce off your head as your friends laugh manically as it's happening.

There are several methods of rejection. The flavor(s)s of choice for teenagers are isolation and ridicule. Those seem extreme at first, but if you think of the dynamics of teenage interaction, it's easy to see those tactics have been used right in front of you. If you have a daughter, you have sat with her as she explained how the most popular girl in her group has instructed the other girls to ignore her. Save a loyal longtime friend or two, suddenly your daughter has been cut off, and it could be for any number of reasons. She wore the wrong Ugg Boots… isolated. Wore pink when the group was explicitly told by the group leader to wear red, á la Regina George in *Mean Girls*... isolated.

Boys often go the route of ridicule, but it is also a strong weapon for females as well. Teenage boys seem to be constantly making fun of each other. This is both a way to establish a hierarchy order in their groups and reject those that do not meet expectations. Fear of rejection via isolation and ridicule—which often crosses the line into full-on bullying—pushes teens to act out to gain the acceptance of their friends.[6]

Your son is a great kid when at home, with family, or in social situations. He's polite and will help others, and shockingly, he can even hold conversations with older people who aren't family. Crazy! Right? But recently, when at school, he has been getting into trouble. That is a clear sign he is making sure he stays a part of the friend group of his choice. He could also be finding himself suddenly in the sights of the school bully or the leading popular group.

Alright, so we now know one of the reasons your child may be getting into trouble at school. All we must do now is tell your child that you know why they are acting out, have a *Full House*, Bob Saget-esque fatherly or motherly talk with them, and then all will be right in the world. Right? RIGHT?

Sadly, that most likely won't solve the issue entirely.

Why? As adults, we are not only competing with the feelings our teens have when they fear they may be rejected by their peers but also against their very own brains. When rejected research has found that the teenage brain activates a network that taps into the same regions we all feel when experiencing negative emotions and actual physical pain.[7]

To the teenage brain, being rejected is the same as having a broken ankle. Their brains scream at them that something is off, not right, broken, and they should be aware. Being rejected is that powerful. It is not just a social issue or our teens being sensitive. Being accepted is a vital achievement teen brains need and doggedly pursue. So, when your teen switches music preferences or suddenly has some crazy fashion choices, they have not lost their minds, they are working to be accepted, to find their place, and to figure out who they are. All are worthy pursuits but also difficult for us as adults to watch and be a part of. The best advice I can give is to be Batman during this time. Watch from the shadows and rooftops, and when there is trouble or the Bat-Signal lights up the night sky, swoop in to protect and guide them.

See! You didn't think you would get to be Batman when you first started reading this book, did you?!

It's all in the eyes

The human eye is a marvelous part of our anatomy. It conveys emotion, even when our thinking brain may not want it to. It also tracks the slightest movement to make sure we are prepared for any activity. The pupil and how it reacts to situations is also unique because it is tied to both the emotional and cognitive regions of our brains. This means that while we are processing something, our pupil is reacting to that information and also reacting to how our emotions are interpreting the event. Very cool, huh!

Working off of how the pupils react to stimuli, a group of researchers created an interactive chatroom experiment where they tracked the dilation of teenage pupils based on the interactions in the interactive chatroom. The experiment went like this: teens of different age brackets were asked about things they were interested in (ex. soccer, movies, dance, video games, types of music, etc.), and they were then grouped with other teens who were said to like the same things. They were then shown pictures of the teens they were grouped with based on their shared interests (these pictures were all of teenage actors or teens who agreed to be photographed). Once they were grouped, the teens were then shown that another teen, whose picture was in the bottom left of the screen, would select either the participant's picture or another teen to discuss one of their shared likes. The experiment was set up to have the participating teen be rejected twice and accepted twice in random order, of course. When they were rejected, a gray X would be put over their picture saying that the selecting teen would rather discuss the shared interests with the other person. All the while, the infrared cameras were tracking how their pupils dilated and reacted to the outcomes. The teens were eventually told that they had been interacting with a preprogrammed computer system and asked to also state how they felt during the selection process.

Science is so cool y'all!

The findings revealed how teens feel about being either rejected or accepted by their peers (even if they were strangers online). The subjects' pupils dilated at a higher degree and for longer when they were rejected by the imaginary teen in the interactive chatroom than when they were accepted. Their brains were trying to process the fact they were rejected while also working through the emotions—and pain we discussed earlier—of the fact that in their minds they were found "unworthy of being interesting enough to talk to."

Teens in the study also reacted more positively when they were selected by the same gender as themselves, which revealed that they were also subconsciously hoping to be found "interesting" by teens like them. To teens, this meant that they fit in with people of their age groups and interests. We all feel this anytime we put ourselves out there to be judged. Very few people are comfortable being labeled as different than others, or as the teens themselves would put it, "a weird kid."

Avoiding the different or "weird" label also proved to be a source of worry, and dare I say anxiety, for teens in this study. The reaction of the pupils of teens who felt less connected to their peers in real-world interactions reacted at a much higher rate to rejection than teens who felt more connected. Simply put, if teens feel that they struggle to connect with their peers in their day-to-day lives, their brains react more when rejected, confirming the worry they carry every single day. To these teens who want to fit in—at least with some group that is like them—but struggle to say the right thing or act how others would want them to, their second backpack holds the weight of fear of being rejected by peers. It can even create fears of interacting with others at all. At a certain point, being a loner is easier than living with constant anxiety and fear of rejection.

What follows is the heartbreaking part of this study. I know that research studies are supposed to be very serious and sterile, but when I read the following fact and did follow-up research, I had to stop because it really did break my heart. Recall how this study displayed a small picture of the imaginary teen selecting which person they would like to chat with in the bottom left corner of the screen and the pictures of the two participants—one being the subject, and the other a fabricated picture of a teenage actor—being selected larger and in the center of the screen?

Well, when our subject teens were accepted and chosen as who the selecting teen wanted to talk to, their gaze was tracked by the computer. Once they were accepted, their gaze lingered on the displayed picture of themselves. Why, you may ask? The answer is the very reason for the title of this chapter. The teenage brain is constantly self-evaluating itself as it develops. This new data stemming from a social situation and culminating in peer acceptance allowed the teen to say, "See, I am worthy of others wanting to talk to me!" This is the equivalent of smiling at yourself in the mirror after you have had a major victory in your life. Don't be bashful, we have all done it after a good day.

Now to the sad part. Teens, when the gray X appeared over their picture indicating that they had not been chosen, avoided looking at their picture. Their eyes darted from the selecting teen's photo in the bottom left corner to the teen that was chosen. Their eyes scanned this other face while they contemplated what features may have made them more desirable to interact with, their brain feverishly making connections with those features. Maybe their smiles were bigger, teeth straighter, perhaps I should copy their hairstyle and clothing choices. Ugh! They have high cheekbones, and my cheeks are chubby, their skin is clearer than mine, and the assessment goes on and on.

This may sound vain and overly dramatic to you, and without context, who could blame you for thinking that? But remember, in the prehistoric world our brains were designed for, to be rejected was to be cast out. To be an outcast was to die either violently, or slowly from starvation, thirst, or the elements. Death was the result regardless. To a developing brain, unlocking the key to acceptance from their peer group means a longer life and the avoidance of a horrific death. This is far from vain; it's the reason our species survived.

You may think that I am overly sensitive, but that really hit me in the "feels." Think of the contrast between being accepted or rejected. Accepted teens gazed longer at their own photo, taking themselves in and assessing everything their peer—even if their peer was a computer program developed by researchers—may have seen and thought about to find them worthy of acceptance. A wry smile of success, confidence, and most likely relief spreading on their face as they gaze at their own picture, self-evaluating and putting everything they learned from being picked into the proper mental compartment.

When rejected, teens avoided looking at themselves, afraid to face the pain of that rejection. Alone in a room, awash in the light of the computer monitor, shoulders slumped, and head slightly tilted down, their eyes scanning the face of the teen who was accepted but those same eyes avoiding their own face. Not being able to look at yourself in the mirror is a cautionary tale we tell ourselves to explain that shame is often the worst punishment of all. These teens feel that shame when rejected, often through no fault of their own.

But, as sad as avoiding their own picture is, science provides us with a bright spot in this whole process. Looking away from their own picture may allow teens to avoid the negative emotions tied to rejection. It's a natural hack to avoid being flooded with negative emotions. Averting their gaze from their picture keeps their brain from applying the same negative social data to their constant self-evaluation. If they were to stare at their photo, their brain would calculate all of the features that made them undesirable. You could imagine how depressed we all would be if this happened daily. The brain in its wonder creates systems to protect itself from itself.

This also tells us a lot about our interactions with teenagers. How many times have we become angrier because the teen we are talking to, be it our child or a student, refuses or makes very little eye contact with us? As a parent or teacher, our approval still carries meaning and weight to teens. Even if they would rather cast themselves into the fires of Mount Doom before they admitted it! Could it be that they avoid our gaze to keep from seeing disappointment in the faces of the adults whose opinions they value?

Try your own little experiment next time you find yourself in a situation where you are correcting a teen's behavior, decisions, or lack of respect. Instead of becoming angrier if they seem to be avoiding eye contact, stop and let them know you care about them, that it was a mistake, and it's going to be okay. Their initial behavior still needs to be corrected, but you could help stem the shame they may be feeling, or avoiding feeling, which will help your message sink in.

This study and others have also found that teens with better social skills are actually more sensitive to peer rejection.[8] This may seem a bit out of place when you first think about it. Wouldn't a kid who is better at seeing social cues, norms, and interacting feel less anxiety and stress if they face rejection?

In fact, they responded the same way that teens with less confidence in their social skills reacted. Having more social skills meant these teens had a greater fear of losing their established social status. As with all of us, teens who seem to have it all together may be struggling beneath the surface. While some teens' second backpack may be filled with anxiety about being rejected or not being part of a group, other teens who seem to be thriving may have the fear of losing their status weighing them down. The second backpack is nebulous and different for every teen. Knowing how teens feel about and deal with peer rejection allows us to assess our teens and see what group they fall into.

Where to belong?

At the beginning of this chapter, we discussed the teenage need to belong. Now we must ask the question of where they seek and need to belong?

Teens are looking for a home. Don't be offended. Your home is their home, and TRUST me, they feel safe and a belonging there. Even if they, once again, would rather be thrown into the fires of Mount Doom than admit it.

They have their childhood home, a type of Fortress of Solitude. Like Superman, they can return here when they feel lost, overwhelmed, sick, or need advice. Teens are looking for a home for their values, beliefs, and personalities that will help them grow as people while finding a place in this world. That noble pursuit does beg to ask exactly what is meant by "home" though.

Is home the place that sustains us and makes us better through nurturing and care? Is it the thing you make right here and right now, growing as life changes? Is it somewhere else, an undiscovered place we all will wander into and make better than the places before? Is it something hard-crafted and wrought from our memories to mimic our childhood home, creating the safety and expectations we are familiar with? Or could it be the place we did not know we needed but then realize that we cannot let go of, finding ourselves back there again and again?

This is the journey our teens are on. They are not seeking a different place to live; that exciting journey for them, and heartbreaking truth for parents, comes later. Teens are looking for a home for their personality, values, and expectations. They want that feeling of satisfaction in the knowledge that their group ensures they are always part of plans or included in discussions. They want to know exactly where to sit in the cafeteria and to see the smiles of their friends as they approach the table. Teens, purely and simply, want to belong, and the school they attend helps to chart that path.

School: A second home

Our teens are at school almost as much as they are at home, especially if you take away our sleeping hours. It makes sense then that school is a vital part of teenagers feeling like they belong and in their social development. School plays a major role in many of the key moments in our lives. How many of you are now thinking of both fond and embarrassing memories from your days in school right now? Maybe a first kiss underneath the bleachers at a football game or making and carrying out an amazing "promposal" where the girl of your dreams (at least back then) said yes. Or maybe you are thinking of the time some mean girl made fun of your outfit in front of everyone and you fled to the bathroom as your peers laughed. All of those memories helped to form and shape you, and for good or for bad, they took place within your school.

Teenagers who feel they belong in their school, and therefore their social habitat, perform greater in academics, have stronger social and emotional adjustment, and are more involved in both the classroom and school activities.[9]

How do we make sure this sense of belonging is happening?

There are three main tent posts in the circus of teenage belonging: parents, teachers, and peers. The cool part is most of the different tent posts may be reading this book at the same time, which means we could all be moving toward the same goal at the same time. Fingers-crossed!

Parents

Parents, you are the easiest to explain of the three, and why not? You have raised, reared, praised, taught, disciplined, cried, supported, and loved your children, so of course you are important. And trust me, we all have felt like we are not. I too have felt the twinge of pain in my heart as the loneliness of the highway sets in and feelings of inadequacy as a parent creep into the silence of the road.

You matter and are important! Say it out loud if you must in those moments because it is true!

Let me say that again so we can all internalize it and hopefully smite those mental demons that tell us that we are not enough, don't do enough, and will fail ourselves and our children.

Parents: you are enough, you matter, and you are so very important!

When it comes to our teens' belonging, how parents react to and interact with their school affects their feelings of belonging as well. The involvement of parents at their child's school, and the attitudes of those parents toward the school, can positively affect the sense of belonging for teenagers.[10] When a student feels supported socially and academically by their parents, they become more motivated to engage in school activities and perform better academically.

My mother tells the story of when she was running track for her school in the 8th grade. Neither of my grandparents attended her meet, and when she returned home, her mother yelled at her for failing to finish her chore of ironing. In response, my mother held up a handful of medals from her dominant performance that day. My grandmother, clearly shocked and embarrassed, stated, in a manner and deadpan tone that only a parent can, "Good job. Now make sure to finish the ironing."

My ironing consists of throwing any wrinkly clothes into the dryer with a damp washcloth, so I had to ask several follow-up questions to this story when I first heard it, and it still baffles me that her bi-weekly chore was to iron everyone's outfits for the remainder of the week. Wouldn't be me!

The days of parents not attending award ceremonies, athletic events, or school functions are long past. Our teens today need that guidance. They are pulled in too many directions, and if parents show that school is important and something they want to share in, that tells our teens school, and success in school, is important to all of the adults they interact with regularly.

I know this seems like another thing on your plate as a parent, but it is a very important thing to have on your plate. Be involved in your children's school. Many of us do a great job when our kids are young. We go to "Pastries with Parents" and little plays, book fairs, and all the events elementary schools provide. But, as our children slip into the uncertainty of their teenage years, parents start to fade from the school realm. A huge part of that is the new social feelings your teens feel. I mean, it is hard to know when you should be there—sports and performances aside—when your child acts as if you just told them that you are all moving to a secluded island with no phone service or indoor toilets whenever you ask them what is going on a school so you could be a part of it.

Another issue with that is that as the middle school years begin, many of the parent-centered activities start to fade as well. This is why many schools are now really working to up their community involvement programs. The easiest way to be involved is to make sure to go to any games or performances they have. Even if you wave at your 8th-grade football player, and of course they barely acknowledge you, they care you are there. Hidden within that glance—if you are lucky, you may even get a head nod, or… *GASP* a return wave—is the fact that they looked, and if you weren't there, they would scan the crowd hoping to see you, saddened when they didn't.

Another method of involvement is communication with their teachers. Email, call, send snail mail. I don't care how you do it but reach out to them. As a teacher, I cannot tell you how many times my perceptions of a student, or strategies to reach them, have completely changed merely due to a quick communication with a parent. You can make sure your child knows you are speaking with their teachers, which makes a world of difference in their classroom behavior and their grades. It also lets us teachers know what your child needs, doesn't need, or is good at in class. It also helps to grow another tent post of belonging in school: the relationship with their teachers.

Teachers

Concerning feelings of belonging at school, teachers were the glue between the three tent posts that allow students to feel they belong.[11] The relationship between teens and their teachers sets the stage to foster belonging to the school as a whole. Teachers create an environment where our teens feel cared for and welcomed.

Especially first-period teachers. If teens are greeted happily and asked about their weekend, or a game they took part in, the sense that they are seen and they matter begins to take hold. Therefore, teachers, just like parents, may have to put another thing on their plate. I know from years of experience it is difficult at times to put on a smiling face when the reality is that you are staring down a day of 120+ different teens and all their antics. The importance of teenagers interacting with someone who cares as soon as they enter the building is a challenge we can all take head-on. So, fire up a pot of extra-caffeinated coffee, or get that treadmill time in that helps you feel energized and put on your best "Open House" face!

The positive relationship with teachers also helps to aid in teenage adjustment. We discussed how teens feel as if they are trying to leave their parents behind to find their role models and examples, and they are in a sense. Teachers can act as very strong non-parental role models for proper adult behavior. Now, does this mean that they won't think that you are lame as a teacher? That is a big fat, "NO!" You can plant the seeds, though. You can show them that the things their parents are saying about hard work, proper behavior, etc. are all true. You can also show them that an adult can still require hard work and good behavior, but care for them throughout it all. In fact, when surveyed, both boys and girls listed their teachers as the most important factor for a sense of belonging at school.

Some of the students who were the most difficult to have in class, whom I believed hated my guts, ended up being the students who cared for me the most and needed me in their lives. That is hard to realize for many new teachers. It is so easy to get caught up in the unreasonable pacing expectations, constant requests from principals or the state, public scrutiny—ironically against the one group, other than parents themselves, who genuinely care about all of their students—and "backseat teachers" who feel that since they went to school twenty years ago they are educational experts, ignoring your several degrees in the field.

But all of that is just noise. It's about the kids! Always has been and always will be.

Communicating with parents is important for teachers as well because it provides dual-sided support for our teens. Much like if mom and dad are on the same page at home, if teachers and families are in communication, negative behaviors can be avoided. A lot of support can also be created from that communication as well. Imagine the belonging a teen may feel if they have always felt a bit on the fringes of their peer group and school community and their parents inform them their teacher emailed them. Their stomach would sink, they would start sweating, and excuses would begin to flood their brain. But, as their heart rate increases their mom or dad smiles and says, "I didn't know you liked English so much that you wrote such a great short story! We are proud of you!"

Wow! Imagine the feeling that child now feels. Their work and its quality caught their teacher's eye and then he or she took the time to tell their parents. Their parents feel proud and encourage their child to write and express themselves in that way now they know their level of skill. A single email, out of thousands of emails sent yearly, could have very well changed that student's life. At the very least it made them, and their parents, feel good for a time. And that, my friends, is not nothing.

Finally, teachers can help teens feel that they belong by making their classroom one of equality and commonality. When a classroom is one where all students feel they have a voice and those voices are protected by the classroom management of the teacher, peer acceptance becomes the norm and less bullying occurs. When students are quickly shut down if they try to tease a student who is talking, then those students know it is not acceptable and will try it less all over the school. Care is a contagious, powerful thing. If that is the vibe of the classroom, bullies are often stopped in their tracks by students on the same social tier as the wannabe bully.

It makes me so mad when I see rampant bullying on television or movies and the teacher either ignores it or just tells them all to be quiet. I have never been a part of that in a classroom, and it's just not how classrooms function. I often wonder if any of the creators have been in a school since the mid-1980s. If they haven't, then give me a call, and for a small consulting fee I will make sure classrooms function as they should in your movies or shows.

Peers

Having acceptance of their peers is what this chapter is all about. Teens crave it and will go through some mind-numbing efforts to achieve it. When it comes to belonging in their second home of school, peer acceptance leads to high self-esteem, personal development, academic confidence, and fewer negative behaviors.

Check, check, check, and check. All the things we all want for our teens and children.

Having a lack of peer belonging can make students apathetic toward both their grades and school events. Having a group of friends to be excited about school events with is crucial to taking part in them. When students don't feel they belong, they tend to fade away at school. They are the students looking annoyed during pep rallies, or not participating in fun activities. Those same students are seldom present for any after-school events.

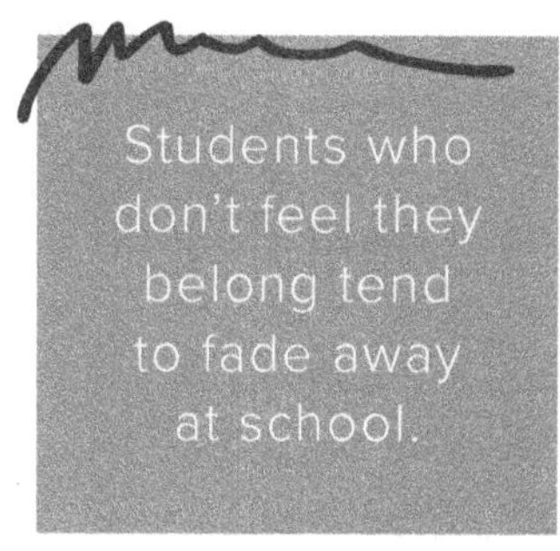

And what are they doing if they are not at school events? Most likely doing everything we as adults don't want them to do. Sitting in front of their TV playing video games, sucked into their phones, or teamed up with other non-engaged friends getting into trouble. It's easy at times, in our busy lives, to be relieved when our children say they don't have anything going on after school. Let's take the time though to check the school website—Lord knows we are already checking several others… Amazon, Temu, Facebook, TikTok, Instagram—and go with our students or offer to take them to games and events. It is building a foundation for their success.

Parents, teachers, and their peers all help and work together to make the place where our teens spend most of their time other than home a place of belonging. If you are a teacher reading this, make your class a place of positivity and equality. DON'T be like Hollywood portrays us (I know you don't behave that way because teachers work hard and are obsessive about their calling), allowing any student to be picked on. Ask questions, support them, be involved, and your students will feel at home.

Parents, get involved in your child's school. Volunteer. Go to any event that supports your student, even if they act as if you posted all of their tubbie-time photos from when they were toddlers online when you tell them that you are going. Positively communicate with their teachers. Make sure that the only time the teacher hears from you is not just when something negative happens with your child. You and their teacher are on the same team, and not a single teacher is "out to get" your kid. We do not have the time to carry personal vendettas against minors. (As I typed that sentence, the absurdity of it shocked me, the fact that some people actually believe it happens consistently.)

Be involved with their peers and encourage them to join clubs, sports teams, school papers, honor societies, and anything that helps them be involved in the school and interact with peers who desire to be involved. Be their support and cheerleader because our teens mimic us; therefore, if you act as if school is just a destination for your kid to go to kill some time so you can go to work worry-free, their feeling of engagement and belonging at school will mimic those sentiments.

We all desire for our children to feel they belong. We can be powerful agents for that desire, let's gain the knowledge and put in the work to make it happen!

Final thoughts on peers

Our teens are moving away from us, and that is a natural and healthy thing. They are not leaving us though; they are practicing the steps to leave our safe little nests and eventually venture into the world on their own. This is a good thing, even though it can make our hearts hurt at times.

The world is a difficult place, filled with rampant division, ignorance, and loneliness for many people. Modern teenagers are carrying more and more in their second backpack into that world, and in an utter stroke of cruelty, the world does not give their troubles a "gap year." Once they make it through their teenage years, often tattered and a bit more jaded than before, the same world then adds adult stressors into their bulging second backpack.

The goal of this book is to help us as parents, adults, teachers, and even teens themselves identify what could be in that second backpack, allowing us to lighten the load. If we have a better understanding of their need to belong, why they strive for acceptance of their peers, why they hurt so deeply when they are rejected, and where they can feel they belong, then we are doing something that has been overlooked for most of modern history.

That is a damn fine accomplishment if you ask me!

Peers are not only the annoying neighbor kid who is always at your house raiding your chip cabinet; they are a sounding board for the values, beliefs, romantic feelings, and positions on new and challenging topics our teens are now being exposed to. Understand that, speak to them, ask them questions, and be a friend and supporter as well.

Let us not forget; every Woody needs a Buzz Lightyear, so, "You've got a friend in me."

8

The Good, the Bad, and the Ugly: Social Media and Technology

"I have a thousand friends [online], and not a single person to feed my cat!"

—*Esther Perel*

You, and I, are currently existing in a previously unimaginable time. Humans, in this very moment, have the greatest ability to connect to each other that has ever occurred. Technology has made it possible for my thoughts, feelings, and opinions to be shot around the world at the speed of light.

But what is connection?

I can reach out and speak to someone in Europe, China, or Australia instantaneously. The question therefore begs to be asked: are we in this period of global communication and social media communicating more but connecting less?

We have a bad habit of getting the two very different forms of expression confused or merged. To communicate, we share information, but to connect is so much more. Connection is the heart of humanity. It is seeing, hearing, and feeling, even for the briefest of moments, the inner thoughts of another. Texting, and to my younger readers, sending the perfect meme at the perfect moment, is FAR from all that I just mentioned.

You may be pouring your deepest fears, highest ambitions, or a moment of paralyzing anxiety via text to another, and they are replying in turn. They may also be replying to these raw and vulnerable moments of yours lying flat on their back while binging a season of *Making a Murderer*.

"I think my husband is having an affair."

"Oh, no sweetie! Say it isn't so!?!"

"Yeah. He is just so detached lately. He is always wandering around checking his phone."

"Ugh! It breaks my heart, but I just don't see it!"

"He got that new job, works late, and now is a different person."

"Girl, flat out let him know you think something is up!"

"Yeah. I'm just so scared. And what if I'm wrong? He will hate me!"

"I know it's so hard. I'm always here for you, you know?"

"Yeah, I know."

Sound familiar? How many of us have had texts or dms, hopefully different in topic, but similar in style?

Because you are in the throes of your pain, fear, anxiety, or excitement, you may read the replies from your friend as caring and engaged. But when you read them detached, as you just did, you could feel something was missing.

Connection. That's what is missing.

The replies, while good intentions, were coming from in-between pairs of underwear to be folded or shocking revelations on their favorite TV show. Consider an interaction on the other end of the spectrum. I can send my wife a text in the middle of the day exclaiming how much she means to me and how much I love her. She sees the data of my message and knows it to be true and feels good. But she is missing the connection that makes expressions like that special and long-lasting.

She didn't *hear* my tone.

She didn't *feel* my touch.

She didn't *see* my pupils dilate.

She didn't *feel* my heart race and my skin become hot.

She didn't connect *with* me.

If we are just reading and interpreting different forms of data but not really connecting on a meaningful level, are we turning ourselves into the very machines and algorithms that we triumphantly declare are connecting us more?

I haven't even talked about modern teens yet!

A fifteen-year-old teen has never lived in a world without the internet, smartphones, social media, and all the apps one can imagine. Their personal, meaningful connections have come from a VERY small group. (See why I chose to inform you how important peers were before I tackled social media and technology?) They are that one friend of yours when you were younger who was always only putting three dollars of gas in their car, and invariably always on "E." Teens hate in-person conversations and then wonder why they feel alone, depressed, or anxious. Their connection tank is always on "E." They are interacting and communicating more than any generation ever but are low on connection.

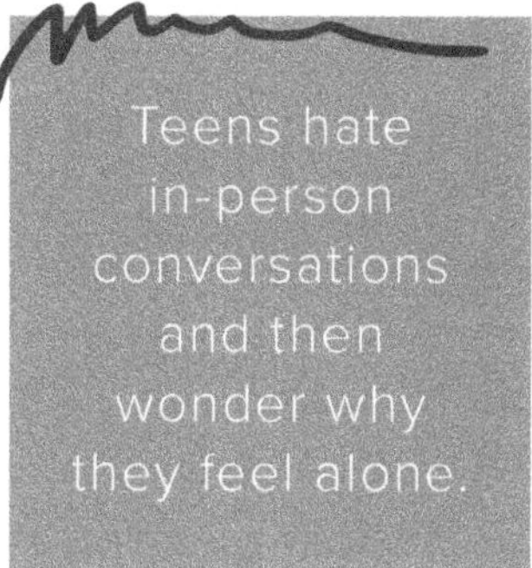

Okay, let's get this over with... phones

I am not a Luddite by any means. Being a millennial myself, I am a part of the generation that has walked both sides of the phone line—see what I did there?—having spent my childhood without a phone but getting one when I was sixteen. Current social media sites such as Facebook, YouTube, and Instagram burst onto the scene during my college years. Like everyone else, I am pretty much on my phone constantly but having had device-free conversations at dinner and having hung out with friends without a phone, I feel that I can put it down and out of mind during important moments of connection.

The pull to scroll is real though.

Any time I am with a group of friends and the conversation turns to a topic I am not active in the allure of quickly checking BlueSky, which is my personal favorite app—and seeing any breaking news, politics, sports updates, or hilarious memes is dangerously strong. I have been chastised by my wife for disengaging while in groups. Much like a teen, in those moments, I feel that since I am not personally involved in the conversation, what is the harm in looking at my phone? The problem though is twofold: once a phone is opened, they have a magical ability to make time move faster, and scrolling with a phone in hand has a distinct look of disengagement or boredom.

For our teens who have never known a time without phones, they simply have not been required to create their own entertainment. A fully curated and instantaneous entertainment supercomputer is conveniently located in their back pocket. They are barely required to hold one-on-one conversations. One student I asked about this very fact flatly stated to me that having personal conversations wastes so much time because they can ask similar questions to their friends via text and field the answers when they choose. To teenagers, this is much more efficient than sitting down and looking into their friends' eyes.

As I said, connection is severely lacking!

The Pew Research Center estimates that 95 percent of teens have access to a smartphone, with 45 percent of teens reporting that they are always on their device.[1] Teens believe that phones are a taken-for-granted element of our daily lives. They are no longer a novel tool in their pockets, they are now seen the same as earlier generations and their wristwatches. An item that when forgotten at home, you feel naked without.

Phones at home

How many times with your teens have you gotten into an argument over their phone usage or had to discipline them because of their phone? If your teen is normal, most likely A LOT! You probably feel that you are a bad parent, but fret not because you are not! Even the very famous Dr. Spock, in all of his parenting books, could not foresee the invention and challenges of our children having a personal entertainment device, which also just happens to be a supercomputer in their pockets!

For Gen X and Millennial parents, phones have encroached upon areas of home life that our parents didn't even have to think of. Dinner time is one of those areas. Maybe your family all sat at the table for dinner, or maybe you all gathered around and ate near the TV, but you were all together. For the parents of Gen X and Millennials, the biggest dinnertime concerns were the kids bickering at the table or establishing rules that you were not excused until all of your food was finished or the whole family was finished.

Modern teens can physically be at the table, but they have something to distract them from the interaction. How many of you have a "no phones at the table" rule? If you don't, then you should! They will complain and think it is unfair, but that time is actual connection time, and deep down, they do value it. Use that time to ask questions and to get to know them and their current state of life.

This rule also counts for AirPods! Don't let them have them in because they still are not fully engaged with you and the family. And DON'T fall for the ol' "I don't have anything playing in them!" ploy because they do and are only half engaged. And if they show you that they don't have anything playing, then why on Earth would they have them in?

The same goes for restaurants. Make rules that while at a restaurant as a family, phones should not be a part of the equation. It always breaks my heart when a family is sitting, and all of them, even the parents, have their heads in their phones until the food comes. You are not tired from cooking, and you choose to share this time while spending your hard-earned money at a restaurant. Take the time to talk, learn, and laugh together. Those are the moments bonds are made.

Remember, with our teens trying to find themselves and moving more toward their peers with every passing second, we need to take every one of those seconds that we can get to strengthen that bond. It is an incredibly sad thought that without working for that connection it is very possible—and happens more than we would all like to believe—that some parents may go several days without having a conversation consisting of more than three or four sentences with their child.

That breaks my heart! Let's all agree not to do that to our relationships with our children.

Phones at home can also lead us to discipline our teens over something they may have done because of their phone, on their phone, or their phone may be the punishment for some behavior of theirs. Since they are so tied to their phones, the punishment is often days without it. Now, when you take their phone away, they will have a meltdown similar to the character Sadness in the Pixar movie *Inside Out.* (If you have seen the film, you know exactly what scene I am referring to!)

But shortly after their Sadness-esque meltdown, you may start to notice some subtle differences in them. Maybe they emerge more from their lair to spend time in family common areas. Maybe they don't eat dinner with the family as fast as possible so they can be excused and make it back to their phone. And maybe you notice that they don't seem on edge as much as they used to be.

My eldest son got into some trouble at school during his freshman year of high school. His punishment was that we would take his phone for a week. He was very upset at first, and we felt bad because the last thing we wanted to do was to damage him mentally. We could tell he was panicking that he may lose connection with his friends or miss something—a serious case of teenage FOMO—that his friends were discussing on their social media sites he no longer had access to. The first day or two he was irritable, almost walking the tightrope between irritability and full-fledged panic.

In no way do I mean to make light of addiction because it is a beast with side effects, I would wish no parent to need to see in their children. But the closest description I can use is that he was much like an addict who was coming down from their addiction. But a day or two later, we saw the changes I mentioned above. A teen who would come home, go into his room, come out for dinner, and then back to his room, was suddenly hanging out with us as we cooked. He ate dinner and then stayed out with us and watched some of what we were watching. My wife and I were shocked. We had become accustomed to feeding our kids and then, the older two especially, watching them disappearing back into the shadows. Now we were asking what he would like to watch just to try to keep the magic happening.

We had forgotten how much we had missed him. We saw him every day and always made an effort to ask about his day, events going on in his world, his friends, and even any news on girls. But this was different. It was like he was nine years old again. He needed us again. And we were eating it up. It was very similar to when you are experiencing an amazing dream but something wakes you up before your alarm, so you immediately gather up the covers and attempt to plunge back into sleep, hoping to recapture that dream. It rarely works. The sweetness of that dream was made for that moment, and that moment had passed.

We knew this moment would pass as well. Terms had been set for when his phone would be returned, and to change those terms would only breed resentment. When the week was up, we returned his phone, and he resumed the same patterns he had followed prior to the punishment. Back to the shadows he crept, and our sweet moments crept with him. To quote the incredible Stephen King, "And why not? For if the sweetness of life did not depart, then there would be no sweetness at all."[2]

The knowledge that his phone and the teenage drive to stay connected, even if that means engaging in online drama, were the main culprits that caused the changes we had seen did provide some relief.

Why would that provide relief, you ask?

That meant that we had the power. And as adults we do have the power. A power that is to be wielded for the good of our children and not tyrannical oppression. Many either forget that fact or believe using it automatically means we are being oppressive as parents. That is completely untrue. We are the ones who make rules, and children crave that structure.

Make rules for their phones for dinner, restaurants, family movie night, social events, and especially downtime and bedtime. Do not let your teenagers have their phone at night. You may be an amazing parent who makes your teens go to bed consistently and at a reasonable time, but other parents may not. I cannot tell you how many times I have been awoken around midnight or later, on a school night, by the constant buzzing of one of my kids' Facetime group calls going off. If the phone would have been in their room, they would wake up and want to be a part of the call—FOMO, remember.

If you are consistent with these rules and expectations, your teen will still be connected but not a constant phone zombie, and that is best for everyone involved.

Phones at school

Cell phones at school are a distraction in every classroom, hallway, and cafeteria. I understand that as a teacher that can sound very biased but think through the issues we discussed at home with just one or two teenagers. Think of how difficult it can be to try and get your teen to listen and remember something when you are sitting at the dinner table. Now add twenty-five more teens to that equation. That is the state of the modern classroom. One teacher, trying to get students to focus on the content of their class, and every student fighting off the pull of their phone and the world of opportunities it promises.

At school, the classroom teacher must first deliver the content and then manage student behaviors to make sure that every student has a chance to succeed. Dealing with standard teen behaviors can take enough of a teacher's time, but now the distraction of phones has made classes too short to finish assignments. In the past, a student may have been slower on a given assignment because they did not understand what exactly to do or they just worked slower than their peers. Both of those issues are still viable scenarios, but now we must add the variable that on top of being slower workers, they were distracted by their phones during the first five minutes of independent work time.

A major uptick in phone usage and issues within the classroom first arose following the Covid-19 pandemic. Who could blame teens for being even more locked into their phones considering for most of 2020, that was the only way we could communicate or take ourselves outside the bubble of our homes and families? Prior to 2020, phones were still an issue, with one or two students attempting to sneak onto them during independent work time, or for the more brazen, scrolling while you are actually up talking to the class as a whole.

I tell all of my students this at the beginning of the year—it is always amusing to me that they still believe they can get away with it after I tell them—that when I am speaking to the class, only one to two seconds passes where I am not looking at one side of the room, therefore, nothing is more telling… and creepy, than a student staring down at their crotch with a grin or angry look illuminated by the eerie glow of their phone. BUSTED!

Phones within the classroom have used up a large portion of teachers' classroom management capital. They have become the thing we are fighting the most within our classrooms on top of the typical behaviors of teenagers. Policing phones in class has become a full-time job for teachers. In fact, across our country, one-third of teachers reported that phone distraction is a "major problem in their classroom."[3] Teachers are feeling more exhausted dealing with all of these issues to the point where some schools are taking steps to limit or completely ban phones during school hours.

One school decided to pilot their entire ninth grade "digitally detoxing" by not allowing their students to have their phones the entire school day. Teachers had become fed up with not only attempting to police phone usage but also asking students to appropriately split their attention between learning and the constant notifications their phones received. This is often a lost idea when considering phones in schools. Many students may want to keep it away, but a constant buzzing of notifications often is too much of a temptation to avoid.

And once the phone is out, we all know how easily it can pull us in. I can't tell you how many times I have honestly intended to look one thing up, and I found myself down a BlueSky or TikTok wormhole where 30-plus minutes had passed.

The "detox" started as you would expect, with the students being visibly grumpy that their phones were no longer accessible, but that quickly subsided. Often the issues with attempting to stop phone usage in the classroom is either students have "burner" phones or the parents of the students get angry that the phone they paid so much for is not available. Parents are often more upset that their communication with their kids has been cut off.

Yes, even your angelic teen may have a burner phone to use when you or a teacher take their phone away. One year I even caught students paying another student ten dollars a day to borrow a burner phone to pop their sim card in and use. And this was the most beat-up phone you have ever seen. You do have to give them props for their entrepreneurial spirit.

Parents being upset over phone restrictions is a more difficult task to manage, however. It baffles me that parents who grew up without phones and survived their teenage years at school still constantly text their children during school hours. Just to be clear, in that moment, YOU are the distraction. If you made it to practice without a reminder, then your child can manage the same task. If you need to tell them about a change in plans, figure out when they are at lunch and send it then, or follow the same strategy as every parent since the invention of the telephone and call the front office! I once had a student try to run out of the school building because his mother texted him that she and her boyfriend got into a fight that became physical. He wanted to drive home and take matters into his own hands. It took five teachers and the administration to calm him down and keep him in the building.

That is an extreme example, but I have also had parents text their child at school to fuss at them for forgetting a morning chore or some other issue, dashing their concentration and commitment to learning. Don't be that parent.

Even the students understood though, even if they didn't want to admit it, that phones were a distraction.

> "They [kids] knew that when a problem arose with their work—when things got hard—it was easier to infinitely scroll than it was to productively struggle."[4]

That right there, my friend, is the crux of the issue with phones in school. They not only offer entertainment or social escape, they also provide a way to avoid difficult situations. In the past when a student would be struggling, they would either ask for help or start to misbehave, which would quickly be fixed and their work focused on. Now, they can quietly avoid that struggle. The problem is that struggling is very important in learning. You have to work through the material and find the answer. It is how we grow, often creating leaps in understanding once a student struggles and then succeeds.

The students at this school eventually started reconnecting. During down time, they would play simple card games together or laugh, just talking. That is connection, and that is important.

The issue has become so pervasive that the second largest school district in the nation located in Los Angeles, with over 429,000 students, brought a cellphone ban policy to its school board and won approval via a 5–2 vote and will go into full effect by January of 2025. The policy cited curbing classroom distractions and protecting students' mental health as the reasons the ban is needed.

Although phones do connect us, all the evidence shows that they are another item weighing down their second backpack. How could we say something that drags their attention away or steals time from them via a connection vortex is not affecting their behavior and adding more fire to the draconian statement, "I just don't understand teenagers!"?

Now we have to shift to the drug inside the phone, slowly stealing more and more of our teens and weighing their second backpacks down like a lead brick: social media.

The bad: Social media

Phones can change the behavior of our teens and be a major distraction both at home and in the classroom. Whether it is texting, FaceTiming, playing a game, doom scrolling through TikTok for WAY longer than you intended (*raised hand emoji* guilty as charged for this author), or using a photo editing app, the amazing invention of smartphones has provided us with constant and instantaneous connection, entertainment, or work and time management abilities.

Those are the good parts of the phone when used in moderation and within the appropriate setting. The bad part, for our teens especially, is the monolith of social media. Social media as a concept is not particularly bad. The ability to connect is a very positive thing. I am still able to speak to many people I grew up with, even as I now live several hundred miles from my hometown. That is awesome and important. But I am an adult. I know that my life exists outside of that world. I can comment on a high school classmate's trip to Disney with their children and I can post my own family and interests. I know that I have value outside of those things because I have lived, struggled, triumphed, and meh'd (pretty sure I am the first to use "meh" as a verb!) during my days on this little rock hurtling around the sun.

Our teens have not.

In Chapter 7, we discussed the importance of peers to teens, and social media quite literally puts all the pressures and strains of that teenage dynamic right in their pocket 24/7. And subsequently, directly into their second backpack. The same things that terrified me about going to school when I was a young teenager, the modern teenager has to deal with day and night. If a girl I was interested in and talking to huffed passed me in the hallway or never showed up to her locker where I was waiting, I was stressed and very distracted the rest of the day. Modern teens not only have to worry about those very same interpersonal interactions but they also have to fear the dreaded "being left on read" or their romantic interest not liking one of their posts or commenting on the post with an embarrassing message for the whole world to see.

For those who don't know, "being left on read" means the recipient read your text message, DM, etc. but never sent any form of reply. Basically a DEFCON 1-level emergency for teens!

And again, it is constant.

I have watched teens laughing and talking but constantly pulling out their phones to see if someone has replied, only to have a crestfallen expression fall over their faces before they re-engaged with the conversation. I have played catch with my sons and watched as every other time my eldest threw one of us the ball he would instantly whip his phone out of his pocket to look for a reply or "likes" notification. And I have seen the look on his face every single time his phone came up empty. He would catch the ball, sigh, and listlessly toss it back.

With 95 percent of teenagers having a smartphone, social media has become their life. Our teens are navigating both a physical and digital life. It is very different than how we manage our digital lives as adults where we use it as a distraction or leisure activity. To our teens, it has as much power and potency as the digital wing of a political campaign. The wrong like, ill-advised post, or laying on too thick can have disastrous effects.

They are juggling all of this on top of EVERYTHING else we have already discussed, including that good ol' undercooked prefrontal cortex.

WOW! That second backpack is bursting at the seams!

If I'm not seen online, do I even exist?

Sadly, the section title above is a sentiment I actually overheard one of my students saying to her friends. She was sharing this disturbing idea while realizing that she could not post pictures on Instagram or keep up her streaks on Snapchat because her parents recently took her phone away.

Let me tell you all… END OF THE WORLD stuff right there.

A major issue has been revealed here: our teenagers think about their lives only having true value based on their connection to social media. They operate and live in a dual reality of our physical world and a digital life. Posting online allows teenage peers to see who they could be interacting with.

Teens love the ability to interact and visualize their social realm through a collection of profiles on various social media sites.[5]

Through social media, our teens can construct and curate their existence and therefore the social perception of themselves. How they pose in a picture and the content of their posts displays to the world who they are in that space. Our teens are creating a type of "digital body" to present to the world.[6] Females attempt to show that they are "cute" and fun, while males attempt to display how adventurous, manly, or physically fit they are.

On a family cruise to the Bahamas, we disembarked for an afternoon and visited a beautiful beach on one of the islands. As my children played, my wife and I sat, talked, and took in the sunshine and breathtaking scenery. Approximately 30 yards from us near the shoreline were two 18 to 20-year-old females. I am not kidding when I tell you that they spent almost an hour taking pictures of each other in various poses with the ocean and beach in the background. By the time they finished, the clouds had moved in—tropical islands get numerous pop-up rain showers daily—and it began to rain.

While my wife and I huddled under our umbrella, our kids played in the water unbothered by the rain; our two photogenic friends quickly packed up and headed back to the ship. While they managed to get some wonderful pictures, I am sure, they ultimately spent all that time at the beach without ever taking in the beauty of where they were. They missed the actual beauty of where they physically were at the moment for the opportunity to curate the perfect social media post to exhibit their "amazing" trip.

I find myself wondering if their memories of that beach trip would stem from the moment and the feelings they were physically a part of or from the photos they took. If it is the latter, sadly, they have become analogous with their social media followers: viewing their memories through online posts. Our memories are largely composed of the emotions experienced during an event. If these memories only exist with the aid of a sterile curated picture, then are they honestly legitimate memories?

Going further, has the social media explosion created a pseudo community memory-bank allowing us to live through each other without cultivating the varied emotions of an experience? I believe that is exactly what we have created. A digital Frankenstein's Monster that, once loose, cannot be brought back to heel. There is no wonder then as to why the pressure to present a covetous digital life is so extreme.

Creating social media personas, and the videos and pictures that define said personas, all follow the same purpose: attracting friends, followers, and of course, the sex they are attracted to.

Story Time: Filter culture—two different people at once

A school I previously worked at had a wonderful reward for students near the end of the first semester. Eligible students were taken to the local mall, allowing them to Christmas shop for their family, friends, or themselves. The students loved it, mostly for the food court and the freedom of walking around the mall with their friends, but it was wonderful to provide them with the opportunity to shop for loved ones.

As a man over 30, it was odd to walk around the mall during the middle of the day. If you think teachers and adults can't feel bullied by the looks of teenagers which scream, "Who is this creeper walking around all by himself?!" I am here to tell you that you are VERY wrong! I felt old… and weird. I even managed to make it worse a few times by awkwardly informing staring groups of teens—who were not students from my school—that it was all good because I was a teacher. Which of course made it even creepier.

For any teens reading: you never really stop feeling embarrassed or embarrassing yourself, so your middle school years weren't that bad!

After taking some shopping time for myself and dodging those judging looks of the youth, I did what any red-blooded American at the mall does. I promptly purchased a soft pretzel with cheese sauce and found one of those massage chairs to people-watch.

From my relaxation oasis, I had a clear line of sight to the first floor of the mall. Particularly the table and bench-laden sitting area in the center of the first floor, which I assume is set aside for wayward husbands who have had their fill of shopping and just want to sit. I like to imagine that on a crowded day of shopping it would be filled with men who also had a soft pretzel, complete with cheese sauce, and a desire to relax.

As the human drama of people watching unfolded around me, I noticed a solo teenage girl, sitting at a table with her back to a circular plant atrium. She looked dejected, near tears, with one palm under her chin and her elbow on the table propping her head up. Her other hand held her phone outstretched in front of her. If you teach, or have teenagers of your own, this is a very common posture that usually follows a full-on sob-fest.

As I wondered why this student was alone, and what happened to make her seem so dejected, she pulled her phone closer to her face, as if making sure what she was reading was true. She then straightened up, checked her background, held her phone at the official "selfie angle" and then smiled the most radiant smile you had ever seen. I assume she took about three or four different selfies—the tilting of the phone, peace sign, and duck lips gave the multiple selfies away—and then she slumped back into her "I'm sad" posture.

This may seem a bit of an overreaction, but seeing it in real time was jarring, and as someone who studies teenage development and behaviors, I was naturally curious of the reasoning behind the drastic shift.

I knew that I could not ask what the situation was because approaching a teenage girl who is alone in the mall as an adult is the quickest way to earn a ticket to the backseat of a police cruiser. As I was about to chalk it up to a brief curiosity that would never be answered, a group of my actual students walked by and asked me what I was doing. I told them that I was just sitting and people-watching, but before I could tell them about the sad/happy selfie girl one of the girls in the group blurted out, "Dr. Lauer, did you see that girl who looked like she was about to cry or fall asleep pop up and take a professional-looking selfie and then look all sad again?" I could only chuckle and let them know that I did and how curious I was.

Of course, with teens, one of the girls said she would go ask. I told her that if the other girl seemed upset not to pry and come back, but as she approached, the sad/happy selfie girl looked up but did not move much and started talking to my student.

When my student came back, she informed us all that the girl was extremely sad because her school was doing a similar reward trip as ours was, but her school went to an indoor trampoline park, but she was failing math so she didn't get to go. Apparently, the girl's mom agreed to let her come to the mall instead since all her friends were not at school, and she was hoping that a few of them would have skipped the trampoline park and come to the mall instead. Sadly for her, all of her friends opted for the trampoline park.

This was all an interesting backstory but still did not answer my main question about how she went from depressed looking to jubilant. I asked my student if she asked about the selfie, and of course, the selfie came up in a teenage girl compliment style that really is attempting to get information. Teenage girls are experts at this tactic, and I should not have been surprised.

The sad/selfie girl's response was a true encapsulation of the social media dual reality our teens live.

Sad/selfie girl's response: she was very sad no one came with her and she was at the mall alone, but she wanted to take selfies that looked like she was having fun to send back to her friends when they sent her a picture. That makes sense for a teenager, but the next part of her answer was the most telling.

She also explained that if she took good selfies, she could post them on "Insta" and "Snap" and get some likes because she "skipped" the trip and is shopping alone, which made her look cool and rebellious. She added that the large-leafed plants behind her helped because, "With the right filter I can make it look like I went somewhere tropical and get a lot of likes and comments."

There it is my friends! The idea of living two separate lives and being part of the filter culture. In reality she was sad and lonely. In her digital life, she was rebellious and adventure seeking, skipping the trip to roam the mall. She also would increase that adventurous persona by adding a filter to her pictures to make the mall plants appear as if she was on some tropical island, most likely adding a hashtag of #Blessed, or #TropicalLife.

The point was to get likes, followers, and comments while in the same instant she was sad and very alone.

She was two very different people at the same time.

To attract friends, followers, and of course, the sex they are attracted to, our teens must constantly choose between "lame or cool." This creates one of the "bad" aspects of social media: if teens want to be seen as cool and popular, they often have to fall in line with what has been deemed cool or exciting by their peers. Even if those aspects are deemed "cool" but are against our teens' tastes, they must fall in line or risk being forced into a smaller niche group that will never achieve the follower or "likes" count they are dreaming of.

As adults we may say, what is the problem with them being in a smaller digital group if it means being who they really are? With your fully developed PFC, and most likely, a distaste for even the idea of adding more people to your life than you already must try to fit in your busy schedule, this is spot on. But, to modern teenagers, with their undercooked PFC and the natural desire to pull toward peers, being pushed into a small group is akin to exile.

And here is a utterly terrifying and fascinating aspect of the digital duality our teens live in: your peers can determine your worth on social media sites by just clicking on your profile page and seeing how many followers you have.

That is terrifying!

Imagine if you were in a job interview and the interviewer flatly states that you won't get the position because, after browsing your social media accounts, you clearly don't have enough followers. The old-fashioned and introverts among us would be walking the streets penniless. But as terrifying as that concept is, I must say that I have been guilty of something similar in the digital world. If I am on X and someone posts something intriguing or controversial, I often do two things before I either comment or internalize their statement. First, I check to see if they have the blue check mark next to their name to state they are verified—although now that you can pay to be verified, that aspect has lost a lot of its power—and second, I go to their profile to see how many followers they have. In the social media world, large numbers of followers shows they have a level of trust.

To teens, likes and followers are a social currency, and just like actual currency, there is a hierarchy stemming from who has the most. They all want to reach that level and often are willing to take part in trends that may be against who they have been or are even silly or dangerous.

All of this is adding to their second backpack. The pressure of having a peer group meeting possibly 24/7 while also judging who they are based on their posts, likes, and followers has created a stress that adults never had to even imagine as they were teens and struggle to really understand. If we can start to understand their thoughts and feelings toward social media and the pressures they may feel to fit in the social media world, we can help guide them through that unique ecosystem and the feelings they may have about it.

Remember as we discussed in Chapter 3, we are driving their development, and we can lighten the load of the second backpack by not fighting against the idea our teens live in in both our physical world and a highly scrutinized, well curated social media world, but rather guide them through and monitor both of their realities.

The ugly: addiction and cyberbullying

The technology that dominates our teens' lives also has an ugly and dark side. Like anything, well-meaning teens can be drawn into that darkness by all manner of dark and insidious forces. We hope, pray, and often deny that any of these things could be happening to our children but to not understand the dark side of social media, phones, and the internet that our teens spent several hours a day on is too dangerous to ignore.

Are the behaviors we see in our teens normal or are they slowly careening down the digital slope into the darkness? Many of us have to guess, and for good reason, because how do you ask a fellow parent or family member if their teen is acting the same way because of their technology without appearing that you are not getting this whole parenting thing? And deep down, that is every parent's fear: "I am not doing a good job."

You ARE doing a good job!

You are here, reading this right now hoping to understand. That means you want to be even better. Know that you are a good parent and know that working to understand is not weakness. It is the greatest strength: vulnerability to gain insight and deeper knowledge.

Let us stare into the abyss so hopefully we can keep our teens from being pulled into it because, as we know, it eventually stares back.

FOMO: Addiction disguised as a funny acronym

Fear of missing out, or FOMO, is a popular term that everyone experiences. Have you ever had to work late, causing you to potentially miss a gathering of friends? Many people attempt to cram some work in or work late into the evening just to be able to make sure they can meet their friends and be a part of the group. That is FOMO. You don't want not to be a part of a possibly amazing night, even while being well aware that the occasion might be as mundane as any other event can be. But none of us want to be the one reading the group texts about the amazing hijinks our friends got themselves into while we were doing something else.

For our teens, and especially their lives in the social media world, missing out does not only mean they missed out on some good times. To them, it means being left behind in the world. According to a meta-analysis of multiple studies performed by Cornell University, five different studies reported that social media distracted students from their studies, kept them from spending quiet time alone without constantly checking their phones, and kept them up too late due to its 24/7 nature.[7]

So, teenagers have an undercooked PFC, and now we are adding the pressure of not missing out on what their peers are doing on various social media accounts on top of them possibly losing sleep because of the constant buzzing from messages, likes, FaceTime Calls, and all the notifications social media can provide.

That is… A LOT.

Parents, one of the best things you can do is to have your teenager keep their phone at night either in your bedroom or some common area so it's not keeping them awake. If you let them keep it, they are constantly in a state of semi-sleep, anxiously waking up with the notification buzzes to check a text, comment, or new Snap Chat from a friend. According to the Pew Research Center, 56 percent of teenagers reported that social media gets in the way of their sleep, and 59 percent reported that it has also reduced their attention span at school or while trying to focus on something non-digital.[8]

So social media is making our teens sleep less, which adds to emotional distress and moodiness, while also making it more difficult for them to concentrate, when many, especially males, already struggle with that?!? Cool… cool.

One evening, my eldest son's phone was plugged in on our kitchen counter. He had already gone to bed, but I was still up—much later than I wanted to be—and I kept hearing a noise over the television. I finally got up and searched out this sound which led me to his phone. It was 12:30 in the morning, he was in eighth grade, and a group FaceTime call kept coming across his phone, plus all of the Snapchats that were being sent between the members of the call. I counted the notifications: in the three hours since he went to bed, there were 109 notifications. Most adults wish to ignore other humans, especially if they attempt to interfere with their precious sleep. But let's pretend we were still teens. Imagine the constant buzzing next to your head and the temptation to turn over and look every time you hear one.

This scenario also meant that there were many other eighth-graders awake texting, calling, FaceTiming, and snapping each other at 12:30 a.m. on a Tuesday. Teens need sleep to develop, and these teens were doing everything but sleeping.

Make your teen take their phone somewhere other than their room so they, and other teens, can rest.

I call this an addiction, not to sound like an old man shaking my fist at something I don't understand, but because due to the pressures of needing to be constantly available and creating their ideal social media persona, teenage behaviors mirror addictive behavior. Teens will constantly check a post they made to see the number of likes. If it is high, they get a dopamine dump and feel amazing, causing them to check the post even more frequently to get that dopamine hit. If the number of likes is lower than expected, they feel awful but still continue to check if the number has improved.

Constantly checking to see how many likes or followers you have achieved, coupled with the natural desire to continue or exceed those numbers, not only is addictive behavior but also leads to the source of the "silent struggle" within our teenagers.

Anxiety.

Anxiety has always existed, and there have always been teenagers who have it. It is much more common now as research has shown that it may be several of the causes for teen behavior, especially newly emerging behaviors such as not wanting to leave the house and panic over being around large groups. But it is getting worse and more prevalent in teens who have very little previous history of it.

Social media is making the very natural fear of peer assessment, or judging if you will, and evaluation greater due to more comparisons by ever-growing groups. All but the most self-assured teenagers and even adults have a natural fear of being judged by their peers. For teens and social media, this fear has increased to the magnitude of inducing high levels of anxiety.

Every single demographic of our teens is frantically comparing themselves with their peers. And thanks to our own naturally built-in self-doubt, which is made even worse via the chemicals surging through our brains during puberty, they are finding the results of this comparison distressing and anxiety-inducing.[9] Our teens are obsessively—similar to an addict—responding to texts, posting to social media, and constantly following highly filtered and curated exploits of their peers.

How could this not cause anxiety? The anxiety it produces is twofold: it first affects how they believe their peers are viewing and assessing them, and second, social media provides a false escape because teens believe they can control their digital life by curating followers, friends, and what they see and decide to like. Believing social media is an escape to a *Truman Show*-like world harms our teenagers, though, because life is not curated, and they run the risk of never learning how to roll with the punches and deal with who they meet.

Anxiety on top of all the struggles modern teens deal with is not something we want to both ignore and unknowingly promote. It very well could be the cherry on top of the whirlwind of negative factors social media and the way our teens use it add to their second backpack.

A bully that follows you home and never sleeps

A constant, gnawing, insidious fear for any parent is that your child will become the victim of a bully. We walk a tightrope of fear and how we tell them to handle it. The fighting side of us tells them that they should "sock" any bully who lays their hands on them. But the rational side understands that they will get into the same amount of trouble at that moment as their bully for fighting. These bullies can be seen and pointed out to parents, teachers, and principals. Social media and the new level of connectedness that our teenagers have has created a bully who follows you home and never sleeps.

Cyberbullying is new to our digital age. It crawled out of the depths of the internet to harass and threaten our children. It is a monster that cannot be seen, located, or planned for. It may be someone from your teen's school, a teen jerk from across the country, or a 40-something keyboard warrior who finds joy in the pain of children.

We have all trained our children how to deal with bullies. Stay away from them, stand up for yourself and others in the moment, and tell an adult when they see it elsewhere or experience it themselves. But with cyberbullying, there are millions of potential bullies hiding in the shadows of the places our teenagers spend most of their time.

When I was in third grade, I was bullied constantly during lunch and in the hallways by a classmate who found it easy to get some laughs at my expense. This made me dread lunch and any time in the hallway, but I learned how to avoid certain areas and to stand up for myself. I could only do this, though, because I knew the bus and my home were safe places. I knew exactly when and where the bullying would end, and that allowed me to gather my strength and maintain some sanity.

Modern teens do not have these safe zones without some form of parent intervention. Maybe you make your teen put their phone somewhere as soon as they get home. Maybe you are very open about the fact that you will look through their messages and posts to sus out any negative items. (To this I would advise to be aware your teen may have a "finsta," which is a fake Instagram account, made to deceive family and to hide their true posts… or a separate "burner" phone. It really does happen a lot!)

Most likely you do not do these things. That is not a failure on your end because, my friends, it is a hefty undertaking to monitor the tsunami of social media options. The same bully—because in the end they are all the same weak, scared, insecure people—that tormented me can now follow your teen into your home, into their bedroom, and harass them twenty-four hours a day. Even the posts your child is proud of could be torpedoed by one anonymous comment aimed at bringing them down.

I have seen entire X accounts made to post and bully a single student. A VPN (virtual private network) was used; therefore it was nearly untraceable. Before the bully tired out, that very same account had over 400 followers. Think about that. Four hundred people who followed this account solely to see one sentence posts aimed at making fun of someone at least half of the followers did not know.

That is the potential toxicity of social media and the internet, summed up in one sentence, my friends.

Harassment and cyberbullying can be so distressing that many teens make the conscious decision to take a temporary break from their social media simply to get away from the constant barrage. And, unsurprisingly, the worst part of humanity finds its way to our teens' posts and comments online. Of the teens who actively decided to try to escape the bully that follows them everywhere they go by taking a social media break: 48 percent were black, 47 percent were Latino, and 30 percent were White according to Common Sense Media.[10]

Let's think about this for a second; almost half of Black and Latino teenagers were bullied online so frequently that they stepped away from the very place where the majority of their connection to their peers happens. In any other situation, that would be a huge red flag as a sign of depression and possible self-harm. Imagine just ignoring if suddenly your son or daughter just didn't want to go to basketball practice or the school dance they have been talking about for weeks. You would be very worried, but since it's online we don't even think what may have happened to get them to step away!

Cyberbullying and harassment also affect teens with previous symptoms of depression in shockingly high numbers. Teens with depressive symptoms took a temporary break from social media to escape bullying more than twice as often (58 percent) than teens without symptoms of depression.

In the words of Pete Campbell from AMC's *Mad Men*, "NOT GREAT, BOB!"

To put it simply, some of the most vulnerable segments of our teenage population encounter cyberbullying to such an extent that large percentages of them take breaks from social media just to get away. This is not good for the development of our teenagers and adds so many different negative items to their, at this point, already bursting second backpack.

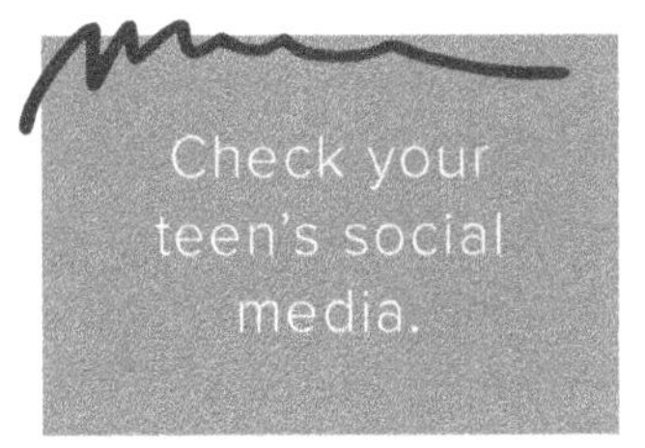

Parents, teachers, family, and friends, check your teens' social media! Use your age, experience, savvy, and care for them to spot threats they may not see. Sit down with them and explain to them that they do not need to keep silent if they are being harassed and bullied online. Help them stay safe in their digital world from predators and bullies and lighten the load of their second backpack.

The very ugly: Sexting

It is very weird to discuss this issue. It is uncomfortable and easy to sweep under the rug, hoping it's an issue that we all personally never need to come face-to-face with. But the purpose of this book is to identify all the issues that fill modern teens' second backpacks and weigh them down. And this is an issue that even though the teenager in your life may never actually take a part of, we would be beyond naive to assume they are not dealing with pressure from someone in their lives to share something. I know this because I have had countless students, mostly females, explain to me that often after a few exchanges of texts, teen boys will send a one-word question just to see how it lands.

What questions do they send you ask?

Often, they only need to send one single word, "Nudes?"

The boldness of that is astounding! As we discussed previously though, the lack of face-to-face contact makes it a 50–50 shot that they may get something, and the worst that can happen is the person says no or stops talking to them. At that point, they are able to move on to another person they are interested in online.

Why does this work, though?

Why are our teens even willing to share these types of intimate photos?

First, let's define sexting. This practice is sending either a picture or video of yourself, or receiving one, that is either nude, semi-nude, or performing some sexually suggestive act. Applying this definition, the numbers reveal that sexting is a very common practice of modern teenagers.

Twenty-five percent of teenagers aged twelve to sixteen have been sent some form of sext, and approximately 7 percent have sent some form of sext to a peer themselves.[11] When you think of the ages I listed, those numbers are shocking. What are the reasons our teens engage in this type of activity? Especially when they are well-aware that items in the digital world can be copied and reproduced, and at that point, they exist on the internet forever.

Breaking down many of the reasons teenagers participate in sexting, the research has found that there are three types of sexting.[12]

> **1. Exploratory**—In this form, teens are still in the peer discovery mode where they are seeking out acceptance from people their age. In this case, they are finding their sexuality and acceptance from their peers in that realm. Basically, they send the picture as a way of asking the question without asking the question, "Does my body meet the standards my peers are seeking?" and "What do you think?" Both questions help to place themselves where others believe they belong.

I know what you are thinking. You are telling yourself right now, "I'll just make sure to tell my teen that they are beautiful and need no one else's approval!" That is great, and you absolutely should share that message with your teen. Remember from Chapter 7 though, they will internalize your message, but at this moment in their development, you are not someone they believe when it concerns "what their friends think." They have to make the decision by themselves to care or not to care, and to share or not to share.

> **2. Sexual Agency**—This category of sexting stems from teenagers attempting to break from the world we have crafted for them. The values and the beliefs of their parents have been what they are led by, but wielding their own sexual agency is a way of having a very personal, private—hopefully—mini-rebellion that they can control and feel they are their own sexually powerful person. In this form of sexting, our teens are loudly stating, "I am a sexual being and I like how I look!" or "I like how it feels to share myself."

This form is uncomfortable to think about and to discuss with good reason. It is difficult to think of our teens as these types of sexual beings. We all hope that sexuality is something that will magically kick in for our teens once they go away to college or move out. But is that really fair?

Let's think back to when we were teenagers living at home. We all were having sexual thoughts, figuring out which boy or girl we thought was cute, why we thought that, and what the possibilities of a romantic relationship with them could be. Now, our teens have the ability to reach out to them instantaneously and to possibly send nude pictures to both play out the exploratory reason for sexting and the sexual agency reason. To both sexes, it feels good when someone sees you in your most natural and vulnerable form and either becomes more interested or replies with praise.

Recall previously how much teenagers crave novelty. What could be more novel than sharing such an intimate secret as seeing, and being seen, naked by someone you care for? And what could be more exciting than feeling like an adult partaking in adult activities? Both teens now share a secret and have seen something no one else has (if it is their first time sexting).

Our children naturally become less innocent as they age. It can be heartbreaking, but it is a very normal part of growing and developing. They desire to have control, and their body and who gets to see it is the most complete control they can have in life.

And to be completely candid, saying something you know and may even be thinking, but do not want to admit: even your super sweet, quiet, polite, boy or girl teen in your life gets sexually aroused… and probably a lot. That is so awkward to say and to think about because we as adults and parents are biologically not supposed to think of them that way, but it is true. If your daughter, who is basically a saint, starts sharing with you the celebrities, sports stars, or boys at school she thinks are "hot," you better believe she is also having sexual thoughts.

Our job is to ensure those sexual thoughts (I know it's weird, but, YES, sexual thoughts are happening in your teen's mind, and, NO, you cannot make them stop having them!) and the natural desire of teenagers to have agency over their bodies are not preyed upon by peers wielding the third form of sexting: Pressure-based.

> **3. Pressure-based**—This type of sexting is all about either a current romantic relationship they are in or one they are trying to create. To teens, it can bc a way to show that the relationship is serious and adult in nature. And let's remember that teens are like the Lost Boys in Peter Pan. They want to be both an adult and still a child—even though they would NEVER admit the latter point—and they will lunge for any type of activity that will make them feel "grown." It is pressure-based because typically one of the members of the relationship will use sexting as a way to prove their commitment to each other, and if the one being pressured have strong feelings for their partner, they typically will oblige to ensure they do not lose the relationship. Many females also believe that sending an intimate picture/video will also up the level of affection shown by the male that she has now show her commitment and loyalty.

Both sexes carry out pressure-based sexting. The pressure often arrives disguised as a sharing of trust. One of the members of the relationship sends an unrequested nude picture and then expects one in return to show that they can trust each other. It's a modern take on the classic, "I'll show you mine if you show me yours." The pressure applies here, though, because in the classic scenario, it's possible to say "no" and shut the whole process down. But when a nude photo unexpectedly appears in your Snap Chat notifications, it is near-impossible to say "no" considering they already sent something to you.

"I shared this with you, so you can trust me or should now trust me."

Or it can be used as a way to make one of the members of the relationship prove how they feel toward the other. "If you feel how you say you do about me then you would send me a nude." (Teens now refer to most sexual pictures as "nudes.")

This type of pressure is a lot for their developing brain, hormones, and desire to feel and be seen as an adult, but both genders often have different motivations for taking part in this type of activity. Females often do it to keep the male interested, of course aided by pressure or subtle hints from her man that there are other fish in the sea that may be more willing to share themselves. Males often do it to confirm their girl truly likes them at the same level they like her or to collect trophies of their exploits, and sadly, as is the purpose of a trophy, to show them off to their friends.

But if they care about the girl, why would they want to show a very intimate picture of her to their friends? That goes back to the pull of peer acceptance from the previous chapter. To show they are one of the guys and to avoid a barrage of homosexual jokes and slurs from their peers, they will show that they, first, are straight, and second, that they are cool enough to get a girl to send them a sexual picture.

They are just boys being boys: Gender bias

There is a darker side to sexting, and the pressures that teens feel. The darkness lies in a gender bias woven deeply into our society. It stems from the same cultural belief concerning boys where many of their behaviors are brushed aside as just "boys being boys." This idea has started to be less accepted, especially concerning sexual behaviors, thank goodness, but is still a common line of thinking concerning boys and their behaviors. Mix this gender bias with current media and pop culture trends of the sexualization of female and male bodies on top of the availability of cell phones and social media, and we have created a perfect storm for sexting to be a common trend and stressor weighing down their second backpack.

To be as clear as possible, there are fewer repercussions for boys if they are caught sexting than there are for girls, both with parents and their own peers. Girls can receive negative attention from their peers solely from rumors that they may have sexted someone. This comes in the form of calling them a "slut" or a "whore," also known as "slut-shaming". The double-standard females often face rears its ugly head very clearly here as females can also receive negative attention from the group asking for their nudes: boys.

Boys will also engage in "slut-shaming" a girl if they find out she sent nude pictures or videos to another male. They do this out of jealousy, anger, or a desire to manipulate the female. They hope that the girl will leave whomever she sent the nudes to and then sweep in themselves, hoping that at some point she will also send them something or do something with them she now has a reputation for being open to. This negative attention is amplified when their nudes get leaked or shared.

I cannot tell you throughout my years of teaching how many girls have been sobbing in the hallway only to find out that they were so upset because either an angry ex-boyfriend or someone who her nudes were shared with leaked them online or to other students. An act that was done either out of care, sexual agency, or pressure becomes a heartbreaking lesson that pilfers many of our female teenagers' innocence.

Boys do not have as much to worry about when they send nudes, other than some teasing by their friends. Let's be honest, that happens anyway about almost anything they do. When a girl gets caught by adults engaging in sexting, there is disappointment, shock, anger, and a hefty amount of scandal. A boy may get grounded, or his phone taken away, but it is often thought of as a stupid act but one not to be surprised by.

Why the difference between the sexes?

We struggle with seeing females, especially teenagers, as sexual beings (ALL humans are) who have sexual agency and are feeling and learning how to manage those thoughts, wants, and urges.

Don't believe me? Just think of a 17-year-old boy saying a sexual joke in a classroom, not overly explicit, just a joke about either sex or a girl's body. The teacher would roll their eyes, forcibly tell them to stop, maybe even write them up, but it's taken as par-for-the-course for teenage boys and moved on from quickly with a head shake from the teacher. Now imagine if a girl did the same thing. Silence would befall the room only to be broken by the shattering of the teacher's coffee mug upon the floor. Then an explosion of noises from the students who have now worked through their shock that a girl would say something like that.

Why the difference? We expect boys to want and talk about sex. We expect girls to be pure, demure, and reserved with their sexual thoughts and desires. Television and movies point this out to us frequently. The older teenage son hooks up with a girl and the dad celebrates, but the mom has to remind him that this is not a good thing. Conversely, when a girl even gets a boyfriend, the dad and often mom become overly protective and are crushed if they find out she has been intimate with him.

This bias we have in our culture filters into our teenagers, making sexting often a double-edged sword for girls and a pursuit of trophies for boys. This plays out in research, where when asked, teenage boys explained that sending, receiving, and sharing sexts from girls is a common occurrence. It is even one where boys can increase their status and be rewarded from both their peers and other girls.

I have heard firsthand accounts from teachers and even teens themselves that some boys will just send several females a nude pic of themselves—at the same time!—in the hopes that one of the girls will strike up a conversation and send something back. Can you imagine the names a girl would be called if she used the same tactic? I'm not even sure Urban Dictionary would help in deciphering some of the awful things she would be called. Boys can do this because their male peers will applaud them for their brazenness, and maybe other than a little bit of teasing from some girls, they will either be successful or have very few social repercussions. Girls, on the other hand, stated the same activities were considered risky behavior that could torpedo their status and negatively follow them throughout their school career.[13]

The pressure to sext and the societal gender bias built in to that practice has one other shocking feature. It has become so normal for boys to ask girls for nudes that if a boy uses threats to attempt to get those nudes, both boys and girls did not see this as harassment.

Can you imagine this?!

It is so normal for boys to pressure girls that they do not even see threats of making up rumors, leaking previous nudes, or embarrassing them as some form as harassment. Anyone of us would run immediately to our human resources department and most likely watch the next day as that person was walked out of the building by security. In the teenage world, it just doesn't work that way.

What can we do?

As always, the best way to combat sexting and potential harassment is to be open and talk with your teen. I understand it can and will be beyond awkward—it was so awkward to write this section of the chapter I almost scrapped it but it is too important—but those moments of awkwardness are far superior to finding that nude pictures of your daughter have been spread across the internet to live in perpetuity!

Tell them their sexual feelings are natural, but if someone really cares about them, they will never pressure them to do anything, especially something like that. Then—take a deep breath and brace yourself—talk to them about their sexual agency and how if they want to send someone a sext without being pressured, they should wait until they are in a committed relationship but that their feelings are valid, real, and their body is their own. I know it is weird to be acting as if you are lending them permission, but if we have learned anything, teens will do what they feel is best for them. It is our job to lay out all of the possible alternative routes they can take.

Also, create a relationship where they understand that you are protecting them, and part of that may be to monitor their social media accounts until whatever age you feel it is best. Clearly with many of these discussions, I am referring to older teenagers. The "your body is your own" speech is not appropriate for a thirteen-year-old, but a seventeen-year-old will only rebel if you treat them as if they are thirteen.

Open communication works. Being there for your child in any moment works even better. If your teen sexts and gets caught, tearing into them does nothing but add more pain to what they are feeling. The often-consistent punishment by their peers will do more than your grounding ever will. Love them and gently explain that when you share something like that with someone who is not committed to them (and I mean actually committed, not the high school committed like "We have a Snapchat streak of a hundred days and of the fifty people I text, I text them the most") but a true meaningful commitment, these types of embarrassing things can happen. And tell your boys that it is NEVER okay to pressure a girl for something like that. You get a girl to like you because of who you are, not how much you can embarrass them if they don't do what you are asking. That is toxic, and we have the chance to take the toxicity from our teenage boys if we have the hard conversations, support them, and take it.

Social media, phones, sexting, and all the new things we cannot even imagine yet are here and are not going away. These elements add to their second backpack and put them in impossible situations which in turn drive their behaviors and can shape them for the rest of their lives. See these items, know they are in the backpack and take the steps to help to take them out. Changes in society often weigh the heaviest on our youngest and least worldly, but by first seeing their second backpack and secondly knowing that these items are there we can protect and enlighten our teens, so they do not regret hitting send on something twenty years later.

As with most things, there is a good, bad, and an ugly side. Let's keep the transformative technology that phones and social media are on the good side and acknowledge and bar from our teens' lives the bad, and especially the ugly.

The Second Backpack is Open

"Never let the odds keep you from doing what you know in your heart you were meant to do."

—*H.Jackson Brown Jr.*

We did it!!!

Well… you did it, but I'm excited for both of us regardless!

You have acknowledged the second backpack, learned some of the items that fill it and weigh down our teens, and now have a blueprint to work with to help the teenager in your life. In the same process you also now have the knowledge needed to understand your teen on a deeper level, which hopefully will enrich your relationship with them, now being one built on understanding and openness.

Those are not small things!

Feel good because you have done what so many have not. You dared to look, to see, and to ask the question: What is the teenager in my life carrying beyond what I can physically see that may be affecting their development and driving their behaviors?

This effort came from fifteen years of teaching and caring for teenagers of various ages. From listening to them, looking through their eyes, and trying to understand – meaning to fully reach -,and connect with them.

As I was writing this book, putting all of my experience, anecdotes, and hours of research to ensure every detail was as accurate and based in truth as much as humanly possible, a stark realization hit me.

Understanding teenagers is **HARD**!

It will take work for all of us.

I am a parent myself, a teacher who is immersed in the lives of teenagers every single day of the school year for every single year of my career. I have letters after my name to show my research and creative prowess, I have researched this topic and each chapter for hours upon end until they were completed. And after all of that, I still screw up and find myself not living out the various strategies I have provided for you.

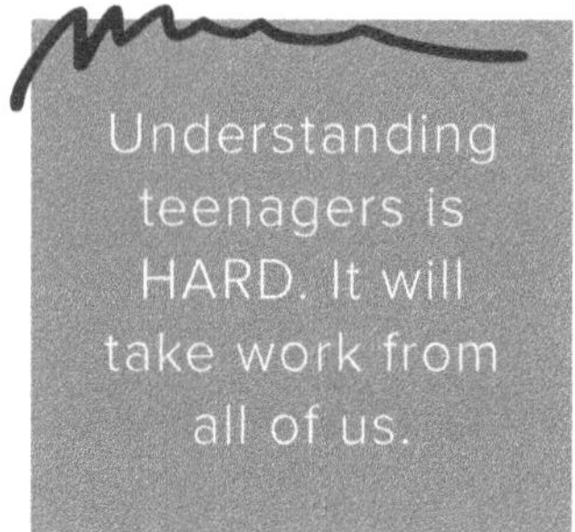

I don't say any of these to brag or to make you feel what you have read won't work or is not worth your time. I say this to clearly show that even when we are focused on a specific pathway or task, we can find ourselves drifting off course.

That is okay.

It is human, and so are you. You are allowed to say to yourself, "I know what to be doing right now and I haven't been doing it. Time to set my feet and dig back in!"

Sometimes we have to take stock and reset. Remember, as soon as we think we have something figured out, a curve ball will be thrown our way. And there we are, standing at the plate of life with our jaw almost on the floor and the bat, unmoved, resting on our shoulder.

My curve ball, my doubt

After graduating college, I decided my destiny lay in forging my own path, so I planned to move far from everything I had come to know. I applied for teaching jobs all around the city I was now going to call home. It was not going well. I would get home from my little summer job, hop on my computer, and apply to any position that matched my teaching license. I had been striking out all summer and had resigned myself to the fate of possessing a shiny new degree, but working at PetSmart.

One evening I followed my nightly routine of getting home, hunting for teaching jobs, applying, and then joining my parents on the front porch to enjoy the summer evening. I love my parents, but I began to fear this pattern would be my norm for the rest of my days. Shortly after I took my position on the front porch, my phone rang showing an area code from the area I was applying for. I shot out of my rocking chair into the house to make sure I could take the call with little interruption. I answered, and on the other side was a principal asking if I would be available for an interview. I was elated and immediately said that I would love to interview! There was one little hiccup though; he wanted to interview me tomorrow around 11 a.m., and the school was approximately six hours from my childhood home.

Being a freshly minted college graduate I lacked true negotiating skills and was afraid to say "no" to the one successful hit I had gotten in my job search. Oh, I may have forgotten to mention that we were nearing the end of July. My time to work in my chosen profession was running out. Being an eager and excited young man, I told my parents the good news, loaded up my truck with extra clothes and anything I may need for the interview, and prepared to leave bright and early. The sadness I noticed in their eyes at the possibility I could be moving hours away still hurts my heart to this day, but being young and excited, I barely registered it at the time. Our lack of knowledge and awareness is really one of the more stupid and hurtful parts of youth. Everything went smoothly; I arrived, interviewed, and was offered the job right there on the spot! My chest puffed with pride: one interview, one job offer! In that moment, I simply assumed I was quite possibly the world's best interviewer. But you know how sometimes people will just give away something they no longer have any use for or just want to get rid of it as long as whoever wants it comes and gets it? Well, that pretty much sums up that position. It was a very difficult school, and an enthusiastic first-time teacher who had not yet found a position was the perfect mark.

The job also came with another little hiccup that should have set off alarm bells in my brain but sadly did not. Remember how we have discussed that teenagers and males approximately twenty-four years old do not have a fully cooked pre-frontal lobe? Yep, this twenty-two-year-old version of me never bothered to think, or check, that other states may have different start dates for their school year.

Hi, it's me. I'm the problem, it's me! (Ask a Swiftie you know, and they will explain that line.)

After I officially accepted the position, my new principal informed me that he was happy I applied because the first day of new teacher orientation was tomorrow and he didn't want a vacant position to start the year. That is right folks, I had less than twenty-four hours until my first teaching job started.

Where I grew up, school did not start until after the Labor Day holiday. This was not the case in the state where I was now working. Teachers started the last week of July, and students showed up at our doors around August 1st. Being broke and not wanting to ask my parents for help in my very first non-college solo venture into the world, I slept in my truck the first two days of my new job. Needless to say, with the way I was offered the job, lack of research on the school (that one is solely on me, and I chalk it up to capricious youth), and how my first few days started, I should have seen the red flags and signs from the universe that it would not be the smoothest of career beginnings.

After that school year ended, I had to look for a different school. My first year teaching was a nightmare. My school had chronic absenteeism, drug activity, and several active gangs. I found myself injured within the first few days and a couple of times after that throughout the year, just breaking up large fights, and I am not a small person. Around Christmas break, I was so spent that I was ready to change careers. I would have a nice office job with a cubicle where I could work with my headphones in, a little plant I could water with a spray bottle, and I would only have to talk to people at meetings or a quick trip to the water cooler. But I pressed on for many of the students who needed me. Teaching is a profession of the soul, and I cared—as all teachers do—about my students. As the year ended and my students moved on to summer break and their next grade, I needed a change for my own physical and mental health.

I now had a year of teaching experience and was interviewed for a position at a local middle school—middle school itself scared me, but it could not be any worse than what I experienced my first year teaching—teaching seventh grade and being the head football coach.

A week after the interview, I was sitting in a hotel room in Bowling Green, Kentucky attending a summer Advanced Placement training, and I received a call from the county's human resource department offering me the position. I was informed I needed to make my decision quickly because summer football practices were beginning soon and they wanted to have a coach in place. I weakly informed them that I would let them know soon.

I sat on the hotel room bed feeling happy I was offered the position, but a swell of pressure wrapped around my chest like a bear hug from Thor. I called my dad and told him about being offered the position. After a few minutes of congratulations, I unexpectedly burst into ugly raw sobs. I played football my whole life and had been an assistant coach during my first year teaching. But this was different. I would be the head coach, leading the team, and dealing with all the things head coaches deal with—especially at a middle school—in a new town, at a new school.

I loathe not doing well at whatever I take on. I always try to work hard to ensure my success. This had so many variables and I was so young. I did not want to fail. I am beyond blessed to have parents who have never tried to push a specific way of thinking or behaving, other than proper behavior of course. I was not above getting disciplined if I acted up as a child—they both accepted and expected emotions and struggles. I have made it my goal to be the same with my sons. There was no toxic masculinity in my home growing up, and there will be none in my children's home, and that is a very good thing.

I knew I could let it all out with my dad, and of course, he listened and reassured me. He knew what I did not in that moment. I was expectedly nervous about being so young and taking on a bigger role. My sobs, however, were not about the job.

I was letting out the entire past year. I had moved far from my entire support system, started a new career, had a difficult year in that new career, and was now starting over again not knowing what would happen. Life had come at me fast, but my real error was that I had allowed all of those emotions to become a gateway for doubt to creep in. Remember, fear and anxiety are not the afflictions themselves. They are the warning bells our brain is sounding when something else is affecting us. In this emotional moment, I was mixing flight and flop from my fight-or-flight response. Doubt was using the emotions I was experiencing as a way to seep into every part of me and steal my confidence and power.

Once I let the emotions out, I found my resolve and pushed the insidious doubt away. The position I emotionally broke down over ended up being one of the best decisions of my life. I made lifelong friends and met my wife, to whom I freely give every ounce of credit for the beautiful things that have happened to me since that day.

The work to understand and maximize your connection with your teenager is an emotional and stressful endeavor. Do not hold in the emotions. Lean into your support and even share with your teen how you are feeling (once you have calmed down of course). Find your resolve and keep working at it, because it will be one of the best decisions of your life.

Know the curve ball is coming, be ready to swing. Don't let doubt win.

Your assignment, should you chose to accept it

We have to have faith in ourselves and our abilities. Every situation varies, and every single teenager is different, often from moment to moment.

I am asking you to take a new look at the teenagers in your life. Even deeper, I hope the information in this book changes your very thoughts about our teenagers. I hope it allows us stop confidently declaring the same things about them that were said about you and even your grandparents.

Bucking the status quo is hard. Rewiring your brain is hard, especially when you are attempting to do it against the emotional storm that can be the teenage years.

As we discussed in Chapter 3, as a parent or teacher, you are driving our teenagers' development. Your assignment is to be their de facto frontal lobe by taking either the "guardian" role, where clearly established boundaries are shared and understood, or the "coaching" role, acting as an external conscience and helping them through mistakes and trying times after they experience them. Choose the role best suited for your family dynamic and each personality. As much as they may fight and rail against it, deep within their brain they crave that guidance. Don't doubt that you can do it. You can, and you have the tools now.

Bolster yourself for the emotions of this stage of life. I called it an emotional hurricane because when it happens, the winds can shift through the entire array of emotions. Your frontal lobe is developed and theirs is not. Those emotions are an ancient defense system, not a true reflection of their feelings. They can, and often will, say some of the most hurtful things you could ever imagine. Sticks and stones, right? It is the same as a cornered animal lashing out. They hope their hurtful words will cut you deep enough that you abandon the fight and slink out of the room, a last-ditch effort to protect their own vulnerability.

Weather this storm and be there with and for them during the cleanup.

Anger in our teenagers, and within ourselves as we guide them through this stage of life, is always hiding behind the scenes. As discussed in Chapter 5, anger is an action emotion. It is based on fear and is a major component of the fight-or-flight system. Anger sets social norms and allows us to show that we believe unfair treatment or outright villainy has been inflicted upon us. It is our version of the threatening growl of a bear or the raised hair and hiss of a cat.

As much as it seems to be, it is important for us to remember that anger is neither good nor bad. It simply is. It has a function to protect us from harm by lashing out first and making ourselves as terrifying as possible to any potential predators. Anger exists and WE chose how to use it. You have many more years of experience than the teenager in your life. The anger launched at you is often the effect of some other actor, possibly an issue with a friend, some stressor at school, or the need to pull away from the members of their family to find out who they are. It is not about you. This is one of the hardest accomplishments we can master as parents or teachers. It is natural to meet anger with anger, especially when the anger comes from a child.

It is hard for us to get out of our own way. How could someone who we have given so much time to and have sacrificed so much for just blatantly throw it into your face with such disrespect? In that moment, thinking along those lines, you have just fallen into their unknowing trap. If we as the adults respond with anger in turn, we become everything they have thrown at us. Set the model for them so they can have positive and healthy relationships as they grow.

Finally, the teenage battle against their need for acceptance from their peers and social media will always be added weight to their second backpack. These issues can cause them to behave as someone you barely know. Clothing styles, attitude changes, strange tastes from everything to music and food will suddenly be your new norm. Taco Tuesday was a staple in your home. Nope, your little girl who loved tacos is now a vegan. You loved listening to country music on your ride to school. Now, if there is any conversation at all, your son asks if you would play Lil Baby. Our teens adapt to find who they are as well as finding acceptance in their social sphere.

Their peers are not only annoying, food-stealing ninjas, coming in and out of your home at their own apparent whims. They are a sounding board for the values, beliefs, romantic feelings, and positions on new and challenging topics our teens are now being exposed to. Understand that, speak to them, ask them questions, and be a friend and supporter as well.

Watch and guide them and know as much as they push away—even though they would spontaneously combust if you were able to make them admit it—they need us. Social media can very well be the monster under the bed or in the closet. Your job remains the same as ever. Teach them where the real danger is and be the protector for them. It all starts, as this entire book aimed, to help aid your relationship. If our teens feel they can openly come to you with everything—without losing our parental authority or power—then they will. Teach them the good, the bad, and the ugly of social media and the pressures we have discussed. If teachers, parents, family, or friends merely hope and pray the very ugly corners of social media will not come for them, we are setting ourselves up for failure. Have the conversation with them, endure the awkward, and ugly, and prevent shame, embarrassment, and social exile to be the newest and most heart-wrenching items added into their second backpack.

If you swoop in from the shadows to provide help and support, does that not only build the positive way they think of you but also models what type of parent they should be? The long-term development and lessening of the weight in their second backpack is the main goal. Let them venture out for a while with the demands of their social world while keeping a close watch. Even Andy took a moment to sit and play with Woody and Buzz as an adult.

> The second backpack is open, but the journey is far from over.

We all come home again.

The second backpack is now open, but the journey is far from over.

The remaining steps on this journey are to use your tools of patience, discussion, empathy, and understanding of teen development that you hopefully either learned, sharpened, or reinforced from reading this book. The topics covered within are many of the most universal and broad in nature. Each issue discussed here can be broken into thousands of sub-issues. And there are many more that could be weighing down their second backpack.

My hope

Hope, the most human gift ever bestowed. It allows the meekest of us to conquer empires and cure diseases that would otherwise ravage our world and allows us to put our feet on the ground, raise our heads high, and move forward through our darkest trials.

Hope is the motivation for this work.

I hope it brings knowledge and understanding.

I hope it brings deep conversations.

I hope it brings reform.

I hope with all of my heart that it makes a teenager sitting alone in their room feel seen.

I hope it is a step and leads to more steps so we can build together and leave a century-long malaise of understanding teenagers in the past.

This hope opens the path to where as a people, society, and adults we can begin to harness teenager creative, social, and emotional powers. After all, teens are the unmolded clay of our species. They are the best part of us, existing in a time and space every single one of us has also existed.

They were you when every new day held promise and novelty. Where every joy consumes us, triggering the ancient part of us where we ponder if humans can actually fly, because feeling that amazing and free could only mean we can conquer any challenge we desire. . . even gravity.? And they were you when every heartbreak destroyed us. Shattering our very spirit upon the jagged rocks of the shoreline; broken to the point that ever being whole again seems as elusive as trying to grasp at the edges of a quickly fading dream.

They are us, and they long to be heard and seen.

Let's lighten and help carry that second backpack together.

They are waiting.

Conclusion

Bridging Generations

Fifteen years in the classroom have shown me that every group of teenagers is both wildly different and strikingly the same. They struggle, they grow, they make mistakes, and they figure out who they are—just as we all did. The teenage years are a multi-cultural rite of passage that we all must journey through. But today's teenagers are navigating challenges we never had to face. Their world is shaped by social media, instant communication, and an overwhelming flood of information. They are growing up in a time when anxiety and pressure are at all-time highs, and yet they are often dismissed as lazy, entitled, or overly sensitive.

The truth is they are none of these things. They are resilient. They are resourceful. They are searching for guidance, even when they push adults away.

Throughout this book, I have explored the complex factors that shape the modern teenager—their brain development, their emotional volatility, their friendships, their struggles with identity, and their relationship with technology. These are not excuses for their behavior but explanations that provide a path to understanding. If there is one lesson I hope to leave you with, it is this: *teenagers do not need us to control them—they need us to guide them.* They need adults who are willing to listen before they lecture, who are curious about their world instead of dismissive of it, and whom are patient enough to teach them how to navigate the chaos. They need us to understand the items carried within their second backpack and how those items weigh them down.

As educators, parents, mentors, and role models, we are the bridge between their world and the one they will step into as adults. The more we seek to understand them, the more we can help them become the best versions of themselves.

So, the next time a teenager rolls their eyes at you, stays glued to their phone, or reacts with an intensity that seems over the top, take a deep breath. Remember that they are still figuring things out. You are the most important factor in helping them figure everything out, and they will mimic and copy how you react because that is all they know. If you still carry hurt from the way your parents may have handled an issue, this is your chance to smother that hurt and keep it from extending into another generation. We have the ability to master of our fates, to mold and shape them as much as we can. And most importantly, remember that they still need you—whether they say it or not.

The conversation continues

Teenagers will keep changing. The world will keep evolving, for good or for bad. We do not know what items may be placed into the second backpack of our children's children, but we will have laid the path of understanding. And our job, as the adults in their lives, is to keep learning right alongside them.

Notes

Chapter 2

1. Sapolsky, R. M. (2017). *Behave: the biology of humans at our best and worst.* Penguin Press.

2. *Ibid* chapter 6, p. 2

3. Siegel, D. J. (2010). *Mindsight: The new science of personal transformation.* Bantam Books.

4. Psychology Tools. (n.d.). *Fight or flight response.* Psychology Tools. Retrieved January 10, 2024, from https://www.psychologytools.com/resource/fight-or-flight-response/

5. Schauer, M., & Elbert, T. (2010). Dissociation following traumatic stress. *Journal of Psychology*, 218, 109–127. https://doi.org/10.1027/0044-3409/a000018

6. Rape Crisis England & Wales. (n.d.) The 5 Fs: fight, flight, freeze, flop and friend. Retrieved February 2024 from https://rapecrisis.org.uk/get-help/tools-for-victims-and-survivors/understanding-your-response/fight-or-flight/

7. Queensland Brain Institute. (n.d.). *The limbic system.* The University of Queensland. Retrieved February, 2025, from https://qbi.uq.edu.au/brain/brain-anatomy/limbic-system

8. Baddeley, A. (2001). The concept of episodic memory. *European Journal of Neuroscience*, 13(6), 495–500. https://doi.org/10.1098/rstb.2001.0957

9. McDonald, H. (2015). Building a better time machine. *Psychology Today.* https://www.psychologytoday.com/us/blog/time-travelling-apollo/201512/building-better-time-machine

10. Payne, R. (2018). *Emotional poverty in all demographics: How to reduce anger, anxiety, and violence in the classroom.* Aha! Process, Inc.

11. Baker, L. (2010). Metacognition. In P. Peterson, E. Baker, & B. McGaw (eds.), *International Encyclopedia of Education* (3, 204–210). Elsevier.https://doi.org/10.1016/B978-0-08-044894-7.00484-X

12. Willis, J. (2010). The current impact of neuroscience on teaching and learning. In D. A. Sousa (ed.) *Mind, brain, and education: Neuroscience implications for the classroom*. Solution Tree Press.

13. *Ibid* Chapter 3, p. 49

14. *Ibid* Chapter 3, p. 50

15. Peterson, J. B., (2021). *Beyond order: 12 more rules for life*. Random House Canada. p. 121.

Chapter 3

1. Van de Werff, T. (2017). The human sciences after the decade of the brain. In J. Leefmann, & E. Hildt (Eds.), *Being a good external frontal lobe: Parenting teenage brains* (pp. 214-230). p. 215. Elsevier Inc. https://doi.org/10.1016/B978-0-12-804205-2.00013-6

2. Giedd, J.N., Blumenthat, J., Jeffries, N.O., Castellanos, F.X., Liu, H., Zijdenbos, A., Paus, T., Evans, A.C., & Rapoport, J.L. (1999). Brain development during childhood and adolescence: A longitudinal MRI study. *Nature Neuroscience*, 2(10) 861–863.

3. Sapolsky, R. M. (2017). *Behave: The biology of humans at our best and worst*. Penguin Press.

4. Sapolsky, R. M. (2017). *Behave: The biology of humans at our best and worst*. Penguin Press Chapter 6, p. 1

5. Van de Werff, T. (2017). The human sciences after the decade of the brain. In J. Leefmann, & E. Hildt (Eds.), *Being a good external frontal lobe: Parenting teenage brains* The Human Sciences after the Decade of the Brain (pp. 214-230). p. 218. Elsevier Inc. https://doi.org/10.1016/B978-0-12-804205-2.00013-6

6. Van de Werff, T. (2017). The human sciences after the decade of the brain. In J. Leefmann, & E. Hildt (Eds.), *Being a good external frontal lobe: Parenting teenage brains* The Human Sciences after the Decade of the Brain (pp. 214-230). p. 218 Elsevier Inc. https://doi.org/10.1016/B978-0-12-804205-2.00013-6

7. Perrin, J., Hervé, P. Y., Leonard, G., Perron, M., Pike, G. B., Pitiot, A., Richer, L., Veillette, S., Pausova, Z., & Paus, T. (2008). Growth of white matter in the adolescent brain: Role of testosterone and androgen receptor. *Journal of Neuroscience 28*(38) 9519–9524. https://doi.org/10.1523/JNEUROSCI.1212-08.2008; Paus, T., Nawaz-Khan, I., Leonard, G., Perron, M., Pike, G. B., Pitiot, A., Richer, L., Susman, E., Veillette, S., & Pausova, Z. (2010) Sexual dimorphism in the adolescent brain: Role of testosterone and androgen receptor in global and local volumes of grey and white matter. *Hormones and Behavior, 57*(1), 63–75. https://doi.org/10.1016/j.yhbeh.2009.08.004; Arnsten, A.& Shansky, R.(2004). Adolescence: Vulnerable period for stress-induced prefrontal cortical function? Introduction to Part IV. *Annals of the New York Academy of Sciencse, 1021*, 143–147. https://doi.org/10.1196/annals.1308.017; Moore, W., Pfeifer, J. H., Masten, C. L., Mazziotta, J. C., Iacoboni, M.,Dapretto, M. (2012). Facing puberty: Associations between pubertal development and neural responses to affective facial displays *Social cognitive and affective neuroscience,7*(1)35–43. https://doi.org/10.1093/scan/nsr066; Dahl, R. (2006, Jan. 12). *Adolescent brain development: A period of vulnerabilities and opportunities* [Keynote Address] *Annals of the New York Academy of Sciences, 1021*, 1–22. https://doi.org/10.1196/annals.1308.001

8. Sapolsky, R. M. (2017). *Behave: The biology of humans at our best and worst.* Penguin Press.

9. Crone, E. A (2016). The Adolescent Brain: Changes in learning, decision-making and social relations (1st ed.). Routledge. https://doi.org/10.4324/9781315720012

10. Crone, E. A. (2008). *The adolescent brain.* Bert Bakker.

11. Shultz, C. L. (2023, July 11). *Alabama officials now say they incorrectly linked boating deaths to TikTok trend.* People. https://people.com/four-people-die-after-attempting-tiktok-boat-challenge-7558550

12. Watson, S. (2021). *Dopamine: The pathway to pleasure.* Harvard Health Publishing.https://www.health.harvard.edu/mind-and-mood/dopamine-the-pathway-to-pleasure

13. Waters, J. (2021). *Constant craving: How digital media turned us all into dopamine addicts.* The Guardian. https://www.theguardian.com/

global/2021/aug/22/how-digital-media-turned-us-all-into-dopamine-addicts-and-what-we-can-do-to-break-the-cycle

14. Willis, J. (2010). The current impact of neuroscience on teaching and learning. In D. A. Sousa (Ed.), *Mind, brain, and education: Neuroscience implications for the classroom.* Solution Tree Press. pp. 45–65.

15. Galvan, A., Hare, T. A., Parra, C. E., Penn, J., Voss, H., Glover, G., & Casey, B. J. (2006) Earlier development of the accumbens relative to orbitofrontal cortex might underlie risk-taking behavior in adolescents. *Journal of Neuroscience, 26*(25) 6885–6892. https://doi.org/10.1523/JNEUROSCI.1062-06.2006 (this is also the source of the figure in the text). A demonstration of dopaminergic response to different reward sizes as more linear and accurate in adults: Vaidya, J., Knutson, B., O'Leary, D. S., Block, R. I., Magnotta, V. (2013). Neural sensitivity to absolute and relative anticipated reward in adolescents. *PLoS ONE, 8*(3) e58708. https://doi.org/10.1371/journal.pone.0058708

16. Sapolsky, R. M. (2017). *Behave: The biology of humans at our best and worst.* Penguin Press.

17. Steinberg, L. (2007). Risk taking in adolescence: New perspectives from brain and behavioral science. *Current Directions in Psychological Science, 16*(2), 55–59. https://doi.org/10.1111/j.1467-8721.2007.00475.x

18. Moutsiana, C., Garrett, N., Clarke, R. C., Lotto, R. B., Blakemore, S., J., & Sharot, T. (2013). Human development of the ability to learn from bad news. *Proceedings of the National Academy of Sciences of the United States of America, 110*(41) 16396–16401. https://doi.org/10.1073/pnas.1305631110

19. Sapolsky, R. M. (2017). *Behave: The biology of humans at our best and worst.* Penguin Press. Chapter 6, P. 6

20. Chein, J., Albert, D., O'Brien, L., Uckert, K., & Steinberg, L. (2011). Peers increase adolescent risk taking by enhancing activity in the brain's reward circuitry. *Developmental Science, 14*(2) F1-F10. https://doi.org/10.1111/j.1467-7687.2010.01035.x

21. Van de Werff, T. (2017). Being a good external frontal lobe: Parenting teenage brains. In J. Leefmann, & E. Hildt (Eds.), *The human sciences after the decade of the brain, 14*(2), pp. 214–230. Elsevier Inc. https://doi.org/10.1016/B978-0-12-804205-2.00013-6

22. O'Connor, C., & Joffe, H. (2013). How has neuroscience affected lay understandings of personhood? A review of the evidence. *Public Understanding of Science, 22*(3), 254–268. https://doi.org/10.1177/0963662513476812

23. *Ibid* p. 258

24. Altikulaç, S., Lee, N. C., van der Veen, C., Benneker, I., Krabbendam, L., & van Atteveldt, N.. (2019), The teenage brain: Public perceptions of neurocognitive development during adolescence. *Journal of Cognitive Neuroscience, 31*(3) pp. 339–359. https://doi.org/10.1162/jocn_a_01332

25. Van de Werff, T. (2017). Being a good external frontal lobe: Parenting teenage brains. In J. Leefmann, & E. Hildt (Eds.), *The human sciences after the decade of the brain, 31*(3), pp. 339–359. Elsevier Inc. https://doi.org/10.1016/B978-0-12-804205-2.00013-6

26. Horsthuis, A. (2008). Lach, luister, voel mee en wees helder. *J/M Puberspecial*, 2, 11–15.

27. Pardoen, J. (2008). Teenagers have no choice but to be teenagers. Leef! Magazine, October/November, pp. 8–10.

28. Van de Werff, T. (2017). Being a good external frontal lobe: Parenting teenage brains. In J. Leefmann, & E. Hildt (Eds.), *The human sciences after the decade of the brain, 31*(3), pp. 339–359. Elsevier Inc. https://doi.org/10.1016/B978-0-12-804205-2.00013-6

29. Sanvictores, T., Mendez, M. D. (2022). Types of Parenting Styles and Effects on Children. In: *StatPearls*. StatPearls Publishing. https://www.ncbi.nlm.nih.gov/books/NBK568743/

Chapter 4

1.Young, P.T. (1963). [Review of the book *Emotion and personality*. by M. B. Arnold]. *The American Journal of Psychology, 76*(3), 516–519. https://doi.org/10.2307/141980

2. Payne, R. B. (2018). *Emotional poverty in all demographics: How to reduce anger, anxiety, and violence in the classroom*. Aha! Process Inc. p. 22

3. Mnich, K., (2022). *The inner self: How social psychology can help you understand you*. Kinga Mnich. https://kingamnich.com/2022/12/27/the-inner-self-the-social-psychology-of-you/

4. Schaefer, M., & Northoff, G. (2017). Who am I: The conscious and the unconscious self. *Frontiers in human neuroscience, 11*, 126. https://doi.org/10.3389/fnhum.2017.00126

5. Erikson, E. H. (1968). *Identity: Youth and crisis.* Norton & Co.

6. Payne, R. B. (2018). *Emotional poverty in all demographics: How to reduce anger, anxiety, and violence in the classroom.* Aha! Process Inc. p. 26

7. Elkind, D. (1967). Egocentrism in adolescence. *Child Development, 38*(4), 1025–1034.

8. Elkind, D. (1967). Egocentrism in adolescence. *Child Development, 38*(4), 1025–1034.

9. Payne, R. B. (2018). *Emotional poverty in all demographics: How to reduce anger, anxiety, and violence in the classroom.* Aha! Process Inc. p. 29

10. Payne, R. B. (2018). *Emotional poverty in all demographics: How to reduce anger, anxiety, and violence in the classroom.* Aha! Process Inc. p. 31

11. Graves, R. (1985). *Greek myths.* Pelican. p. 113

12. Cherry, K. (2023). *What is attachment theory?: The importance of early emotional bonds.* Verywell Mind. verywellmind.com/what-is-attachment-theory-2795337

13. Bowlby, J. (1969). *Attachment and loss.* Basic Books.

14. Payne, R. B. (2018). *Emotional poverty in all demographics: How to reduce anger, anxiety, and violence in the classroom.* Aha! Process Inc. p. 38

15. Lyons-Ruth, K. (1996). Attachment relationships among children with aggressive behavior problems: The role of disorganized early attachment patterns. *Journal of Consulting and Clinical Psychology, 64*(1), 64–73. https://doi.org/10.1037/0022-006X.64.1.64

16. Payne, R. B. (2018). *Emotional poverty* in all demographics: How to reduce anger, anxiety, and violence in the classroom. Aha! Process Inc. p. 42

17. Hazan, C., & Shaver, P. R. (1994). Attachment as an organizational framework for research on close relationships. *Psychological Inqiry, 5*(1),1–22. https://doi.org/10.1207/s15327965pli0501_1

18. Schneider, M., Obsuth, I., Szymanska, M., Mathieu, J., Nezelof, S., Lyons-Ruth, K., & Vulliez-Coady, L. (2022). *BMC Psychology, 10*,112. https://doi.org/10.1186/s40359-022-00821-9

19. Szymanska M., Monnin, J., Tio, G., Vidal, C., Girard, F., Galdon, L., Smith, C. C., Bifulco, A., Nezelof, S., & Vulliez-Coady, L.. (2019). How

do adolescents regulate distress according to attachment style? A combined eye-tracking and neurophysiological approach. *Progress in Neuro-Psychopharmacology & Biological Psychiatry, 89*, 39–47. https://doi.org/10.1016/j.pnpbp.2018.08.019

20. Pickhardt, C. (2023). *Parenting adolescents and the tyranny of now.* Psychology Today. psychologytoday.com/us/blog/surviving-your-childs-adolescence/202311/parenting-adolescents-and-the-tyranny-of-now

21. Pickhardt, C. (2017). *Telling the start of adolescence by how parents can change.* Psychology Today. psychologytoday.com/us/blog/surviving-your-childs-adolescence/201706/telling-the-start-of-adolescence-by-how-parents-can

Chapter 5

1. Mooney, C. G. (2009). *Theories of attachment: An introduction to Bowlby, Ainsworth, Gerber, Brazelton, Kennell, and Klaus.* Redleaf Press.

2. Kashdan, T. B., Goodman, F. R., Mallard, T. T., & DeWall, C. N. (2015). What triggers anger in everyday life?: Links to the intensity, control, and regulation of these emotions, and personality traits. *Journal of Personality, 84*(6), 737–749. https://doi.org/10.1111/jopy.12214

3. Bennett, K. (2024). *Did anger evolve to make us happy? Anger's function may be to promote fairness and discourage exploitation.* Psychology Today. psychologytoday.com/us/blog/modern-minds/202403/did-anger-evolve-to-make-us-happy

4. Kashdan, T. B., Goodman, F. R., Mallard, T. T., & DeWall, C. N. (2015). What triggers anger in everyday life?: Links to the intensity, control, and regulation of these emotions, and personality traits. *Journal of Personality, 84*(6), 737–749. https://doi.org/10.1111/jopy.12214

5. *Ibid* p. 740

6. Madigan, T. (2013). *Sisyphus rocks!: Tim Madigan looks at the meaning of life for Albert Camus.* Philosophy Now. philosophynow.org/issues/98/Sisyphus_Rocks

7. Acker, B., Ahdieh, R., Angleberger, T., Blacker, B., Brown, J., Brown, P., Cabot, M., Carson, R., Christopher, A., & Córdova, Z. (2017). *Star Wars: From a certain point of view.* Del Rey, an imprint of Random House, a division of Penguin Random House LLC.

8. Griffin, C. (2020). *Star Wars: 10 archetypes of the main characters.* ScreenRant. screenrant.com/star-wars-archetypes-main-characters/

9. Pickhardt, C. (2024). *Parents, adolescents, and the management of anger.* Psychology Today. psychologytoday.com/intl/blog/surviving-your-childs-adolescence/202312/parents-adolescents-and-the-management-of-anger

10. *Ibid* p. 3

11. Bennett, K. (2024). *Did anger evolve to make us happy? Anger's function may be to promote fairness and discourage exploitation.* Psychology Today. psychologytoday.com/us/blog/modern-minds/202403/did-anger-evolve-to-make-us-happy

12. Pickhardt, C. (2024). *Parents, adolescents, and the management of anger.* Psychology Today. psychologytoday.com/intl/blog/surviving-your-childs-adolescence/202312/parents-adolescents-and-the-management-of-anger

13. Sell, A., & Sznycer, D. (2023). Societal institutions echo evolved human nature: An analysis of the Western criminal justice system and its relation to anger. *Evolution and Human Behavior, 44*(3), 21–221. https://doi.org/10.1016/j.avb.2011.04.013

14. Nangle, D. W., Hansen, D. J., Erdley, C. A., & Norton, P. J. (Eds.). (2010). *Practitioner's guide to empirically based measures of social skills.* Springer New York. https://doi.org/10.1007/978-1-4419-0609-0

15. Lochman, J. E., Powell, N., Clanton, N., & McElroy, H. (2006). Anger and aggression. In G. Bear & K. M. Minke (Eds.), *Children's Needs III* (p. 115–133). National Association of School Psychology.

Chapter 6

1. King, S. (2012). *The wind through the keyhole: A Dark Tower novel.* Scribner

2. Peterson, J. B. (2021). *Beyond order: 12 more rules for life.* Random House Canada.

3. *Ibid* p. 134

4. *Ibid* p. 115

5. Spielberg, S. (Director). (1991). *Hook* [Film]. Tri-Star Pictures.

6. Stosny, S. (2023). *For parents of angry teenage boys.* Psychology Today. psychologytoday.com/us/blog/anger-in-the-age-of-entitlement/202304/for-parents-of-angry-teenage-boys

7. Hendriksen, E. (2019). *Failure to launch syndrome.* Scientific American. scientificamerican.com/article/failure-to-launch-syndrome/

8. Pickhardt, C. (2024). *Parents, adolescents, and the management of anger.* Psychology Today. psychologytoday.com/intl/blog/surviving-your-childs-adolescence/202312/parents-adolescents-and-the-management-of-anger

9. Bailen, N. H., Green, L. M., & Thompson, R. J. (2019). Understanding emotion in adolescents: A review of emotional frequency, intensity, instability and clarity. *Emotion Review, 11*(1), 63–73. https://doi.org/10.1177/1754073918768878

10. Eisenberg, N. (2020). Findings, issues, and new directions for research on emotion socialization. *Developmental Psychology, 56*(3), 664–670. https://doi.org/10.1037/dev0000906

11. Otterpohl, N., Wild, E., Havighurst, S. S., Stiensmeier-Pelster, J., & Kehoe, C. E. (2021). The interplay of parental response to anger, adolescent anger regulation, and externalizing and internalizing problems: A longitudinal study. *Research on Child and Adolescent Psychopathology, 50*, 225–239. https://doi.org/10.1007/s10802-021-00795-z

12. Lengua, L. J. (2006). Growth in temperament and parenting as predictors of adjustment during children's transition to adolescence. *Developmental Psychology, 42*(5), 819–832. https://doi.org/10.1037/0012-1649.42.5.819

13. Shenk, C. E., & Fruzzetti, A. E. (2011). The Impact of Validating and Invalidating Responses on Emotional Reactivity. *Journal of Social and Clinical Psychology, 30*(2), 163–183. https://doi.org/10.1521/jscp.2011.30.2.163

14. Onion, A., Sullivan, M., & Mullen, M. (2018). *First trenches are dug on the Western Front.* History. history.com/this-day-in-history/first-trenches-are-dug-on-the-western-front

15. LoBraico, E. J., Brinberg, M., Ram, N., & Fosco, G. M. (2019). Exploring processes in day-to-day parent-adolescent conflict and angry mood: Evidence for circular causality. *Family Process, 59*(4), 1706–1721. https://doi.org/10.1111/famp.12506

16. *Ibid* p.4

17. *Ibid* p.13

18. *Ibid* p.13

19. Almeida, D. M., Wethington, E., & Chandler, A. L. (1999). Daily transmission of tensions between marital dyads and parent-child dyads. *Journal of Marriage and the Family, 61*(1), 49–61. https://doi.org/10.2307/353882

20. Larson, R. W., & Almeida, D. M. (1999). Emotional transmission in the daily lives of families: A new paradigm for studying family process. *Journal of Marriage and the Family, 61*(1), 5–20. https://doi.org/10.2307/353879

21. Huddleson Jr., T. (2023). *Child psychologist shares the No. 1 way to help your kids become "happier" and "more successful": Stop yelling at them.* CNBC. cnbc.com/2023/12/17/psychologist-how-yelling-at-kids-affects-their-happiness-success.html#:~:text=The%20lasting%20negative%20effects%20of

22. *Ibid* p. 5

23. Stosny, S. (2023). *For parents of angry teenage boys.* Psychology Today. psychologytoday.com/us/blog/anger-in-the-age-of-entitlement/202304/for-parents-of-angry-teenage-boys

24. *Ibid* p.3

25. Payne, R. (2018). *Emotional poverty in all demographics: how to reduce anger, anxiety, and violence in the classroom.* Aha! Process, Inc.

Chapter 7

1. Roberts, J. (2001). *Baboons smarter than we thought?* CBS News. cbsnews.com/news/baboons-smarter-than-we-thought/

2. Sapolsky, R. M. (2017). *Behave: The biology of humans at our best and worst.* Penguin Press.

3. Pickhardt, C. (2024). *Adolescent growth and peer group membership.* Psychology Today. psychologytoday.com/us/blog/surviving-your-childs-adolescence/202112/adolescent-growth-and-peer-group-membership#:~:text=Social%20growth%20in%20adolescence%20is

4. Sapolsky, R. M. (2017). *Behave: The biology of humans at our best and worst.* Penguin Press.

5. Adolphs, R., Tranel, D., & Damasio, A. (1998). The human amygdala in social judgment. *Nature, 393,* 470–474. https://doi.org/10.1038/30982

6. Masten, C. L., Eisenberger, N. I., Borofsky, L. A., Pfeifer, J. H., McNealy, K., Mazziotta, J. C., & Dapretto, M. (2009). Neural correlates of social exclusion during adolescence: Understanding the distress of peer

rejection. *Social cognitive and affective neuroscience, 4*(2), 143–157. https://doi.org/10.1093/scan/nsp007

7. Lieberman, M.D., Eisenberger, N.I., Crockett, M.J., Tom, S. M., Pfeifer, J. H., Way, B. M. (2007). Putting feelings into words: Affect labeling disrupts amygdala activity to affective stimuli. *Psychological Science, 18*(5), 421–428. https://doi.org/10.1111/j.1467-9280.2007.01916.x

8. Masten, C. L., Eisenberger, N. I., Borofsky, L. A., Pfeifer, J. H., McNealy, K., Mazziotta, J. C., & Dapretto, M. (2009). Neural correlates of social exclusion during adolescence: uUnderstanding the distress of peer rejection. *Social cognitive and affective neuroscience, 4*(2), 143–157. https://doi.org/10.1093/scan/nsp007

9. Uslu, F., & Gizir, S. (2017). School belonging of adolescents: The role of teacher-student relationships, peer relationships, and family involvement. *Educational Sciences: Theory & Practice, 17*(1), 663–682. http://dx.doi.org/10.12738/estp.2017.1.0104

10. *Ibid.* p. 75

11. Osterman, K. F. (2000). Students' need for belonging in the school community. *Review of Educational Research, 70*(3), 323–367. https://doi.org/10.3102/00346543070003323

Chapter 8

1. Pew Research Center (2022). Teens, Social Media and Technology 2022

2. King, S. (2012). *The wind through the keyhole.* Scribner.

3. Nguyen, T. (2024, June 18). Los Angeles school district bans use of cellphones, social media by students. *USA Today.* usatoday.com/story/news/nation/2024/06/18/los-angeles-school-district-cellphone-social-media-ban/74144479007/

4. Kay, M. (2024, September 1). A classroom without cell phones. *EL Magazine, 82*(1). ascd.org/el/articles/a-classroom-without-cell-phones

5. Boyd, D. (2007). Why youth (heart) social network sites: The role of networked publics in teenage social life. In D. Buckingham (Ed.) *MacArthur Foundation Series on Digital Learning—Youth, Identity, and digital Media Volume.* MIT Press.

6. *Ibid.* p. 13

7. Ma, L. (2021, October 16). The Pros and cons of social media for youth. *Psychology Today.* psychologytoday.com/us/blog/evidence-based-living/202110/the-pros-and-cons-social-media-youth

8. Madden, M., Calvin, A., & Hasse, A. (2024). *A double-edged sword: How diverse communities of young people think about the multifaceted relationship between social media and mental health.* Common Sense. commonsensemedia.org/sites/default/files/research/report/2024-double-edged-sword-hopelab-report_final-release-for-web-v2.pdf

9. Denizet-Lewis, B. (2017, October 11). "Why are more American teenagers than ever suffering from severe anxiety?" *The New York Times Magazine*, pp. 39–51, www.nytimes.com/2017/10/11/magazine/why-are-more-american-teenagers-than-ever-suffering-from-severe-anxiety.html.

10. Madden, M., Calvin, A., & Hasse, A. (2024). *A double-edged sword: How diverse communities of young people think about the multifaceted relationship between social media and mental health* . Common Sense. commonsensemedia.org/sites/default/files/research/report/2024-double-edged-sword-hopelab-report_final-release-for-web-v2.pdf

11. Hunehäll Berndtsson, K., & Odenbring, Y. (2020). They don't even think about what the girl might think about it': Students' views on sexting, gender inequalities and power relations in school. *Journal of Gender Studies, 30*(1), 91–101. https://doi.org/10.1080/09589236.2020.1825217

12. Agnew, E. (2021). Sexting among young people: Towards a gender sensitive approach. *The International Journal of Children's Rights, 29*(1), 1–28. https://doi.org/10.1163/15718182-28040010

13. Ringrose, J., & Harvey, L. (2015). Boobs, back-off, six packs and bits: Mediated body parts, gendered reward, and sexual shame in teens' sexting images. *Continuum, 29*(2), 205-217.

Bibliography

Acker, B., Ahdieh, R., Angleberger, T., Blacker, B., Brown, J., Brown, P., Cabot, M., Carson, R., Christopher, A., & Córdova, Z. (2017). *Star Wars: From a certain point of view.* Del Rey, an imprint of Random House, a division of Penguin Random House LLC.

Adolphs, R., Tranel, D., & Damasio, A. (1998). The human amygdala in social judgment. *Nature, 393*, 470–474. https://doi.org/10.1038/30982

Agnew, E. (2021). Sexting among young people: Towards a gender sensitive approach. *The International Journal of Children's Rights*, 29(1), 1–28. https://doi.org/10.1163/15718182-28040010

Almeida, D. M., Wethington, E., & Chandler, A. L. (1999). Daily transmission of tensions between marital dyads and parent-child dyads. *Journal of Marriage and the Family, 61*(1), 49–61. https://doi.org/10.2307/353882

Altikulaçc, S., Lee, N. C., van der Veen, C., Benneker, I., Krabbendam, L., & van Atteveldt, N.et al. (2019), The teenage brain: Public perceptions of neurocognitive development during adolescence. J Cogn Neurosci Journal of Cognitive Neuroscience,. 2019 March O1; 31 (3): pp. 339-–359. doi: https://doi.org/10.1162/jocn_a_01332Arnsten, A.& Shansky, R.(2004). Adolescence: Vulnerable period for stress-induced prefrontal cortical function? Introduction to Part IV. *Annals of the New York Academy of Sciencse, 1021*, 143–147. https://doi.org/10.1196/annals.1308.017

Baddeley, A.. (2001). The concept of episodic memory. *European Journal of Neuroscience*, 13(6), 495–500. https://doi.org/10.1098/rstb.2001.0957

Bailen, N. H., Green, L. M., & Thompson, R. J. (2019). Understanding emotion in adolescents: A review of emotional frequency, intensity, instability, and clarity. *Emotion Review, 11*(1), 63–73. https://doi.org/10.1177/1754073918768878

Baker, L. (2010). Metacognition. In P. Peterson, E. Baker, & B. McGaw (eds.), *International Encyclopedia of Education* (3, 204–210). Elsevier. https://doi.org/10.1016/B978-0-08-044894-7.00484-X

Bennett, K. (2024). Did anger evolve to make us happy? Anger's function may be to promote fairness and discourage exploitation. *Psychology Today.* psychologytoday.com/us/blog/modern-minds/202403/did-anger-evolve-to-make-us-happy

Bowlby, J. (1969). *Attachment and loss.* Basic Books.

Boyd, D. (2007). Why youth (heart) social network sites: The role of networked publics in teenage social life. In D. Buckingham (Ed.), *MacArthur Foundation Series on Digital Learning—Youth, Identity, and Digital Media Volume.* MIT Press.

Chein, J., Albert, D., O'Brien, L., Uckert, K., & Steinberg, L. (2011). Peers increase adolescent risk taking by enhancing activity in the brain's reward circuitry. *Developmental Science, 14*(2), F1-F10. https://doi.org/10.1111/j.1467-7687.2010.01035.x

Cherry, K. (2023). What is attachment theory?: The importance of early emotional bonds. verywellmind.com/what-is-attachment-theory-2795337

Crone, E. A. (2008). *The adolescent brain.* Bert Bakker.

Crone, E. A. (2012). *The social brain of the adolescent.* Bert Bakker.

Dahl, R. (2006, Jan. 12). *Adolescent brain development: A period of vulnerabilities and opportunities* [Keynote Address] *Annals of the New York Academy of Sciences, 1021,* 1–22. https://doi.org/10.1196/annals.1308.001Denizet-Lewis, B. (2017, October 11). Why are more American teenagers than ever suffering from severe anxiety? *The New York Times Magazine*, pp. 39–51. www.nytimes.com/2017/10/11/magazine/why-are-more-american-teenagers-than-ever-suffering-from-severe-anxiety.html.

Elkind, D. (1967). Egocentrism in adolescence. *Child Development, 38*(4), 1025–1034.

Eisenberg, N. (2020). Findings, issues, and new directions for research on emotion socialization. *Developmental Psychology, 56*(3), 664–670.

Erikson, E. H. (1968). *Identity: Youth and crisis.* Norton & Co.

Galvan, A., Hare, T. A., Parra, C. E., Penn, J., Voss, H., Glover, G., & Casey, B. J. (2006) Earlier development of the accumbens relative to orbitofrontal cortex might underlie risk-taking behavior in adolescents.

Journal of Neuroscience, 26(25) 6885–6892. https://doi.org/10.1523/JNEUROSCI.1062-06.2006

Graves, R. (1985). *Greek myths.* Pelican.

Griffin, C. (2020). *Star Wars: 10 archetypes of the main characters.* ScreenRant. screenrant.com/star-wars-archetypes-main-characters/

Giedd, J. N., Blumenthal, J., Jeffries, N. O., Castellanos, F. X., Liu, H., Zijdenbos, A., Paus, T., Evans, A. C., & Rapoport, J. L. (1999). Brain development during childhood and adolescence: A longitudinal MRI study. *Nature Neuroscience, 2*(10), 861–863.

Hazan, C., & Shaver, P. R. (1994). Attachment as an organizational framework for research on close relationships. *Psychological Inquiry,* 5(1), 1–22.

Hendriksen, E. (2019). *Failure to launch syndrome.* Scientific American. scientificamerican.com/article/failure-to-launch-syndrome/

Horsthuis, A. (2008). Lach, luister, voel mee en wees helder. *J/M Puberspecial,* 2, 11–15.

Huddleson Jr., T. (2023). Child psychologist shares the No. 1 way to help your kids become "happier" and "more successful": Stop yelling at them. *CNBC.* cnbc.com/2023/12/17/psychologist-how-yelling-at-kids-affects-their-happiness-success.html#:~:text=The%20lasting%20negative%20effects%20of

Hunehäll Berndtsson, K., & Odenbring, Y. (2020). They don't even think about what the girl might think about it': Students' views on sexting, gender inequalities and power relations in school. *Journal of Gender Studies, 30*(1), 91–101. https://doi.org/10.1080/09589236.2020.1825217

Kay, M. (2024, September 1). A classroom without cell phones. *EL Magazine, 82*(1). ascd.org/el/articles/a-classroom-without-cell-phones

Kashdan, T. B., Goodman, F. R., Mallard, T. T., & DeWall, C. N. (2015). What triggers anger in everyday life? Links to the intensity, control, and regulation of these emotions, and personality traits. *Journal of Personality, 84*(6), 737–749. https://doi.org/10.1111/jopy.12214

King, S. (2012). *The wind through the keyhole: A dark tower novel.* Scribner.

Larson, R. W., & Almeida, D. M. (1999). Emotional transmission in the daily lives of families: A new paradigm for studying family process. *Journal of Marriage and the Family, 61*(1), 5–20. https://doi.org/10.2307/353879

Lengua, L. J. (2006). Growth in temperament and parenting as predictors of adjustment during children's transition to adolescence. *Developmental Psychology, 42*(5), 819–832. https://doi.org/10.1037/0012-1649.42.5.819

Lieberman, M. D., Eisenberger, N. I., Crockett, M. J., Tom, S. M., Pfeifer, J. H., & Way, B. M. (2007). Putting feelings into words: Affect labeling disrupts amygdala activity to affective stimuli. *Psychological Science*, 18, 421–428. https://doi.org/10.1111/j.1467-9280.2007.01916.x

Lochman, J. E., Powell, N., Clanton, N., & McElroy, H. (2006). Anger and aggression. In G. Bear & K. M. Minke (Eds.), *Children's Needs III* (p. 115–133). National Association of School Psychology.

LoBraico, E. J., Brinberg, M., Ram, N., & Fosco, G. M. (2019). Exploring processes in day-to-day parent–adolescent conflict and angry mood: Evidence for circular causality. *Family Process, 59*(4), 1706–1721. https://doi.org/10.1111/famp.12506

Lyons-Ruth, K. (1996). Attachment relationships among children with aggressive behavior problems: The role of disorganized early attachment patterns. *Journal of Consulting and Clinical Psychology, 64*(1), 64–73. https://doi.org/10.1037/0022-006X.64.1.64

Madigan, T. (2013). Sisyphus rocks!: *Tim Madigan looks at the meaning of life for Albert Camus.* Philosophy Now. philosophynow.org/issues/98/Sisyphus_Rocks

Ma, L. (2021, October 16). The pros and cons of social media for youth. *Psychology Today.* psychologytoday.com/us/blog/evidence-based-living/202110/the-pros-and-cons-social-media-youth

Madden, M., Calvin, A., & Hasse, A. (2024). A double-edged sword: How diverse communities of young people think about the multifaceted relationship between social media and mental health. *Common Sense.* commonsensemedia.org/sites/default/files/research/report/2024-double-edged-sword-hopelab-report_final-release-for-web-v2.pdf

Masten, C. L., Eisenberger, N. I., Borofsky, L. A., Pfeifer, J. H., McNealy, K., Mazziotta, J. C., & Dapretto, M. (2009). Neural correlates of social exclusion during adolescence: Understanding the distress of peer rejection. *Social Cognitive and Affective Neuroscience, 4*(2), 143-157. https://doi.org/10.1093/scan/nsp007

McDonald, H. (2015). Building a better time machine. *Psychology Today.* psychologytoday.com/us/blog/time-travelling-apollo/201512/building-better-time-machine

Mnich, K. (2022). The inner self: How social psychology can help you understand you. Kinga Mnich. kingamnich.com/2022/12/27/the-inner-self-the-social-psychology-of-you/

Mooney, C. G. (2009). *Theories of attachment: An introduction to Bowlby, Ainsworth, Gerber, Brazelton, Kennell, and Klaus.* Redleaf Press.

Moore, W., Pfeifer, J. H., Masten, C. L., Mazziotta, J. C., Iacoboni, M.,Dapretto, M. (2012). Facing puberty: Associations between pubertal development and neural responses to affective facial displays *Social cognitive and affective neuroscience,7*(1)35–43. https://doi.org/10.1093/scan/nsr066

Moutsiana, C., Garrett, N., Clarke, R. C., Lotto, R. B., Blakemore, S., J., & Sharot, T. (2013). Human development of the ability to learn from bad news. *Proceedings of the National Academy of Sciences of the United States of America, 110*(41) 16396–16401. https://doi.org/10.1073/pnas.1305631110

Nangle, D. W., Hansen, D. J., Erdley, C. A., & Norton, P. J. (Eds.). (2010). *Practitioner's guide to empirically based measures of social skills.* Springer New York. https://doi.org/10.1007/978-1-4419-0609-0

Nguyen, T. (2024, June 18). Los Angeles school district bans use of cellphones, social media by students. *USA Today.* usatoday.com/story/news/nation/2024/06/18/los-angeles-school-district-cellphone-social-media-ban/74144479007/

O'Connor, C., & Joffe, H. (2013). How has neuroscience affected lay understandings of personhood? A review of the evidence. *Public Understanding of Science, 22*(3), 254–268. https://doi.org/10.1177/0963662513476812

Onion, A., Sullivan, M., & Mullen, M. (2018). *First trenches are dug on the Western Front.* History. history.com/this-day-in-history/first-trenches-are-dug-on-the-western-front

Osterman, K. F. (2000). Students' need for belonging in the school community. *Review of Educational Research, 70*(3), 323–367. https://doi.org/10.3102/00346543070003323

Otterpohl, N., Wild, E., Havighurst, S. S., Stiensmeier-Pelster, J., & Kehoe, C. E. (2021). The interplay of parental response to anger, adolescent anger regulation, and externalizing and internalizing problems: A longitudinal study. *Research on Child and Adolescent Psychopathology, 50,* 225–239. https://doi.org/10.1007/s10802-021-00795-z

Payne, R. (2018). *Emotional poverty in all demographics: How to reduce anger, anxiety, and violence in the classroom.* Aha! Process, Inc.

Pardoen, J. (2008). Teenagers have no choice but to be teenagers. *Leef! Magazine,* October/November, pp. 8–10.

Paus, T., Nawaz-Khan, I., Leonard, G., Perron, M., Pike, G. B., Pitiot, A., Richer, L., Susman, E., Veillette, S., & Pausova, Z. (2010) Sexual dimorphism in the adolescent brain: Role of testosterone and androgen receptor in global and local volumes of grey and white matter. *Hormones and Behavior, 57*(1), 63–75. https://doi.org/10.1016/j.yhbeh.2009.08.004

Perrin, J., Hervé, P. Y., Leonard, G., Perron, M., Pike, G. B., Pitiot, A., Richer, L., Veillette, S., Pausova, Z., & Paus, T. (2008). Growth of white matter in the adolescent brain: Role of testosterone and androgen receptor. *Journal of Neuroscience 28*(38) 9519–9524. https://doi.org/10.1523/JNEUROSCI.1212-08.2008

Peterson, J. B. (2018). *12 rules for life: An antidote to chaos.* Random House Canada.

Peterson, J. B. (2021). *Beyond order: 12 more rules for life.* Random House Canada.

Pew Research Center (2022). Teens, Social Media and Technology 2022

Pickhardt, C. (2017). *Telling the start of adolescence by how parents can change.* Psychology Today. psychologytoday.com/us/blog/surviving-your-childs-adolescence/201706/telling-the-start-of-adolescence-by-how-parents-can

Pickhardt, C. (2023). *Parenting adolescents and the tyranny of now.* Psychology Today. psychologytoday.com/us/blog/surviving-your-childs-adolescence/202311/parenting-adolescents-and-the-tyranny-of-now

Pickhardt, C. (2024). *Adolescent growth and peer group membership.* Psychology Today. psychologytoday.com/us/blog/surviving-your-childs-adolescence/202112/adolescent-growth-and-peer-group-membership#:~:text=Social%20growth%20in%20adolescence%20is

Pickhardt, C. (2024). Parents, adolescents, and the management of anger. *Psychology Today.* psychologytoday.com/us/

blog/surviving-your-childs-adolescence/202312/parents-adolescents-and-the-management-of-angerPsychology Tools. (n.d.). *Fight or flight response.* Psychology Tools. Retrieved January 10, 2024, from psychologytools.com/resource/fight-or-flight-response/

Queensland Brain Institute. (n.d.). *The limbic system.* The University of Queensland. Retrieved February, 2025, from qbi.uq.edu.au/brain/brain-anatomy/limbic-system

Rape Crisis England & Wales. (n.d.) The 5 Fs: fight, flight, freeze, flop and friend. Retrieved February 2024 from rapecrisis.org.uk/get-help/tools-for-victims-and-survivors/understanding-your-response/fight-or-flight/

Ringrose, J., & Harvey, L. (2015). Boobs, back-off, six packs and bits: Mediated body parts, gendered reward, and sexual shame in teens' sexting images. *Continuum, 29*(2), 205-217.

Roberts, J. (2001). *Baboons smarter than we thought?.* CBS News. cbsnews.com/news/baboons-smarter-than-we-thought/

Sanvictores, T., Mendez, M. D. (2022). Types of Parenting Styles and Effects on Children. In: *StatPearls.* StatPearls Publishing. ncbi.nlm.nih.gov/books/NBK568743/

Sapolsky, R. M. (2017). *Behave: The biology of humans at our best and worst.* Penguin Press.

Schaefer, M., & Northoff, G. (2017). Who am I: The conscious and the unconscious self. *Frontiers in human neuroscience, 11,* 126. https://doi.org/10.3389/fnhum.2017.00126

Schauer, M., & Elbert, T. (2010). Dissociation following traumatic stress. *Journal of Psychology,* 218, 109–127. https://doi.org/10.1027/0044-3409/a000018

Schneider, M., Obsuth, I., Szymanska, M., Mathieu, J., Nezelof, S., Lyons-Ruth, K., & Vulliez-Coady, L. (2022). BMC Psychology, 10,112. https://doi.org/10.1186/s40359-022-00821-9

Shultz, C. L. (2023, July 11). *Alabama officials now say they incorrectly linked boating deaths to TikTok trend.* People. https://people.com/four-people-die-after-attempting-tiktok-boat-challenge-7558550

Sell, A., & Sznycer, D. (2023). Societal institutions echo evolved human nature: An analysis of the Western criminal justice system and its relation to anger. *Evolution and Human Behavior, 44*(3), 210–221. https://doi.org/10.1016/j.avb.2011.04.013

Shenk, C. E., & Fruzzetti, A. E. (2011). The impact of validating and invalidating responses on emotional reactivity. *Journal of Social and Clinical Psychology, 30*(2), 163–183. https://doi.org/10.1521/jscp.2011.30.2.163

Spielberg, S. (Director). (1991). *Hook* [Film]. Tri-Star Pictures.

Szymanska, M., Monnin, J., Tio, G., Vidal, C., Girard, F., Galdon, L., Smith, C. C., Bifulco, A., Nezelof, S., & Vulliez-Coady, L. (2019). How do adolescents regulate distress according to attachment style? A combined eye-tracking and neurophysiological approach. *Progress in Neuro-Psychopharmacology & Biological Psychiatry, 89*, 39–47.

Siegel, D. J. (2010). *Mindsight: The new science of personal transformation.* Bantam Books.

Steinberg, L. (2007). Risk taking in adolescence: New perspectives from brain and behavioral science. *Current Directions in Psychological Science, 16*(2), 55–59. jstor.org/stable/20183162

Stosny, S. (2023). For parents of angry teenage boys. *Psychology Today.* psychologytoday.com/us/blog/anger-in-the-age-of-entitlement/202304/for-parents-of-angry-teenage-boys

Uslu, F., & Gizir, S. (2017). School belonging of adolescents: The role of teacher-student relationships, peer relationships, and family involvement. *Educational Sciences: Theory & Practice*, 17, 663–682. http://dx.doi.org/10.12738/estp.2017.1.0104

Van de Werff, T. (2017). Being a good external frontal lobe: Parenting teenage brains. In J. Leefmann & E. Hildt (Eds.), *The human sciences after the decade of the brain* (pp. 214–230). Elsevier Inc. https://doi.org/10.1016/B978-0-12-804205-2.00013-6

Waters, J. (2021). Constant craving: How digital media turned us all into dopamine addicts. *The Guardian.* theguardian.com/global/2021/aug/22/how-digital-media-turned-us-all-into-dopamine-addicts-and-what-we-can-do-to-break-the-cycle

Watson, S. (2021). Dopamine: The pathway to pleasure. *Harvard Health Publishing.* Harvard Publishing. health.harvard.edu/mind-and-mood/dopamine-the-pathway-to-pleasure

Willis, J. (2010). The current impact of neuroscience on teaching and learning. In D. A. Sousa (ed.), *Mind, brain, and education: Neuroscience implications for the classroom.* Solution Tree Press.

Young, P.T. (1963). [Review of the book *Emotion and personality.* by M. B. Arnold]. *The American Journal of Psychology, 76*(3), 516–519. https://doi.org/10.2307/1419805

Acknowledgments

When I started writing this, I was venturing into an unknown arena. I was a stranger in a strange land, if you grok. Pushing myself to create the narrative I wanted for *The Two Backpacks* was an effort that if I had to go about it on my own none of you would be reading this. So many people helped to keep me on track, edit and read the work, and share their stories, ideas, and anecdotes about teaching, parenting, and living this rollercoaster life. I am thankful to them all. I know that I will leave someone out, and for that I sincerely apologize.

I would first like to thank my wife, Ashley, who has been the greatest friend, cheerleader, and coach throughout all our years together. She witnessed the ups and downs that come along with writing something that is truly important to you. She listened to me yap away when I was excited about a section I had just written and talked me through moments where I felt that everything I wrote was just awful. She read, edited, critiqued, praised, and made sure I was creating something that I would be proud of. I could not have done any of this without knowing she was in my corner, and I hope that I have made her proud. I love you.

My parents, Greg and Jill, have always been the most steadfast supporters in every single thing that I have ever done. The love of a parent is a marvelous thing, especially when you add up how very much and for how long they have been unwavering pillars of support. This book would not be here without their support, encouragement, and the willingness to always show that they will bet on me, even when I wouldn't.

A special thanks to my *Educational Warfare* co-host, Dr. Ryan Jackson. You were all-in on my crazy idea of a podcast and have helped create an awesome platform to discuss education as a profession and various parts of *The Two Backpacks*. He has been a great mentor and friend, and I look forward to continuing working together and helping teachers, parents, teens, and professionals all over the world.

Dr. Colin Hunt deserves so many thanks. He worked with me on a major life goal, been a wonderful friend, wrote the wonderful forward you have already read, helped with my very first rounds of edits and structure adjustments to make sure that I didn't lose the narrative track of the book. I was more nervous than I could explain sending what I had finished at that time to such an amazing writer. Hearing his feedback and positive comments provided me with the confidence that I could continue on this journey and make something important.

Blake Bellamy, an all-star AP Government and U.S. History teacher, also spent countless hours listening and sharing his thoughts and opinions on the first few chapters, and has been a true supporter and listener of my podcast and any other crazy idea I have had. I truly appreciate it.

Dr. Contessa Sanders, Dr. Trace Hebert, Jonathan and Mandy Barry, Josh and Katherine Sykes, Anna Kinnard, Chasity Ragsdale, Webb Williams, Krista Pikilton, Samantha Bays, Steven Kelley, Spencer Hill, Casey and Kristen Sheffer, Dave and Debra Sheffer, Katie Reed, Travis Sheppard, Michael Ford, Chad Harrington, all of my wonderful students who always supported me and cheered (shout-out to AP Euro and the Todds) when I announced that I had finished a chapter, and so many more that I know I forgot some… thank you all!

About The Author

Dr. Jordan Lauer is an educator, researcher, and advocate for understanding the complexities of modern teenagers. With over fifteen years of experience in rural, urban, and suburban schools across diverse socioeconomic backgrounds, he has gained a deep understanding of the challenges students face both inside and outside the classroom.

Throughout his career, Dr. Lauer has served in leadership roles such as RTI2b Tier II Coordinator (student behavioral interventionist), Professional Learning Communities Coach, Ayers Institute Teacher Leader Cohort member, and Data Coach. These experiences have equipped him with the insight to address the unseen pressures weighing on today's students—what he calls their "second backpack."

He earned his doctoral degree in Learning Organizations and Strategic Change from Lipscomb University in Nashville, Tennessee, and has contributed to the field of education through his dissertation, *The Lived Experiences of Tennessee School Superintendents*, as well as his article in *AASA's School Administrator Magazine, Superintendents as De Facto Politicians.*

Dr. Lauer is also the host of *Educational Warfare*, a podcast that tackles the critical issues affecting education today. His work is dedicated to bridging the gap between students, parents, and teachers—translating their concerns into meaningful conversations that lead to real solutions.

He resides in Columbia, TN, with his wife, a fellow career educator, their three children, two dogs, and three cats.

Social Media:
BlueSky: @drlauer.bsky.social
X (Formerly *Twitter*): @jordanlauer54
Website: JordanLauer.com

www.ingramcontent.com/pod-product-compliance
Lightning Source LLC
Chambersburg PA
CBHW022004090426
42741CB00007B/892

* 9 7 9 8 9 9 8 5 7 5 7 1 6 *